The Desert March to Relieve Gordon

The Desert March to Relieve Gordon
The Nile Expedition 1884-5

Too Late for Gordon and Khartoum
A Newspaper Correspondent's Experiences of the Nile Expedition 1884-5

Alex. Macdonald

The Battles of Abu Klea & Abu Kru
A Correspondent's Report of Fighting in the "Squares"

Bennet Burleigh

The Desert March to Relieve Gordon
The Nile Expedition 1884-5
Too Late for Gordon and Khartoum
A Newspaper Correspondent's Experiences of the Nile Expedition 1884-5
by Alex. Macdonald
The Battles of Abu Klea & Abu Kru
A Correspondent's Report of Fighting in the "Squares"
by Bennet Burleigh

First published under the titles
Too Late For Gordon and Khartoum
and
The English in Egypt with the Life of General Gordon (extract)

Leonaur is an imprint of Oakpast Ltd

Copyright in this form © 2014 Oakpast Ltd

ISBN: 978-1-78282-389-6 (hardcover)
ISBN: 978-1-78282-390-2 (softcover)

http://www.leonaur.com

Publisher's Notes

The views expressed in this book are not necessarily those of the publisher.

Contents

Preface	7
Introductory	11
Delayed Departure for Egypt	26
Off at Last	34
A Surgeon's Adventures on Lower Nile	42
Stir at Wady-Halfa	50
Gordon's Plans for Opening River to Khartoum	62
Departure of Marines and Artillery, &c., for Korti	71
Off Again After Wolseley	82
Abu-Falmeh to Dongola	94
Departure from Dongola	106
Gordon's Critical Position	118
Lord Wolseley's Adieu	131
The Crisis of the Expedition and How it Ended	144
First Signs of the Enemy	154
Stewart's Decision and Sunset	161
Dangerous Position of the Naval Brigade	171
The Nile at Last	189
Junction with Gordon's Troops	209

All Lost	227
Gordon's Faithfulness to the End	242
Appendices	255
The Battles of Abu Klea & Abu Kru	271

Preface

The chief object of the author in this volume is to give his readers a more complete account of the recent Nile Expedition than either himself or the Press colleagues who accompanied him were at the time able to supply. Owing to the demand for the rapid despatch of news made by the journalism of the present day, the telegrams of war correspondents take precedence over their letters. These telegrams are unsatisfactory as a medium of information, for they comprise only a synopsis of the most important current events. Under the trying circumstances of the expedition, and owing to the rapidity with which its events followed one another during the period of active operations, it was physically and mentally impossible to take into account in our subsequent despatches by mail, and deal satisfactorily with, the subsidiary events which so largely contributed to the failure of the heroic struggle made by Lord Wolseley and the force he commanded to rescue Gordon and his brave garrison from the fate which befell them. Even his lordship's published despatches were in this respect, and evidently from the same causes, regarded as unsatisfactory.

Upon my return from the Sudan I was therefore met by a widespread demand for fuller information than had as yet been supplied to the public on important points respecting the expedition, and especially on those to which its disastrous failure was due. There were also grave misconceptions prevalent about some of the more serious incidents of our desert march on Metammeh, the battles we fought, and the gallant effort made by Sir Charles Wilson to open up communications with General Gordon. In fact a most unfair attempt was made to fix upon him the blame of what must ever be regarded as a great national disaster.

A desire to correct these misconceptions, and do full justice to the distinguished general who so patriotically undertook at the eleventh hour the conduct of the expedition, and to the gallant forces of which it was composed, was the incentive to the task I have now completed.

In its prosecution I have depended chiefly on my own observations along the whole line from Cairo to Metammeh, and when events had to be noticed with which I was only partially or indirectly acquainted, I have taken every possible care to avoid misstatement. Some questions arose the solution of which caused me, from their gravity, much anxiety. Amongst these were, for instance, the choice of routes for the expedition, the arrest of Sir Frederick Stephenson's preparations for an advance to Dongola at high Nile in the autumn of 1884, and Lord Wolseley's detention at Korti after he had expressed his earnest desire to accompany the desert column. There were also purely military questions which, from their bearing on the movements of various parts of our force, had to be answered in order to explain such incidents as the accident to the square at Abu-Klea, and the late Sir Herbert Stewart's double journey to Jakdul before his advance on Metammeh.

I am under deep obligation to Lord Wolseley, not only for the interest he expressed in the task I had undertaken, but for his readiness to give me whatever information I thought myself at liberty to ask from him. I am further indebted to his lordship for advance copies of maps and plans issued by the Intelligence Department—specially of the battlefield of Abu-Klea.

I am also desirous of expressing my thanks to many of the officers of the expedition for valuable information which either confirmed my own observations and impressions on important points, or enabled me to explain others about which I was uncertain.

Major Dixon's journal, which that officer kindly permitted me to make use of, illustrates, in a manner which no description of my own could, the battle of our troops with the difficulties of their advance up the Nile by the Cataracts. The Misses Janson very kindly placed at my disposal several interesting letters of General Gordon to their late brother, which also throw light upon various points in my narrative.

I have been encouraged by the expressions of many friends, both civil and military, in the task I had undertaken, and by their assurance that as I had accompanied the expedition, a great many things must have come under my notice which have hitherto not been submitted to the public, and that my opinions would have great value as those of an unprejudiced looker-on. But these encouragements deepened the sense of my responsibility in dealing with matters affecting personal and official character and the policy of the rulers of the land, and made me doubly careful in criticising the conduct of the expedition.

I have endeavoured to keep to the title I had chosen, which was suggested to me by one deeply interested in the conduct of the expedition, and for whom as a military commander I have always entertained the greatest admiration and respect.

Alex. Macdonald

London: October 13, 1887.

Late, late, so late! but we can enter still:
Too late, too late | ye cannot enter now
      Tennyson's *Guinevere*

Chapter 1

Introductory

Early in October 1882 disquieting rumours began to circulate in Cairo relative to the state of affairs in the Egyptian provinces in the Sudan. The false prophet, of whose appearance there we had already heard, had, it was said, made great progress since our communications with that region had been interrupted by the rebellion of Arabi, and having gathered round him a number of Arab tribes, he had raised the standard of revolt against the Khedive.

This startling news naturally toned down our elation over the decisive results of Tel-el-Kebir, and made it very probable that more battles would have to be fought before the work we had undertaken for Egypt could be accomplished. A greater than Arabi in many respects had arisen to trouble us in a region whose geographical position made it more difficult to reach than had been the scene of our recent successful military operations. It was also apprehended that after capturing Khartoum he might advance down the Nile and draw after him the whole Mussulman population. And there were good reasons for this apprehension, for subsequent to Arabi's overthrow the masses in Egypt proper were quite open to the seductive influences of a successful native leader, especially if he came clothed with the prestige of the predicted prophet, who when he appeared would revive Islamism and extend it over the whole world.

At first it was very difficult to trace these alarming reports to any trustworthy source, on account of the reticence maintained about them in official circles. They however daily gained strength, and soon their substantial correctness was admitted to the writer by Riaz Pasha, the minister for the interior. Later on it became known that Lord Granville had received a memorandum drawn up by Sir Charles Wilson respecting the Sudan, which described affairs there as being 'in the greatest disorder.' It also included the following telegram from Khartoum, dated September 17:

> Owing to telegrams sent by Arabi Pasha to the Sudan ordering people not to recognise the authority of the Khedive, revolt had broken out in the country, and the pretended *Mahdi* had gained more adherents.... The Governor of the Sudan asks for 10,000 Remington rifles to be sent in order to arm a force under Said Pasha to crush the *Mahdi*.... The *Mahdi* is now two hours from Kordofan (Obeid), and has a large force....

This, Sir Charles says, must be regarded as a favourable account of the state of affairs then existing, and therefore he deemed it advisable to send two English officers to the Sudan to report on the state of the country and the steps which will be necessary to ensure its pacification. He further says that as the *Mahdi* can approach Egypt by routes only traversable by small bodies of troops at a time, a small disciplined force could block him easily; but he adds, 'At present, however, if the *Mahdi* attempts a forward movement, there is no *Egyptian force* to meet him.'

At the very outset of our intervention in the affairs of Egypt we were thus confronted by difficulties of an embarrassing character. As the welfare of the whole country was now seriously endangered by the rebellion which had broken out in the Sudan, it appeared to be the duty of Her Majesty's Government to deal with it as it had dealt with that of Arabi. Unless it did, then the task of pacifying Egypt and reorganising its administration could not be so easily or so satisfactorily accomplished as had been anticipated when it was undertaken.

There seemed so little reason at Cairo at the time to doubt that Her Majesty's Government would shirk the new responsibility which had been thrust upon them, that some of my military friends there busied themselves in arranging the details of a campaign to smash the *Mahdi*.

But these were not the views entertained by the more stolid diplomatists in Downing Street with respect to the scope of British responsibility for the welfare of Egypt, for they denied all obligation to restore order in the Sudan, announcing their intention to pursue a policy of absolute non-interference in its affairs. But the Gladstone Cabinet found it impossible to maintain this position, and the disastrous results which followed their attempts to do so fully justified the warnings they had received on the subject from competent authorities in England and Egypt The events and circumstances which eventually compelled this active interference in the affairs of the Sudan are matters of too recent, (1887), history to require any further reference to them here than may add to the interest of our narrative. It is therefore now only proposed to recall the attention of our readers to such of the incidents in that history as have a direct bearing on General Gordon's last mission to Khartoum, and which not only necessitated the expedition undertaken for his rescue, but also seriously contributed to its failure. Our first reference is to the destruction of Hicks Pasha's army. When the news of this disaster reached Cairo on November 24, 1883, Sir Evelyn Baring informed Lord Granville that General Stephenson and Sir Evelyn Wood with himself were of the opinion that the successes of the *Mahdi* were a source of danger to Egypt, which would be increased if Khartoum fell, and that it now seemed impossible to hold that town.

To this communication Lord Granville replied that Her Majesty's Government could do nothing in the matter that would throw on them any responsibility for military operations in the Sudan.

This despatch from Downing Street was crossed by another from Cairo, telling his Lordship that the Egyptian Government, finding it impossible to hold the Sudan, had decided upon withdrawing their garrisons and falling back on Egypt proper.

It is not necessary here to refer to the discussions which then ensued between Sir Evelyn Baring and Cherif Pasha, and which ended in the Egyptian Government placing itself entirely in the hands of our government, with the suggestion that either Turkish troops should be employed to save the Eastern Sudan for Egypt, or that the whole country should be abandoned to the *sultan*. We come therefore to January 9, 1884, when Sir E. Baring telegraphed to Lord Granville that all doubts about the necessity for withdrawing from Khartoum were removed by the decided opinion of Colonel Coetlogon, late Governor of Khartoum, who recommended an immediate withdrawal from that town, and asserted that if it was ordered at once it could be safely effected.

It was then proposed that Abdel-Kader, minister of war, 'should proceed to the Sudan and superintend the withdrawal of its endangered garrisons, and Egyptian officials and their families.' He agreed to do so on condition that the intention of abandoning the country should not be openly avowed, for in his opinion any such avowal would prevent the success of his mission. Her Majesty's Government not acceding to this request, he declined the task, although General Gordon had already informed them that the moment it was known we had given up the game in the Sudan, everyone would go over to the *Mahdi*.

The name of General Gordon had, early in December 1883, been mentioned in connection with this hazardous undertaking, but Sir Evelyn Baring seems then to have assumed that he would not be acceptable to the Egyptian authorities on account of the movement in the Sudan being a religious one. If appointed to a high office there, he said it was feared the Mussulman tribes who were loyal to the government would go over to the *Mahdi*. It is difficult to ascertain whether this view was that of our able representative at the time or not, for, so far as experience goes, the incompleteness of the despatches published in the Blue Books often puzzles those who devote themselves to their perusal. Still, if General Gordon had then been asked to proceed to the Sudan, he could have reached Khartoum from Palestine, through Cairo, on January 1, 1884, and before the *Mahdi* had had time to take advantage of his defeat of Hicks's army.

When he left London for Khartoum on January 18, 1884, the whole Press of the country, while heartily recognising his mission as a step in the right direction, expressed a unanimous opinion that the late hour at which his mission had been undertaken endangered its success. It was hardly fair, therefore, for Sir E. Baring, in view of the difficulties against which General Gordon had to contend on his arrival at Khartoum, to say that the Press had altogether overestimated his personal influence and the prestige of his name in the Sudan. If his heroic mission was not entirely successful, it was not the man who was to blame, but this fatal delay in despatching him on it.

The instructions which General Gordon carried with him from London were to report to Her Majesty's Government on the military situation in the Sudan, and on measures for the security of the Egyptian garrisons still holding positions in that country, and for the safety of the European population in Khartoum, and further upon the best mode of evacuating the interior of the Sudan, and best securing the safety and administration by the Egyptian Government of the ports on the coast of the Red Sea.

On his arrival at Cairo the Egyptian Government gave full discretionary power to General Gordon to retain the troops then in the Sudan for such reasonable period as he might think necessary, *in order that the abandonment* of the country might be accomplished with the least possible risk to life and property.

Lord Granville, on recapitulating to Sir E. Baring on March 28, 1884,[1] the circumstances under which General Gordon was sent to Egypt, said that:

> Her Majesty's Government, bearing in mind the *exigencies of the occasion*, concurred in instructions *which virtually altered General Gordon's mission* from one of *advice* to that of *executing*, or at least *directing the evacuation* not only of Khartoum, but of the whole of the Sudan, and were willing that General Gordon should receive the very extended powers thus conferred upon him by the *khedive*, to enable him to execute his difficult task.

We have also at the same time this admission, that:

> In a matter involving such complexity and depending so much on local circumstances, it was to be expected that *General Gordon might be obliged to modify and alter his views on his arrival at Khartoum as to the details and even some of the material features of the course to be pursued in order to attain the main objects in view.* Her Majesty's Government have been anxious that in this respect he should have the largest discretion.

Lord Granville, while admitting that the circumstances with which General Gordon had to deal were no doubt difficult, and might change from day to day, thus attempts to qualify the responsibility of Her Majesty's Government towards him, by declaring that:

> It certainly was not in contemplation that the duties to be assigned to General Gordon should be of a nature which would require the despatch of a British expedition to support or extricate him.

Nor did General Gordon himself ask for any such aid or interference on his behalf when he undertook his hazardous mission. For example, when asked by the Government for advice about the Eastern Sudan, after Baker Pasha's defeat, he told them that they should do nothing beyond summoning the chiefs of the tribes to meet him at Khartoum, in order to arrange for the independence of the Sudan. The very day after they had (Feb. 13, 1884) received this communication from him, they gave orders for the despatch of General Graham's

---

1. See Blue Book, Egypt, 13 (1884), p. 5.

first expedition to Suakim, and thus, at the very outset, not only took an important part of the Sudan question out of his hands, but seriously added to the difficulties of his mission by taking from it its pacific character.

Immediately after his arrival at Khartoum, General Gordon informed Sir E. Baring that he found two-thirds of its people terrorised over by one-third; and that, in place of supporting the terrorised majority, 'our undisguised intention was to get the Egyptian *employés* out of the Sudan,' and asks him 'whether this partial evacuation of the Sudan fulfils your desires. *If it does'* he adds, '*then you must act* by Indian Moslem troops by *Wady-Halfa; and do so at once by sending troops there*'

Evidently reasoning from the state of feeling between the one-third terrorisers, and the two-thirds of the terrorised, and the influences from the *Mahdi*'s camp, he further says:—

> You must be aware that a conspiracy up here is more to be feared than any outward revolt.

On February 29 he sends this warning:—

> There is not much chance of improvement, and every chance of its getting worse, for we have nothing to rely upon.'

In March several telegraphic despatches from General Gordon disclose the increasingly dangerous position he then occupied at Khartoum. The rebels, by a daring march to the Nile, had interrupted his communications with Berber, cutting off eight hundred of his troops who were stationed at Halfaya. In one of these despatches, dated March 14, he says:

> Should we even succeed in getting the Shaggiehs from Halfaya, it will be about the utmost we can do beyond annoying the enemy by skirmishing. We can do nothing against the superiority of numbers. Happily you have three steamers at Berber to help any forward movement.

From this it is evident that General Gordon concluded that General Graham had been sent to co-operate with him by reopening his communications with Berber. Others of these despatches show that the mutiny of his soldiers, or the treachery of their officers, might at any moment deliver him and the brave companion of his enterprise, Colonel Stewart, into the hands of their cruel enemies.

Early in April Lord Granville was informed that the number of rebels surrounding Khartoum was increasing, that all the population south of Shendy had joined the revolt, and that the population north of Shendy were ready to do likewise. He was also further informed that the rebels were in communication with the Bishareen Arabs with a view to besieging Berber itself, and that its governor, Hassan Khalifa, had asked for reinforcements. Baring tells Lord Granville that unless these reinforcements are sent to him Berber will fall into the hands of the rebels, and *that this would seriously affect Gordon's position.*

In order to meet this crisis Mr. Egerton informed Lord Granville that, in the opinion of Nubar Pasha and our generals in Egypt, an Anglo-Egyptian force could be sent for the relief of the town, and that in the meanwhile its governor should be encouraged to hold out by the assurance that material British aid would, as soon as possible, be given to him. Instead, however, of acting upon this suggestion, his Lordship instructed Mr. Egerton to send messengers by Berber and Dongola, or by other routes, to General Gordon, asking him to keep Her Majesty's Government informed, to the best of his ability, as to the immediate danger to which Khartoum might be exposed, and informing him that, to be prepared for any such danger, he should advise them as to the amount and composition of the force that would be necessary, under the circumstances, to secure his removal, and as to the route by which it should approach Khartoum, and the time at which its despatch should be undertaken. He was further to be informed that it was not intended to supply him with Turkish or other forces for military expeditions, because these would be at variance with the pacific policy of his mission to the Sudan, and that if with this knowledge he continued at Khartoum 'the government wished him to state to us the cause and intention with which he so continues.'

With the full facts of General Gordon's perilous position staring them in the face, who could suppose that they would have sent such a message to him? No wonder he ridiculed it when it was received.[2] Had he not told them that he was hemmed in by determined men, and could not carry out his mission without some aid from the outside? Was it not clearly enough stated by him in some of the despatches we have quoted, that his way of escape had been closed by the relentless army of the pseudo *Mahdi*? There is sufficient evidence that they did so understand his position at the time this message was despatched to Gordon. Lord Granville, in a communication to Mr. Egerton on May 15, virtually admits they did understand him, for he

2. See Appendix A.

says in that communication:

> It is clear that General Gordon's object in asking for these troops (Turkish) is to effect the withdrawal of the Sudan garrisons by military expeditions, and to effect the collapse of the *Mahdi*.

He even admits that:

> His military operations in the vicinity of Khartoum may be taken to be for the defence of the place.

Why then call in question his good faith by asking from him a virtual pledge that the troops asked for by him will not be used for any other purpose save his withdrawal? Gordon seems to feel this keenly, as will be seen from an entry in his *Journal*.[3] Beneath this message there seems also to lurk the unworthy suspicion that because General Gordon holds certain powers from the *khedive* he will either directly or indirectly perpetuate the Egyptian sway over the Sudan. What other interpretation can be put on this statement in the communication to Mr. Egerton?

> Such a course would involve a reversal of the original policy of the government which was to detach the Sudan from Egypt.

Was ever a noble generous-hearted man so misunderstood as was General Gordon in this instance, or so badly treated? He might perish, and with him the thousands who cling around him as their only hope of escape from the consequences of the policy of the government whose representative he was—but that policy must be maintained.

The instructions about forwarding to Gordon the message referred to were despatched from London to Mr. Egerton on April 23.

On April 25, he informed Lord Granville that he had telegraphed its purport to General Gordon, sending one copy to Berber to be forwarded by messengers, and others to Suakim and Massowah. He also enclosed a copy of a telegram from Mr. Cuzzi, our consular agent at Berber, which stated that it was impossible to send letters or telegrams to General Gordon, as the last messenger sent had returned, saying that it was impossible to go or come to Khartoum with letters or telegrams, and adding, 'The situation is more desperate than ever.'

In no way discouraged by this serious information. Lord Granville continues to press our diplomatic agent at Cairo to renewed efforts to reach Gordon with this message. All efforts for his relief must be sus-

---

3. See Appendix B.

pended until his reply to its enquiries has been received. The knowledge already possessed as to Gordon's position is thus ignored, and Her Majesty's Government are not to be moved from their intentions by the information which is pouring in on them weekly, relative to the increased danger in which he is. Berber falls in June, and Dongola is threatened. The stream of refugees from Khartoum, which had been passing down the Nile since March 10, is practically stopped at the end of May. After a long interval a message comes from Gordon, dated June 22, which clearly indicates his expectation that a force has been sent to relieve him. This reaches Lord Granville on July 21, and on the 24th he issues instructions that this pet message of April 23, with an unimportant addition, should be repeated to General Gordon, if he had not already received it.

In this way, therefore, did Her Majesty's Government deal with the agent they had sent on a hazardous mission, and reply to the appeals made to them through the dangers which were gathering round him. Well might Gordon subsequently ask in a tone of sad remonstrance:

> Is it right that I should have been sent to Khartoum with only seven followers, after the destruction of Hicks's army, and no attention paid to me until communications were cut?

As the facts of Gordon's position became publicly known, the British Press with but few exceptions appreciated its danger, and urged the government to send an expedition for his rescue. Lord Wolseley had, as early as April 8, pressed them on the subject, and doubtless continued to do so until July 24, when he wrote to the Government that he thought no time should be lost in pushing up a small brigade of between three and four thousand British troops to Dongola. He believed that such a force would most probably settle the whole business, adding:

> But you must know time presses. I believe that such a force could be sent from England and reach Dongola about October 15 if the government be in earnest and act at once. Remember we cannot command things, but all the gold in England will not affect the rise and fall of the Nile or the duration of the hot and cold seasons in Egypt. Time is a most important element in this question, and indeed it will be an indelible disgrace if we allow the most generous, patriotic, and gallant of our public servants to die of want or fall into the hands of a cruel enemy because we would not hold out our hands to save him. Don-

gola can be reached without fighting, and our presence there in force might secure for us all the objects we wish to obtain.'

And then follows the eloquent and touching declaration:—

> At any rate I don't wish to share the responsibility of leaving Charley Gordon to his fate, and it is for this reason that I recommend immediate and active preparation for operations that may be forced upon us by-and-by.

The only member of the Cabinet who seems to have sympathised with this appeal was Lord Hartington, but his efforts with his colleagues seem only to have induced them to accept Lord Wolseley's proposition on conditions that virtually rendered it abortive, for the Cabinet were not then convinced that it would be impossible for General Gordon, acting on the instructions which he had received, to secure the withdrawal from Khartoum, either by the employment of force or by pacific means, of the Egyptian garrisons and of such of the inhabitants as may desire to leave.

His success seems to have been limited to inducing his colleagues to ask Parliament for a grant, in order to make preparations for an expedition to Khartoum, should the circumstances of General Gordon—when ascertained—make such a movement on his behalf necessary. All their efforts to obtain a reply from him to their messages of April 23 and May 17 having failed. Lord Hartington says that the opinion of her Majesty's Government then was:

> That the time has arrived when some further measure should be taken for obtaining accurate information as to his position and, if necessary, for rendering him assistance!

In a despatch[4] to General Stephenson of August 8—which is worth the attention of any of our readers who may not have perused it—Lord Hartington mentions to him that he has been advised by competent authorities that the transport of a force of moderate dimensions in small boats, such as those used in the Red River expedition, would not present insuperable difficulties. Therefore Her Majesty's Government have come to the conclusion:

> That the best mode in which they can place themselves in a position to undertake the relief of Gordon, should the necessity arise, would be by the provision of the means by which

---

4. See Parliamentary paper, Egypt, 35 (1884), pp. 14, 15.

such an expedition could be despatched to Dongola, and, as circumstances at the time may render expedient, to Berber or Khartoum.

Lord Hartington, after the above despatch was drafted, had received one through Lord Granville from Mr. Egerton, in which the latter says:

> It is clear that a very critical time has been reached, that the Nile will soon be high, and the time is short within which any river expedition is possible and it is imperative that it should take place at once or not at all.

Under these circumstances Mr. Egerton humbly submits to Lord Granville that English troops should be moved beyond the Cataracts as a means of opening communications with Khartoum either directly or indirectly through irregulars.

Lord Hartington therefore in a telegraphic despatch to General Stephenson, referring to the small-boat plan under consideration, asks him, as he gathers from this despatch from Mr. Egerton that he is prepared to move English troops beyond Wady-Halfa, what he could do in that direction with the force and resources now at his disposal. On August 11, General Stephenson replies as follows:—

> Yours of 7th. Can move to Wady-Halfa 4 battalions, 2,200 bayonets; 2 squadrons, 200 sabres; 1 battery horse or field artillery, 2 batteries mountain, mounted infantry. Small boats proposed not suitable. Can procure large amount water transport locally.

In reply to this communication Lord Hartington informs General Stephenson that, in framing plans for the movement of troops south of Wady-Halfa, the possibility of being obliged to advance as far as Khartoum itself should be included, and form a necessary part of such plans; and that to provide only for moving a single brigade of troops to Dongola would be to ignore the one great object of the proposed expedition. Exception is also taken to another part of General Stephenson's proposition, namely, that it would not be possible for a suitable force to reach Khartoum by water and return to Egypt before the end of the approaching winter if the steamers and native boats now at the disposal of the General were alone to be used; and therefore Lord Hartington says that orders have been given to provide 400 small boats, which it is hoped may be in the water by November 1.

Our experiences in March, April, and June 1885, fully justify Lord

Hartington's fears, for owing to the low water in the Nile great difficulties were then experienced, even in the use of the whalers; and the use of *nuggers* had to be entirely abandoned from the same cause between several points above the fourth cataract. But there can be no justification for delaying the despatch of the expedition on the grounds Lord Hartington mentions, until the small boats decided upon for its transport were ready. Troops could have been sent up on the native craft at high Nile at any rate as far as Korti, and if necessary the small boats could have been used later on for their return to Egypt.

The feasibility of General Stephenson's proposed plan of moving troops to Dongola by the native craft available at the time could not be denied even by Lord Hartington or his advisers. It was fully proved in the following instance.

The 1st Royal Sussex Regiment, which had been sent on from Assouan to Wady-Halfa about the middle of August, arrived there on the 26th of that month, arid were ordered on September 3 to proceed to Dongola and hold it. The regiment went by rail to Sarras, where the leading half battalion, under Colonel Vandeleur, embarked on *nuggars*, sailed thence on the 6th, and arrived at Dongola on the 19th. This journey of 210 miles, which took the troops in the whalers nearly five weeks to perform, was thus accomplished in thirteen days. The second half battalion, under Colonel Tolson, went up the river in the same manner, but took a few days longer owing to breakdowns and unfavourable winds.

Acting under instructions from Lord Hartington, General Stephenson early in the summer secured a large fleet of native boats for use between Assiout and Wady-Halfa, as well as twenty steamers, and a number of *nuggers* to be used on the reaches of open water between the second and third cataracts. He was also ordered to forward commissariat and other stores to Hannek. Unfortunately as the Nile fell these reaches became unnavigable, and consequently the *nuggars* on them were rendered useless. As I rode up the river in December I noticed a number of their wrecks lying high and dry on its rocky shores. Despite these difficulties Sir Evelyn Wood succeeded in getting up three months' food supply for the *Royal Sussex*, and by the middle of July had accumulated 42,000 rations at Hannek and a much larger quantity before the whalers started up the river in November.

All these efforts were, however, brought to a comparative standstill by an order from Lord Hartington on August 22, 1886, to the effect that no more troops were to be sent beyond Wady-Halfa, and:

That having regard to the plan adopted of using boats propelled by their own crews above the Cataracts, it was considered of first and chief importance that the river transport between Assiout and the second cataract should be maintained in a condition of complete efficiency.[5]

No one can read the correspondence to which we have above referred, without excusing Her Majesty's Government for much of the delay which occurred subsequent to August 8 in the despatch of the expedition to Khartoum, for which they had obtained a parliamentary grant. The advice they had received from naval and military authorities was most conflicting, and often they must have been sorely puzzled by it The Cabinet, however, appear to have acted on the counsel of those whose views harmonised with their own cherished policy, of only interfering in the Sudan in so far as the disorder there might affect the peace of Egypt. It was partly on this ground that it rejected General Stephenson's proposition to send the expedition to relieve Khartoum by Suakim and Berber.[6]

It is not our intention to discuss here the question as to the advantages or otherwise of this route over that of the Nile. We only desire to call attention to the fact that its proposition, when it was evident Her Majesty's Government had adopted that by the Nile, was inopportune, and because it seriously delayed the despatch of the expedition by the latter route, as the correspondence on the subject between Lord Hartington and General Stephenson shows.

It is important to notice in this connection that in the opinion of Colonel Kitchener a force half the size of that sent up the Cataracts would have been quite sufficient to accomplish the objects of the expedition. Referring to five short letters from General Gordon, received by him on August 28, he says (Sept. 2, 1884) that there can be no doubt from them but that General Gordon can hold out until the middle of November.

> I do not think, that a large expedition would be necessary from here to Khartoum. A flying column, composed of strong force of cavalry and artillery, and some infantry on camels and on foot—altogether about 4,000—could, I believe, relieve Khartoum in less time than the time required by the road from here,

---

5. Blue Book, Egypt, 35 (1884), p. 58; also p. 46, No. 37.
6. See Egypt, 35 (1884), pp. 14, 16, 32, 34, 36; compare No. 54, p. 45, with No. 66, p. 53, and No. 73, p. 58.

(*i.e.* from Abu-Gus). Gunboats can easily take Berber with small force, as it is quite open to the river, and they have no cannon. Probably *mudir's* force will do for this. If Gordon knows expedition coming, he will hold out, never fear, and co-operate. My opinion is decidedly, send up your troops; there is no difficulty, and one good fight close to Khartoum will see the matter through.[7]

Now this was the opportune advice of an intelligent and energetic officer, well acquainted with the country and the people, and who therefore was in a better position than our military authorities either at Cairo or in London to give an authoritative opinion on the subject. And there was everything in favour of the success of his proposal at the time.

The deserted Mudir of Dongola had by his own energy saved the province for us by the punishment he had inflicted on the enemy at Debbeh in June. There was, in fact, no force of rebels between us and Khartoum then, that could have offered any serious resistance to a disciplined force, and camels could have easily been obtained in sufficient numbers for transport. But he was not listened to, the die was cast, and the relief expedition which Lord Wolseley had first urged upon the government in April, and subsequently in July, was now so planned that it could not move for the relief of General Gordon, whatever might be his danger, until early in November.

Although no time was lost in despatching the troops from England which were selected to take part in the proposed expedition, and in collecting and forwarding to Egypt all the necessary supplies for it, it was only on October 8 that Lord Wolseley received his instructions officially, or a month after his arrival at Cairo. Even on September 17, when he received a reply to his demand for the formation of the Camel Corps, he was informed that, although Her Majesty's Government had agreed to his request, no decision had yet been arrived at by them to send any portion of the force under his command beyond Dongola. They, however, recognised the fact that to put him in a position effectually to undertake such a military operation would probably tend more than anything else to render such an operation unnecessary!

How such a hope could have been entertained in view of all the circumstances of the case it is difficult to understand, for Gordon was

---

7. Blue Book, Egypt, 35 (1884), No. 104, p. 73.

then known to be hemmed in at Khartoum by determined men. Dongola was at too great a distance from Khartoum for the *Mahdi* to be frightened by any such military demonstration there as was proposed. Had it taken place before his troops had invested Khartoum—as Gordon had suggested—there would have been some hope of its success, but now such a result could not be anticipated. This delusive hope threw a damper over the expedition from its inception, and largely contributed to its failure.

In review of the whole circumstances of the case, one wonders at Lord Wolseley consenting, under such a restriction as has been mentioned, to undertake the command of the expedition. If report be true, he did so under protest, throwing the whole responsibility of failure—if it did come—on the government. His anxiety for his friend, 'Charley Gordon,' made him doubtless anxious to avail himself of any opportunity the government could be induced to afford him, to rescue him from the endangered position in which he was convinced he was now placed. From this standpoint how eloquently sad was that part of his address to the troops of the desert column as he reviewed them at Korti after their return:

> It was not your fault that Gordon has perished and Khartoum has fallen.'

Upon whom the blame of failure rests no one can doubt after a careful perusal of the case of the government presented by itself in the Blue Books and parliamentary papers referring to the Sudan and to the Nile expedition. That the latter—despite the difficulties and obstacles primarily placed in the way of its success by those who were responsible for its despatch, as well as others which, as in all mere human efforts, attended its execution—nearly succeeded in its objects, is to be attributed to the skill and indomitable perseverance of its chief and the heroic efforts of the force under his command, to which, with feelings of national pride, we now proceed to call attention in the following pages.

Chapter 2

Delayed Departure for Egypt

There seemed therefore so much uncertainty in London, even up till the end of September, as to the despatch of any expedition at all to Khartoum, that my departure for Lord Wolseley's headquarters was delayed until October 1. It was even supposed that starting then I should be ahead in point of time, and therefore I took matters easily, deciding to go all the way to Egypt by sea. On the date mentioned I sailed from Tilbury Docks in the good ship *Lusitania*, Captain Nixon, of the Orient Line.

This was to me an interesting coincidence, for the last time I had been on board of this steamer was on the afternoon on which she left Alexandria in September 1882 with the Cameron Highlanders for the Suez Canal. She was now, however, bound on a more peaceful mission, for her cabins were not filled as then with men of war off to the fray, but with gentler civilians for the most part returning to their happy homes at the Antipodes or going to push their fortunes there.

Every state-room was full, and when we ran into hot weather, sleeping below became so uncomfortable that many adjourned for the night to the quarter-deck. The table was, as usual on vessels of this admirably managed line, excellent, and the company on the whole agreeable. Nothing particular occurred during the voyage except crossing the Bay of Biscay in smooth water, witnessing the total eclipse of the moon the second evening out from Plymouth, and getting a sight of the rare conjunction of Jupiter and Venus in the early morning.

On the thirteenth day after leaving the Thames we arrived at Port Said, where a delay of a day occurred in shipping cargo and taking in coals. Another day was lost at Kantara, where our progress was stopped by a block on the canal through a steamer grounding ahead of us. Ismailia was reached too late for the train to Cairo on the day of arrival, so altogether the journey from London to the Egyptian capital occupied seventeen days. So far it had been a pleasant sail, but now the hard work involved in my mission would have to be undertaken. In preparing for the second part of my journey, more vexatious delays had to be encountered.

First there was my license as war correspondent to be obtained from the proper military authorities. As Lord Wolseley's headquarters were now at Wady-Halfa, Colonel Swaine as military secretary had to be communicated with on the subject by telegraph; owing to pressure of business over the wires at the moment, some delay ensued. Then the press syndicate, whose correspondent I was, seemed to be unknown up the Nile, for Colonel Swaine sent the following amusing telegram to Colonel Ardagh, the commandant at the base, through whom my application had been made:—

Your 149 never heard of newspaper. Where is it published?

The name of the newspapers forming the syndicate had then to be wired to Wady-Halfa, and five days elapsed before authority was received to supply me with the important document.

The 'Declaration drawn up by the War Office for press correspondents' had to be signed before licenses were issued to them. Upon the whole the rules of conduct it imposed were not unreasonably stringent, but they appeared to me at the time unnecessarily so when the nature of the expedition was considered. At any rate they indicated a respect for the power of the pen by those who wielded that of the sword. Both might be mischievous if not properly used, and hence these stringent regulations might be looked upon as being rather of a preventive character than as an attempt to interfere unduly with the discharge of our important duties.

That the duties which a war correspondent is called upon to discharge are weighty, will appear from a consideration of the following reasons:—

The commander-in-chief of an army in the field assuredly occupies an all-important position, but he only does so in the execution of a duty assigned to him by public opinion, acting through the government of the day. The newspaper correspondent, however, stands alongside of him as the living representative of that public opinion. He is in fact the virtual ambassador of a power stronger than any Government, and one which retains its strength while government after government decays and falls.

The preference, however, given by the War Office for military men, even such of them as have retired from the service, cannot from this point of view be accepted as sound—that is, in the public interest. Far less should officers on duty with an expeditionary force be employed in such a service; for upon such correspondents, however honourably disposed they may be, the public cannot rely for an absolutely independent or impartial account of the events of a campaign.

On the other hand it is of equally great importance that a non-military correspondent should have such a knowledge of military matters as would enable him to understand, and also to describe accurately, the movements of an army in the field. If not, he may so err as to do injustice to the men who for queen and country are risking their lives—or often even seriously mislead public opinion. It was no doubt in view of the danger of such men being employed as war correspondents that this preference for military men was expressed in these regulations for representatives of the press.

In passing I may remark that personally I had but little reason to complain of the manner in which these regulations were enforced. Colonel Swaine and subsequently Colonel Grove were in fact the most amiable and considerate of press censors, being always ready to give us information and interfering very little if at all with the way in which our telegrams were written.

The detention of our telegrams, however, until after those of the commander-in-chief were despatched, was naturally unpleasant. Of course, the line was a military one, and Lord Wolseley had therefore undoubtedly right of way over it. On the other hand, we had this satisfaction, that on all important matters the British public would suspend its judgment until the despatches of the generals of the Fourth Estate had been received.

The licenses of the correspondents did not authorise their transport in the boats of the expedition, not even if room could be found in any of them for an extra passenger. Several of my colleagues, who had preceded me up the river, complained of this in very strong terms. Mr. Cameron in one of his letters to the *Standard*, dated Wady-Halfa, November 3, thus wrote about this prohibition:—

> I had hoped myself to have gone on with the Nassif-el-Khier to Merawi, and although her commandant kindly offered me a passage, Colonel Sir Herbert Stewart at Dongola was obliged to enforce the order which forbids English journalists, whether

there is room for them or not, to put foot on any of the vessels belonging to their country now navigating the Nile. The Mudir of Dongola, an Egyptian clerk, or an officer's native servant might be allowed a passage, but the representative of an English newspaper on no account whatever. As matters stand, should an unfortunate correspondent be chased to the bank by a crowd of howling Arabs, the officer in command of any Government craft, if he did his duty, would be obliged to refuse him refuge, saying civilly, no doubt, but firmly, 'No correspondents allowed on Government boats.' We are thus, in a manner, branded officially as outcasts, although we come neither asking nor receiving medals or honours, but seeking simply, while willing to share the dangers and hardships of the troops, to do our duty.'

When correspondents had provided themselves with transport animals, some consideration should certainly have been shown to them in the matter of fodder. How could they be expected to secure an adequate supply, accompanying an army through what was virtually an enemy's country, except by being privileged to draw it with their other rations? But this privilege was not accorded, and in my own case it delayed me several days in my journey from Wady-Halfa to Dongola. On my return from El Gubat to Korti in February, when I reached Jakdul I had not sufficient provender left to take my camels back to the Nile, and there I should have stuck fast, had I not been, like my colleagues, a man of expedients.

Having secured my license, the next matter requiring attention was the engagement of suitable servants. In accomplishing this, I experienced great difficulty—not lacking, however, in the ludicrous. I was not bound on a pleasure excursion up the Nile, else I could have readily obtained what I needed. Then the demand for interpreters by the military authorities was so urgent, and the prices they offered were so high, as not only to drain but also to 'bull' the market. Every Arab who had ever been employed as a servant, and had a smattering of English, demanded fifteen pounds a month, whereas in other times a third of the amount would perhaps be all he could get. Still, servants I must have, and in pursuit of them these are the things that happened to me.

First an Arab swell came along, highly recommended by himself, of course, and specially on the ground of having been Mr. O'Kelly's servant. As he would not promise to go further with me than Dongola,

I had to decline his offer. Then another turned up bearing the name of Hassan, a cognomen as common among Arabs as Smith is amongst us. Oh, he could cook and would go anywhere with me. The recommendation upon which he relied most was his having been with Mr. Dixon when he shipped Cleopatra's Needle from Alexandria. I demurred to qualifications based upon such grounds, as shipping this celebrated obelisk and going after Gordon to Khartoum were essentially different, and so he eventually found out.

Nevertheless, he consented to go with me, and an appointment was made for next day to sign the usual contract. When he came I traced disaster in his face, for the brightness of his eyes had gone. There had been trouble at home; his wife and friends protested against his risking his life in the Sudan. In fact the Cairo Arabs were deeply imbued at the time with the notion that the *Mahdi* was sure to win, and that our expedition would share the fate of Hicks Pasha's army. So I had to give this Hassan up, and soon a namesake came along, but this time a Syrian Arab. I resolved to begin right with him at once, and my first question was: 'Are you afraid of being shot?' He declared he was not, but, as events showed, he was not able to maintain the courage of this opinion about himself. For two days we negotiated. At 5 p.m. on the second day he called and said that his wife also would not hear of his going to the Sudan.

I was in despair. On the morrow I had either to leave for Assiout or lose four more days waiting for the next steamer. So I decided to go on alone, trusting that somewhere up the river I might be able to pick up suitable attendants.

Half an hour later an elderly man wearing a *fez* accosted me in the street and offered his services for the expedition, producing excellent testimonials from several of our consuls. He was a British subject, and a Christian, and assured me that he was not afraid of being shot, for he had been through the Crimean war and the Abyssinian expedition. These last qualifications rather told against him so far as age went, yet he looked hale and hearty, and from a remark he dropped, it occurred to me that he thought he was quite as able to stand the fatigues of the expedition as I was, so far as age went However I engaged him, and after paying the usual half-month's salary in advance, as a precautionary measure I made him promise to sleep that night at Shepherd's. He turned up after dinner, but begged off until next morning, in order to complete his wardrobe for the trip, and said with amusing earnestness: 'Tank God, sir, that you got me to take care of you and not the—Arabs!' I believe the old fellow meant well, but as it turned out I was more bothered than enough taking care of him. My experience on this and on other journeys in the East agrees with that of Gordon, namely, 'that in these lands you are yourself your only reliable servant'

Michael turned up all right, and with bag and baggage piled into two carriages we reached the Boulac Railway station in time for the 8.30 a.m. train.

The distance to Assiout was 229 miles, which was accomplished after eleven hours' weary travelling.

A commissariat officer and a captain of one of the regiments up the river, now attached to this important department, were my companions.

The carriage in which we rode was a 'veteran,' full of cracks and crevices, through which the fine pulverised soil over which the road passes poured in upon us. At many of the stations at which the train stopped, we found railway servants standing ready with feather dusters to give us a 'brush up.' Before our arrival at Assiout my companions, like myself, were of a yellowish-drab hue.

It was quite dark when the train ran into the station at Assiout, which we found crowded with natives and only lighted by the lanterns carried by the railway officials. How to get through this crowd safely with a lot of baggage and down to the steamer landing a quarter of a mile off was a puzzling question. Happily through the kind courtesy of the late Hon. Colonel Primrose, commandant of the station, a fatigue party, in charge of Lieut. Lindsay of the Cameron Highlanders, took charge of our baggage, loaded it on camels, and despatched it to the steamer, where subsequently I found it and my old man all right.

After being thus relieved of our impedimenta, we adjourned to an hotel adjacent to the station for dinner. The table was nearly full with officers and civilians connected with the expedition. The stores brought up by rail from Cairo and Alexandria as well as the Nile boats or whalers were here shipped for Assouan, and a detachment of the Cameron Highlanders occupied the station.

As the steamer sailed at 1 a.m., we went on board at ten o'clock, escorted by Captain Baker, R.N., who led us down in the thick darkness through devious paths by the aid of lanterns carried by himself and several of the officers with whom we had dined.

The state-rooms of the *Fiod* were below, and all but the one at the stern were very stuffy. Captain D—— and I took possession of the latter, which being open from side to side of the steamer was well supplied both with air and light. At 1 a.m. on October 24, she left Assiout for Assouan—330 miles up the Nile.

The *Fiod*, doing her best, could only score four miles an hour against the current. Her allotted time for making the trip to Assouan was five days, running only by daylight. On the St. Lawrence she would not have been considered good enough for even a tow-boat; but here she ran regularly with the Khedivial mails.

The cabin fare from Assiout to Assouan was 5*l.*, meals being extra. These were served in the saloon on deck, and were a most creditable specimen of Cook's catering for his Nile passengers. In fact they were quite equal to and in some things better than anything served up at Shepherd's. The charges, and specially for wines, were reasonably moderate.

Slowly steaming against the current we tied up to the shore every evening, first at Giirgeh and then at Keneh, but as the steamer got under way before daylight, saw nothing of them. At Edfu, however, where we arrived in the morning and remained several hours, we had an opportunity of revisiting its temple; but as Egyptian antiquities bore no part in the expedition we must refer the reader to the accurate and graphic description of it given in Murray. A more interesting object to us now was therefore Captain Beach mounted on a camel and engaged in purchasing others. He had secured over a thousand at prices varying from eleven to twenty napoleons each. The camels for which he paid the higher figure were designated dromedaries, but only I presume out of courtesy, for they were after all only better camels of the ordinary kind. As purchased they were forwarded overland in convoys to Assouan.

As we proceeded up the river, signs of the advance of the expedition became more and more frequent. All the *dahabiyehs* and Nile-boats met bore the contractors' red signal. With their tall masts and winglike sails they gave a life to this part of the Nile it had never before possessed.

On the second day out from Assiout, we passed a large steamer towing barges conveying our *kroomen* auxiliaries. Fine stalwart-looking fellows they were, jet black, some clad in blue naval suits, and others stark naked enjoying a bath. In passing we gave them a hearty cheer and received as hearty a one in reply.

The Canadian contingent, comprising 370 voyageurs, had preceded us, and had arrived at the foot of the second cataract on October

26. A number of camel-drivers from Aden had also passed up the river some days previously. We tied up to the shore for the last time at Kom Ombo, some twelve miles below our destination, passing Silsilis an hour or so before sunset.

As we approached Assouan the realities, if I may so speak, of the advance of the expedition up the river were visible on all sides, until at length we came in sight of the long line of white tents under the palms along the right bank of the Nile below Assouan, marking the camps of our gathering hosts. Soon followed the inspiriting sound of British bugles where British bugles had never been heard before.

Chapter 3

Off at Last

The steamer landed me at Assouan on the morning of October 29, six days after I had left Cairo. Civilisation and its comforts were for a time now to be abandoned. There were no lodgings or apartments to be let hereabouts, and no Shepherd's hotel, nor any other hostelry opening its doors to the homeless traveller. He had snail-like to carry his house with him. Therefore, until I could find a place whereon to pitch my tent, I was thankful to the Coptic purser of the *Fiod* for permission to make the steamer my home.

During the day, however, I received an invitation from M. Dervieu, who had been my fellow-passenger from Esneh, to make use of his *dahabiyeh* during my sojourn. This gentleman, an Alexandrian merchant, held large contracts with the Commissariat Department for the supply of fresh meat and vegetables to the troops, and also fodder for the camels. The authorities spoke highly of the liberal and prompt manner in which these contracts were being fulfilled. His kind hospitality at this moment of transition from home to camp life will never be forgotten.

Perhaps nowhere else in Egypt is such a motley population to be found as at Assouan, in its mixture of Ababdeh and Bishareéh, Bedouins, Nubians, and negroes of all sorts, Fellaheen, Turks, Greeks, and a few Copts, to which now were added English, Irish, and Scotch soldiers.

The territory of the Ababdeh and Bishareéh extends from Kosseir to Suakim between the Nile and the Red Sea. Ethnologically the latter were as brown as roasted coffee. Although generally small of stature and slender in figure, they were symmetrical in form. The thickness and length of their hair, which covered the head like a brush, and hung in thick plaits down over the back of their necks, gave them a wild and savage appearance. The short and pointed knife each wore strapped on his left arm above the elbow always made me nervous of too close a contact with these barbarians.

The friendship of these tribes had been most sedulously cultivated by our authorities, as their enmity would have seriously endangered our long line of communications. During my stay at Assouan considerable anxiety was caused by the large quantities of grain purchased by these tribes in the grain bazaar. This was construed into a preparation for an attack upon us. The suspicion proved groundless, for, despite all the efforts of Osman Digna or the *Mahdi* to win them over, they remained faithful to the last.

The railway which had been constructed some years ago round the first cataract proved of great service in the transport of stores and troops from Assouan to Philae. This northern terminus was near the shore where all the boats bringing up commissariat and other stores from below were moored. These were landed and piled in sorted heaps ready for shipment by the railway to Shellal, as Philae was colloquially called, thence to be transported by sail-boats or by steamers to Wady-Halfa. Crowds of native labourers, superintended by commissariat officials, were engaged in this work. Amongst the piles figured conspicuously the Nile-boat stores, as they were all plainly labelled. These were not, as the designation might lead one to think, stores merely for the voyage up the river in the whalers, but rations for a hundred days for Camel Corps and all. The cargo of each boat comprised no less than 88 packages of a gross weight of nearly 4,000 lbs., of which 991 lbs. was preserved meat, and 1,001 lbs. of biscuits, tea, sugar, bacon, jam, lime-juice, and preserved vegetables. In fact, never was there an army more liberally and thoughtfully supplied than the force sent up the Nile in this expedition.

The proposed daily ration was as follows: preserved corned beef 1 lb. four days out of six; bacon or boiled mutton 1 lb. one day out of six; biscuit 1 lb. five days out of six; flour 1 lb. one day out of six; tea 1 ounce; sugar 3 ounces, and the other articles, such as pickles, pepper, salt, &c., in due proportion. This distribution was varied occasionally in its minor details. For example, at all the stations on the river and at the permanent camps, fresh instead of preserved meat was supplied, and fresh bread in place of biscuit

Although these stores had to be discharged from the boats on their way up the river, and carried on camels over more than one portage in order to be reloaded, they arrived at their destination in a fair condition. The tea had, however, been very carelessly packed in tin cases and not hermetically sealed, consequently some of it was badly damaged by water. A quantity of the sugar suffered in like manner, and a small percentage of the biscuits was landed in bad condition. The most lamentable thing, however, was the purloining of these stores. This must be partly attributed to the natives engaged in their transport, but painful reports were current that the men of some of the line regiments were not innocent of the charge.

Each boat was supplied with a most effectual water-filter. The cylindrical baskets in which they were kept looked so nice and cosy as they stood piled up in rows, that an officer asked what they were; 'Oh they are *tiffin* baskets for every boat,' was the answer of the waggish officer in charge. The story was believed, and being repeated went the round of the camp at Assouan, much to the amusement of the initiated.

As already stated, the camp was below the town, and along the bank of the river under a grove of palms. The cultivated land it covered was rented from the occupiers, and so little were the inhabitants interfered with, that a weekly subsidy was actually paid to the owners of a water-wheel by the messes of two regiments quartered near it, in order to get rid of its horrid noise at night.

Through the entire length of the camp ran a branch of the Shellal railway, which was of great service in transporting men and supplies to Philae, the point of departure for boats and *nuggars* for Wady-Halfa. The road from the town to the camp was hot and dusty, and was generally traversed on donkeys by the natives, who, at certain hours of the day, mingled with our soldiers riding to and fro on camels.

For the general convenience, the locality of each department and corps in the camp had been marked by sign-boards on the side bordering on the road leading from the town. Strolling along, the first of these that I noticed was 'Rest Camp,' and upon enquiry it was facetiously explained that it was a synonym for 'Casual Ward,' and seriously that quarters were provided here for those not attached to any of the corps then encamped, or while on their way to duty up the river, or *en route* to their regiments, and for officers until otherwise quartered. Then followed the Royal Engineers, the Egyptian Cavalry Regiment, which was subsequently dismounted in order to supply the 19th Hussars with horses. Then came the Guards' Camel Regiment which had been fifteen days on its way from Assiout, then the Cornwall Regiment, the 38th, and at the extremity the Black Watch, isolated for some time on account of smallpox.

The Transport Department had its headquarters near the 'Rest Camp,' and from sunrise to sunset Colonel Furse, whose services to the expedition in the Transport Department were most valuable, was engaged with his subordinates in purchasing camels, branding them with a broad arrow and a number, and in ferrying them across the river to be sent on to Wady-Halfa. The headquarters of the Commissariat Department were in the town, near the steamboat landing. This place, as may be imagined, was the centre of great activity from daylight till dark. The officer in charge, Captain Rogers, had also to deal with the heaps of stores accumulated round the station waiting to be forwarded up the river.

Here and in all the other departments everyone worked as if the whole success of the expedition depended upon his individual exertions.

No one who has never come in contact with the officers and non-commissioned officers of Her Majesty's troops when on active service can have any conception of the hard and often responsible work they have to perform. Their adaptability seems almost unlimited. We all know how well they can fight when called upon to do so; but here they were actually employed in work which required either business capacity or technical knowledge, and they went at it as if they had been used to it all their lives. One general, speaking to me of one of the commandants, said:

> I never met such a man as he is for reports and statements and accounts. If ever I start a bank, I will try and engage him as manager.

The facility also with which all seemed to accommodate themselves to the discomforts of camp life showed that our officers were not mere carpet-knights, but soldiers. At Assouan the change from club to home life was not so great as to be very uncomfortable, as chairs, tables, and a fair menu were then available. But when the force began to move up the river, many of these modern conveniences and comforts had to be given up for rougher fare and accommodation. In place of tables we had boxes of stores, and so uncomfortably piled that no one could say of his guest that he had his legs under his mahogany. With the exception of the commander-in-chief's and one or two other messes, an invitation to dine was always accompanied with: 'Don't forget to bring your plate, cup and spoon, and cutlery.' Still, even then, great as was the contrast between camp and club life, things went merrily as ever at meal-time.

Although the camp at Assouan was picturesquely situated, it was unfortunately very unhealthy. This was, in great measure, consequent upon its having been pitched on cultivated soil near the river—a position which in all warm climates is carefully avoided on account of its unhealthiness. Then its water supply was polluted by the sewage from the Egyptian Fort 300 yards above it, and the filth thrown into the river by the natives of the town. To these causes, and to the forced inactivity of the troops, must be traced the prevalence of enteric fever and dysentery amongst them during their detention here, and from which they subsequently suffered so much up the Nile.

All this, to a very large extent, might have been avoided if proper care had been taken by the Medical Department, who, according to the principles of common sense, should certainly have a voice in the selection of camping ground for troops. I do not know whether it falls by regulation within the duty of that important branch of the service to supervise matters of this kind, but in many instances during our recent campaigns in Egypt no such supervision was exercised. For example, the camp at Ghezeereh, in 1882, was pitched on ground similar to that at Assouan, consequently there were many cases of enteric fever and dysentery.

Hearing of the prevalence of sickness in this camp, I visited it, and found to my astonishment that in this place, where the body, while lying on the ground, drew upwards the moisture from beneath its dry surface, waterproof sheets had not been served out to the troops. Lord Wolseley, a few days later when inspecting them, made a similar discovery, and had this mistake at once rectified. But why, may it not be asked, did not the surgeon-general find this out when the spread of disease was brought to his notice? Subsequently, when the mischief caused had become too apparent, a medical board sat in solemn conclave, and reported the camp at Ghezeereh as being in an unhealthy position. In justice, however, to the medical staff with us on this occasion, and its able chief Surgeon-General O'Nial, in the present case, these criticisms are meant to refer rather to the system than to the men.

Having noticed at Assouan a large proportion of old people amongst its population, in course of conversation with the '*Mammour*' I called attention to the circumstance. He attributed it to the great healthiness of the place, about which he became enthusiastic, backing up his statements by the following illustration.

He said that a man in one of the villages a few miles down the river had lived to be 135 years of age, and that, strange to say, his old teeth were being replaced by new ones, and his grey hair by black! So seriously was this related by the *Mammour*, as to lead one unacquainted with Eastern habits of story-telling to think he believed it. He certainly expected from his manner and tone that I should do so.

Bleeding and cauterising are extensively practised in the Sudan; the latter by the use of red-hot irons, chiefly applied to the back. The barber is the principal medical operator in bleeding, and on several occasions when passing through the bazaar I saw him at work on his victims. It was performed by cupping the back, the blood being drawn off into a glass vessel by a vacuum in it through the sucking of the operator. At Assouan and elsewhere up the Nile, many applications were made to us by suffering natives and their friends for medicines or advice. The cases of some of the sufferers were most painful to witness, and such as it was often impossible in our haste to relieve.

After some hard bargaining and two narrow escapes from being cheated, I succeeded in purchasing three camels in anticipation of a dash across the Bayuda desert to Khartoum. Intending to proceed by steamer I despatched them up the left bank of the river to Wady-Halfa, in charge of two of my men. Owing to the failure of the coal supply I was further detained for three days. On the morning of the third I was informed by the authorities that a steamer would be despatched in the afternoon from Shellal, and that I could have a passage in her. In order to be in time I was directed to leave Assouan by the 1.30 p.m. train. So piling my luggage, tent, and stores on camels kindly supplied me by the Transport Department for the purpose, with my old dragoman I hurriedly started for the station to catch this train.

It was, however, 3 p.m. before it started. On arrival at Shellal I found that the *Fayûm* could not possibly get away before sunrise on the morrow. This 'inevitable' had again to be faced, and so with two of the four officers who were to be my fellow passengers up the river, I decided to take up our quarters for the night on board of the steamer, spending what remained of daylight with them in visiting the celebrated ruined temple on the island of Philae, opposite where the *Fayûm* was moored.

Its present name Philae is a strange misnomer, for in Greek it was originally called **Φιλαί** and in Egyptian '*Pilak*' and '*Ma-n-lak*,' literally 'the place of the frontier.' Nowhere else did Egyptian architects carry out to the same extent their mania for irregularity in their lines and dimensions, and with such beautifully picturesque effects as in this temple dedicated to their god Isis. It had all the play of the light and shade of the Gothic, combined with the massiveness and grandeur of the Egyptian. The building is still fairly entire, and is considered the best specimen of the latter style in Egypt out of Thebes.

The impressions thus made on us by the ruins of the island of Philae, and produced by that outcome of modern art and civilisation, the *Fayûm*, were in painful contrast She was a paddle steamer of the earlier ages in which such vessels had been constructed, had oscillating engines, with boilers so weakened by long use that they could only bear a pressure of 18 lbs. to the square inch. Her decks between the paddle-boxes were heaped up with coals, over which one had to scramble to get aft from her shore gangway to the cabin. This was below, open from side to side, with a state room partitioned off at the stern. A bare wooden divan on both sides was the only furniture it contained.

On the quarter-deck there was a large plain deal table, which with a galley fire was all the accommodation provided on this Nile boat for cabin passengers. In fact, she was but a floating Eastern *khan*, for those who travelled by her had to provide themselves with bed and board. Happily we had come provided for such a contingency, both in servants and provisions.

One of my companions for the night was an officer of the Army Medical Department, of Hibernian descent, and six feet good in his stocking soles. He was the first to retire below to rest, but soon reappeared on deck in a great state of excitement, declaring that the cabin swarmed with mosquitoes, that they were the most vicious insects he had ever been stung by, for they had actually bitten him through his corduroy breeches! This was a dismal prospect. Some means must be adopted to get rid of the insects, else sleep would be out of the question. Smoking and mosquito-nets were therefore promptly called into requisition, and although the venomous gnats occasionally sung their war songs around us and made an occasional assault, tired nature soon rendered even the doctor clad in his corduroys callous to their assaults.

Daylight came, but still the steamer did not move, for her departure had been further delayed by the non-arrival of a detachment of blue-Jackets from Assouan, who were coming to lash together the twenty-four Nile boats she was to tow to Wady-Halfa. They were again expected by the 7.30 a.m. train, but did not arrive until 11 a.m., and consequently we did not get off until 1 p.m., or twenty-four hours after I had hurriedly left my comfortable quarters on M. Dervieu's *dahabiyeh*. But it was a time of war.

CHAPTER 4

A Surgeon's Adventures on Lower Nile

Besides the twenty-four whalers we took in tow a barge crowded with part of the 161 *kroomen* bound up the river with us under the command of Major Tyndal. Another detachment of 109 had started from Shellal the day before in charge of Major Smith. Twenty of these ebony auxiliaries were left at Assouan to aid in getting boats up the cataract there, and useful hardy fellows they were at such work. We had an illustration of this just before we started in the manner in which they brought up the whalers and made them fast to the *Fayûm*. The boats had been lashed together two abreast, with a tow line passed down six pairs and up the other six, both ends of which were intended to be fastened to the barge astern of us. They thus formed a squadron four abreast.

Awkward as such a string of boats must have been to manage in a strong current, the skill and agility of the *kroomen* enabled them to pilot it safely past the two steamers moored to the shore between ours and the place where the boats had been lashed together, and without either a bump or a scratch. And what was most surprising was the quiet and orderly manner in which this difficult operation was carried out.

Major Tyndal, who had gone from Tamaisu to the west coast of Africa to collect these men, gave us an interesting account of the manner in which this had been effected, and of his and Major Smith's early experiences with them.

Only 261 of the proposed 300 men could be obtained within the time given for the work. The President of the Republic of Liberia refused permission to recruit men in his territory, as the policy of the republic was opposed to warlike expeditions. Those secured for the expedition came from Sierra-Leone, Monrovia, Grand Bassa, Bereby, Half-Bereby, Taboo River, and Grand Taboo. The men were engaged for six months or longer, for boat service only, and were paid as follows:—head man, 2s, 6d. a day, second man, 2s., and privates 1s. per day.

When first engaged, saving a cloth round their loins, they were entirely naked. The day after the transport *Shelley* sailed, each man was supplied with a naval rigout of dark blue. Major Tyndal said that the men seemed as much at home in their civilised dress as if used to it all their lives. When their suits had been served out to them, they were most particular about having them properly marked. In their persons they were remarkably cleanly. Whether in putting on the garments of the white man they had become imbued with a desire to assume his colour, this deponent saith not. But if this could be accomplished by washing, they stood a chance of success, for I never went forward amongst them without finding two or three stark naked lathering themselves from head to foot with soap.

The names by which they were known to their officers were very amusing. They had to sign an agreement, and each man had of course to be entered on the pay list. Their native cognomens were, Major Tyndal told me, almost unpronounceable by Europeans. He called several of them aft in order to give us an illustration of this. One said he was called something that sounded like 'Oolah,' and another like 'Wadeh,' and others like 'Kakaua,' 'Biva,' and 'Dabwa.' Most of them on signing had therefore adopted or invented other names, or retained those given to them by the sailors of the vessels trading on their coast.

Looking over the pay list, I found the following:—Tom Teapot, Peter Jim, George, Jack Everyday, Jack Ropeyarn, Peasoup, Tom Twoglass, Sea Breeze, Bottle Beer, Ginger Beer, Go Ashore, Jack Neverfear, Flying Jib, Jack Upside Down, Smart all Day, Black Man's Trouble, Spyglass Jack, and Bag of Rice. One had been named John Bright, but certainly not from any resemblance to the original, and another was named John Wesley.

They had a prince amongst them, a son of the king of Grand Bereby, who bore the name of Bob Ridley. Both their royalties signed the articles with a cross.

After the men were clothed. Major Tyndal said they endeavoured to drill them into something like order, and considering that they had been together but a fortnight, their success was marvellous. One of the difficulties encountered in the drill was teaching them how to distinguish right from left. It was overcome by substantially adopting the plan under similar conditions of the Irish drill sergeant in his 'hay foot,' 'straw-foot' marking of the 'sinister' and 'dexter' extremities of his recruits. In the case of the *kroomen* it was 'smallpox arm' for left, as they had been vaccinated in it, and 'slash arm' for the right, the one by which they used their knives.

Two days before we reached Wady-Halfa, some of the men showed signs of impatience at the length of the journey up the Nile. They had evidently become homesick, and with the others sought consolation from Dr. Bell, R.N., who had come up with them from Assiout, and whose kindly disposition had won their confidence. He had always a smile on his face when amongst them, and a kind word for all. 'Doctor,' they said, 'know ebberyting.' Then they would ask: 'Doctor, how long me go that place?' meaning Wady-Halfa, and then 'When catch that feller?' meaning the *Mahdi*; 'When shove him off; how long stay there?'

The doctor held an hospital *levée* every morning, as a few of the men were suffering from bruises, colds, and other ailments. The first head man was always master of the ceremonies on these occasions. 'Peasoup' and 'Teapot' were among the patients, and it excited some merriment as he called out: 'Hallo! Peasoup, hurry up;' 'Here, Tom Teapot, come along.' The description of their ailments, too, was both characteristic and amusing, but often coarse.

When we tied up to the shore at sunset, the barge of the *kroomen* was cast off and moored to the bank astern of us. After supper they became very lively, laughing, chatting, and winding up for the day with a genuine African sing-song. Their songs were rather monotonous, although not altogether unmusical. The chorus, in which all seemed to join, was lively enough, however, and sounded not unlike the Y'heave ho! of our own sailors.

Some of those on board of the steamer slept on top of the paddle-boxes and of the cabins adjacent. While quietly chatting after dinner one evening, by the light of lanterns—as it was pitch dark—we were startled by the cry of 'A man overboard!' One of the *kroomen* had rolled off his elevated bed into the river between the steamer and the shore, and as quickly tumbled himself out again upon dry land. The major called him aft and administered a glass of grog as a precautionary antidote. Then to our amusement came another cry out of the adjacent darkness: 'Do that again, and you'll get another glass!' There was no mistake as to the quarter from which this suggestion came; and we soon recognised it as having been made by a Tommy Atkins.

Our progress was so slow that it took us from Friday at 1.30 p.m. until 9 a.m. on the following Thursday to reach Wady-Halfa—a distance of 210 miles. Our running time, after deducting the ten hours and a half we tied up every night, was 129 hours, and our speed therefore averaged less than two miles an hour!

Had the steamer and barge been provided with sails, we might have saved a couple of days by taking advantage of the strong north wind, which was then wafting a fleet of sailing craft to our common destination.

A large amount of transport was carried on by the latter, which, aided by their enormous sails and the fresh breeze, sailed up stream at the rate of six miles an hour.

At El-Bab we passed the armed steamer *Saidieh*, commanded by Lieutenant Vankoughnet, R.N., flying the white ensign, and ready to tow a *dahabiyeh* through the Kalabsheh rapids above, or to blaze away with the Gardner gun on his upper deck at any enemy attempting to cut the line of our communications.

At Korosko the Nile suddenly turns to the northwest, and through this reach of the river *dahabiyehs* had often to be towed, as the hitherto fair wind now became a head one. We passed twenty-seven of them flying Cook's signal unable to proceed owing to the armed steamer *Mahmoudieh* employed in this service being out of fuel. Further on we passed two *dahabiyehs* being tracked through this reach by their crews and soldier passengers. One of them carried a detachment of the South Staffordshire regiment, and the other, Surgeon ———, and the cargo of medical stores he had brought up by sail boat all the way from Cairo to Assouan. Not being able to obtain a passage for himself and impedimenta by our steamer, or even a tow by her, he had left Shellal for Wady-Halfa when we did on the *Five*—and here he was now ahead of us—although the odds were in our favour. Before starting he told us how when rowing up the river all alone in a Nile boat he had been menaced by the Arab crew. On several occasions, he said, they had drawn their hands significantly across their throats, but the doctor confessed that he was not sure whether the threat had been aimed at himself or the *Mahdi*!

The people seemed to have been pretty well cleared out of eggs and chickens by our predecessors, for the only reply we could get, when foraging for them, was 'All finish.' This was their English rendering of the Arab word '*Mafish*'—'there is not'—the reply to the Arab question '*Fee*'—'is there?' An amusing instance of this occurred at a village where we tied up one sunset, from which on our appearance all the women had bolted to the neighbouring hills, from fear of the *kroomen*, whom they regarded as cannibals. Going ashore with Dr. Bell, and diligently enquiring for eggs and milk, we found that none were to be had. The Arab for chicken was forgotten, but an imitation of the music of a chanticleer after '*Fee*' brought the house down, but still we could get no supplies whatever here, and our enquiries were finally closed by a smart little Arab sitting with his back to the house, and going over the whole list *seriatim*, with 'Finish' after each item.

Some life was given to the scenery of the river by the groups of people who collected on its banks watching our passing steamer. Sometimes these would assemble under a grove of palms, men, women, and children, then again we would pass some of them at work on the soil recently left uncovered by the fall of the river. This was sown with beans in terraces a couple of feet wide. At one place a well castor-oiled lady, wearing pink and white bracelets on her wrists, was seen grubbing away among these plants. Besides bracelets, this Sudanese lady had a silver ring in her nostril and another in the upper part of one of her ears. Near Tomas, on the left bank, we noticed two white men bathing, who, our *reis* told us, were the only persons of that colour ever born in the Sudan. From their white hair I presumed they were Albinos. All the women wore their hair in very small plaits, and so saturated with castor oil that I could see the shine of it at a considerable distance through my glass.

The cabin of the steamer swarmed with rats. This added very much to our other discomforts. The first night, after I had got comfortably settled and put out the light, I heard them galloping about in squadrons overhead and forward of the cabin. Nevertheless, tired out, I fell comfortably asleep, but was soon aroused by a detachment of the vermin rattling the loose floorboards in their sportive antics. The moment I lighted a match all became quiet, but looking round, I saw one of them, a good-sized fellow with a light grey breast, jump out from behind my *dragoman*, who was sleeping on the divan. When our eyes met, the creature doubled up his back, pricked up his ears, waved his tail, and, after a moment's defiant stare, galloped off into the outer darkness. Next night, shortly after I had dozed off, another fellow deliberately began walking over my legs; waiting until he reached my knee, I gave him a hoist on to the floor. This secured quiet for the rest of that night, but as the enemy seemed inclined to 'push home' he had evidently to be met before he came to too close quarters. The captain being appealed to placed at our disposal a large old-fashioned wooden box trap, temptingly baited. Although we caught no rats in it, it seemed to have had a wholesome deterrent effect on our nocturnal disturbers, for they henceforth abandoned our part of the ship.

The river soon became alive with steamers and sailboats. Some of the latter were bound to Wady-Halfa heavily laden with all kinds of stores for the expedition, while others were drifting empty back to Philae for another cargo. Between November 1 and 11 no fewer than fifty-six freight-boats under sail, and six steamers towing barges with troops and other freight, had been despatched up the river from Philae.

Some of the boats bound up under sail were easily passed by our steamer, but with others the *Fayûm* could scarcely hold her own. When the breeze freshened the sail-boats forged ahead, but when it slackened we caught them up again. At sunset, instead of mooring to the bank as the steamer did, they kept on for some time longer under their heavy press of canvas, as the breeze was always strongest at that hour of the day. We got under way earlier than they did, and so in the long run we beat them in the race.

The north wind, which blows constantly for two-thirds of the year, and heavily during the months of November, December, and January, happened this season to be abnormally fickle and weak. This seriously delayed the transport of both stores and troops between Assiout and Wady-Halfa. Had the coal supply been adequate, it would have to a large extent made up for this deficiency in wind power. In fact, so far as my observations went, and from data obtained at Wady-Halfa, I know that the supply was but a hand-to-mouth affair. The contractors excused this deficiency by stating that the consumption of coal far exceeded the original estimate on which they had tendered. Nevertheless, the fact remains that its inadequate supply was one of the unfortunate causes which contributed to the delay of the advance of the expedition. As such Lord Wolseley includes it in a telegram of November 3 from Dongola, in which he says:—

> Owing to the breakdown of the steamer between Assiout and Wady-Halfa, *to the coal difficulty*, and to the scarcity of native labour, I do not expect to concentrate the whole force about Ambukol until the end of the year.

In several cases steamers, after having discharged their cargo, had to take one another in tow on their return trip from Wady-Halfa to Assouan, in order to eke out the supply of coal on hand at the former place.

We naturally now kept a look-out for crocodiles, as we had been told that hereabouts they were often to be seen. Below Assouan but few of these monsters are now seen, owing to the introduction of steamers in that part of the river. At last we were rewarded by a sight of a monster basking in the sun on a long uncovered shoal near Toski. He lay quite out of the water, and was a tempting shot, though he was a few hundred yards distant from us. Mr. ——, of the commissariat, borrowed a rifle of Colonel Webber's servant, and prepared to bag him. But just as he was about to fire our Irish doctor, who had been taking his *siesta* down below, rushed up and excitedly exclaimed: 'Oh, do stop a moment and let me see him!' That moment's delay saved the crocodile's skin, for just as my friend fired the reptile moved, startled probably either by a sight of the steamer or by the sound of her paddles, then he rolled into the water over the bank of the shoal, with a splash, and disappeared. The bullet struck the spot which the monster had thus hurriedly vacated.

Captain Sir W. Gordon Cumming shot one hereabouts on another shoal, and was fortunate enough to secure the carcase, the skin of which measured twelve feet nine inches.

Opposite Korti I noticed another crocodile for several afternoons, basking himself on a long shoal. He was over twenty feet long and was of a dark bronze-green colour. On my return from El-Gubat six weeks later, I looked, but the shoal had been so entirely occupied as a dockyard for the Nile boat fleet as to leave no room for crocodile-loafing.

Below Ambukol I was told crocodiles were to be found, but, although I and my colleagues wished very much to pay them a visit, the pressure of important impending events prevented our doing so.

At many of the villages on my way up the river from Sarras at which I bivouacked for the night, I found the natives professed very little dread of these reptiles, although some of them told us that occasionally women when filling their water-jars had fallen victims to them.

At El-Gubat we were warned against crocodiles when bathing in the river by Khasm el-Mus and other officers of Gordon's troops. The crowd of afternoon bathers on the shoal of silver sand above where the steamers were moored, however, took no notice of the warning. I thought it was an unnecessary precaution, until one afternoon I noticed part of the heads of several crocodiles peeping out of the water about fifty yards out in the stream. Although one or two cases were reported of accidents from them, I found upon enquiry that not a single case of their attacking our troops had occurred in their passage either up or down the Nile.

CHAPTER 5

Stir at Wady-Halfa

As viewed from the steamer Wady-Halfa appeared to be a very busy place, for the shore was lined with freight-boats, from which a crowd of natives were engaged in removing the precious cargo of stores they had brought up the river—such a motley, curious crowd they seemed. Some were turbaned and others bareheaded, some were clad in light blue, others in black, or in a dingy white, while a few wore not much of anything. Their faces varied also, for some were black as polished ebony, and the others of the various shades from that up to coffee-coloured. They swarmed up the sandbank near the river's edge, carrying boxes and bags to the commissariat *depôt* and railway terminus, and as they went to and fro they chattered and sometimes halted to scold and be scolded by their head man armed with a *courbash*.

The grouping together of various nationalities in the work of this expedition made it ethnologically the strangest the world had ever seen, for it comprised British soldiers and sailors, mingled with Egyptian troops, natives of India, Sudanese, Kroomen, Canadians of several national origins, and including specimens of the American aborigines, mixed up with their counterparts, the Bedouins of the desert.

Piles of stores had accumulated on the bank and around the railway end, and were being hourly increased. Some of the busy multitude were engaged in loading them on trucks for despatch to Sarras, thence to be shipped by the whalers up the river.

Above the freight-boats, and just beyond the railway end, were several *dahabiyehs* moored to the shore. One of these was Colonel Duncan's headquarters as station commandant. Above it was that of Sir Redvers Buller and his staff, above which, on the bank, was the camp of Sir Evelyn Wood and his staff, over which floated his flag as *sirdar* of the Egyptian Army.

My first visit on landing was, as a matter of necessity, to the *dahabiyeh* of Colonel Duncan, in order to secure quarters for myself and camels, when he assigned me a place amongst the paymasters, and conveniently situated near the telegraph office, and only a hundred yards from the railway starting-point. Beyond this was the camp, with its orderly rows of tents, pitched unfortunately, and, as the results testify, also most unhealthily. On the strip of cultivated soil between the desert and the river it was ankle deep in dust, and when the wind blew strongly it raised this pulverised compound of Nile mud and of other more deleterious substances into clouds, which permeated everywhere, contaminating even the very food of the troops.

These were my convictions at the time, and they have been confirmed since by the printed reports of the senior medical officer at Wady-Halfa.[1] In these reports, I venture to say, too much stress is laid on the foul state of the camping ground in consequence of the Egyptian soldiers defecating all over the place, and too little, if anything, said of the unhealthy character of the ground itself. The remarks made about the camp at Assouan apply equally to the site of that at Wady-Halfa. Better would it have been to have pitched it on the hard gravel soil of the desert and put up with the slightly greater distance which would thus have been placed between us and the Nile.

The hospitals were happily placed at the lower or north end of the camp and on the bank of the river; and being to leeward, when the north wind blew, escaped much of the dust which troubled the camp itself. On the day of my arrival they contained 128 sick British soldiers, and the number daily increased until the 30th of the month (November), when it reached 259. Enteric fever was the prevailing disease, and of the 178 patients attacked by it and treated at Wady-Halfa no less than 47 died. Some of the cases were, however, contracted elsewhere, and many of the deaths occurred amongst men transferred from other hospitals. Four times more men died during the expedition from this and other fatal diseases than by the bullets of the enemy, the numbers being—Died from disease, 557; from being killed in action or died subsequently from their wounds, 126. No fewer than 8,953 patients were admitted to the various hospitals during the expedition out of a total force of 10,771, of which the febrile group contributed 2,514, inceluding 760 cases of enteric, with 277 deaths, and 63 invalided in consequence of its attacks.

Unfortunately, the Nile expeditionary force was largely composed

---
1. Army Medical Department Report, vol. xxvi. (1884), p. 281.

of men of those ages most liable everywhere to enteric fever, as tables in the Medical Report for 1884 abundantly show. In one table of 528 cases of enteric fever, 71.59 *per cent*, occurred between the ages of 20 and 24; whilst 115 cases, or 21.78 *per cent*., occurred in men between 25 and 29. In the latter instance 107, or 20.6 *per cent*, (of the 115), had served less than four years. It is therefore evident that for such an expedition, with older and more seasoned soldiers than those of which this one was composed, the death-rate would have been considerably less.

During my stay at Wady-Halfa deaths occurred almost daily. On three successive evenings, at sunset, as I sat in my tent, I heard those ominous volleys which have from time immemorial accompanied the burial of the British soldier. The burying-place was but three hundred yards from the hospital, and if it was sad enough for those in health four times that distance from it to hear these volleys over newly made graves, how must they have affected the patients in them who were suffering from the same disease to which these comrades of theirs had succumbed! Honoured as these funeral volleys may be, under the existing circumstances here they would have been 'more honoured in the breach than in the observance.' So also thought Sir Evelyn Wood and General Buller, who eventually put a stop to this part of the military burial service.

Although my headquarters were very conveniently situated so far as 'the telegraph' and the other departments were concerned, they were uncomfortably near the railway starting-point and the camp. At sunrise a crowd of natives employed by the commissariat and transport people would gather about my tent, squatting round in circles and keeping up a continuous chatter. Sometimes words would run high, and consequently rest was no longer possible. My man managed to get rid of those near enough to be ordered off, but this was only a partial relief. They moved off, but not beyond earshot, and then continued their chatter.

No sooner was this disturbance allayed than it was followed by the snorting and puffing of the locomotives shunting railway trucks for the first train to Sarras One could have put up with that part of the operation, but then came the unpleasant volley of noises which accompanies the concussions between a string of the trucks when either started or stopped.

Then '*réveillé*' at daybreak was not always regarded as so musical a performance as its poetical name might lead the uninitiated to expect.

If a single bugle had been sounded, one might have turned over and had another nap; but this was impracticable when half-a-dozen bugles from different quarters followed each other like echoes of the first. Then came the less musical call for 'rations,' and then 'stables.'

There was nothing therefore for it under these circumstances but to turn out and resolve that next night we should retire when the rest of the camp did.

It afforded some amusement to the cavalry detachments of the camel corps to hear 'stables' sounded by the buglers of the Guards. Remarks were also made by some of them on the absurdity, as they deemed it, of taking infantry off their feet and making cavalry of them. An officer of the 'Heavies' said to me when a detachment of the Guards had come up from Assouan to Wady-Halfa by land, 'Well, what do you think! One of these Guards officers excused his detachment for being so long on its way by pointing to his camel's sore back and asking me what could they do with animals like that? You know,' he continued, 'sore backs among cavalry is almost an unpardonable sin.'

This *esprit de corps* of the cavalry detachments of the camel corps led them at first to conclude that they were to be employed as cavalry through the expedition, and that camels were in their case to take the place of horses. Lord Wolseley, however, put an end to these speculations by a general order at the time, pointing out that all the camels were only intended for transport purposes, and that, in the presence of the enemy, the riders were to dismount and fight on foot.

The Guards camel corps was at the southern end of the camp and only within a hundred yards of my quarters. Looking in their direction one morning, I saw them mounted on camels for the first time, and turned out to see how they would acquit themselves under such novel circumstances. As if on foot, first came the word of command, 'Call your numbers,' and the first time probably in the history of the British Army was this obeyed by the Guards mounted as they were now. The next order was 'Fours right!' Like faithful soldiers, the men tried to obey the command, but the camels, unused to it, hindered such an ordinary manifestation of discipline. Instead of fours right, it was two, three, five, and in one case six.

The peremptoriness of the military command, with the confusion that ensued after it was given, provoked many a smile from officers and men, ending in many a half-suppressed 'guffaw' of merriment. However, they soon got the fours all right, and as they rode past me I was requested by one of the officers to remember that this was but their first drill on camel back, and so I have, for who could forget the fun of such a scene? Things, however, improved later on, for the camel rapidly mastered the intricacies of British military drill. It seemed at length to understand the words of command, and especially the word 'Halt!' or its bugle equivalent, for at its sound the camel would pull up suddenly, like any veteran riding-school charger. They also learned to wheel fairly well, and to move in open column with such a regular pace that a body of 'camelry' when in motion became a most interesting and imposing spectacle.

The camels somehow or other always showed great dislike to kneeling when urged to do so. This led at first to scenes verging on the ridiculous. The signal to the animal used by their Arab masters was a gurgling, guttural sound, not possible to be represented by the letters of any language but a Semitic one. This sound had to be imitated by our men whenever the rider wanted either to dismount or to mount. The failure of this mode of transport, as will be noticed further on, was to a large extent owing to the gravest errors in working these useful animals, and not providing for the consequences that might be expected to follow. Speaking of the camel, *Ensor* says that for short distances, when the state of the camels at the end of the journey has not to be considered, it is possible to travel, on animals in good condition, at their normal pace for sixteen hours a day, and journeys of 250 miles have sometimes been made at this rate. After such a journey, however, the camels will require a rest of ten or twelve days before being again fit for work; and, moreover, many will have died on the road.

On long journeys, when it is necessary to husband the strength of the camels and men, it is always best to work them eight hours per day, and, if the wells are four or five hours apart, to allow them to rest for two or three days. Twelve miles a day, including stoppage at wells and other delays, is generally considered a fair rate of travelling; whereas a rate beyond this will throw the camels out of health and fitness for long and continuous work.

General Gordon says that he considers the powers of endurance of the camel as having been overrated, as it cannot travel more than ten days without being considerably distressed; and that an average of six days' travel may be expected from good camels.

The requirements of a military expedition designed to reach a certain distant point within a given time placed ours in the first of these categories. The state of the camels employed in it, at the end of the journey, should have been taken into consideration, which on this occasion was overlooked. The loss of camels which must thus naturally be expected, should, in the present instance, have been foreseen and provided against. This was not done, and the consequences were most serious, as will be seen farther on. At Assouan I learned that the purchases of camels were ordered and then countermanded by the chief of the staff in the most fitful manner.

The same thing occurred while I was at Wady-Halfa, and I am told that in some cases the owners of camels from whom such purchases were made one day had to be compensated the next, or later, because the camels bought from them were left on their hands. I am not quite certain about the truth of this, but it comes on authority good enough to be recorded here. Any number of good camels could have been had not only in Lower Egypt, but at Dongola, Abu Gus, Debbah, and elsewhere up the Nile. Instead of 7,000 camels, which is about all we had, how much better and safer it would have been to have had, say, 10,000! That they could have been fed above the cataracts cannot, I think, be doubted.

Another singular mistake was made by the staff at Wady-Halfa with respect to camel-drivers. One day I heard that 300 were to be despatched to Dongola. I watched for them, but was told that they would not be sent now, for the expedition would be over before they could reach their destination! How we suffered in January following from the blunder will subsequently appear.

The second and third cataracts, extending from Wady-Halfa to Hannek, interposed the first serious obstacle to the progress of the expedition, as they put an end to the continuous water transport of its stores. This interruption covered, according to the river itinerary supplied to the whalers, a distance of 172 miles.

Between Wady-Halfa and Saye Island there were no fewer than eight cataracts, or rather rapids, two of which were wholly impassable at low Nile and difficult at high Nile. Between that island and Hannek there was only one rapid, but it was seven-and-a-half miles long and impassable for large boats at low Nile.

Upwards from Hannek, for about 225 miles, the river flows generally in a broad stream between banks of the very richest alluvial land in Egypt, and is navigable for large craft the entire distance, excepting at low Nile.

The following reference to the causes which produce the cataracts may not be uninteresting to the general reader, and will aid in illustrating the difficulty encountered in ascending them in the heavily

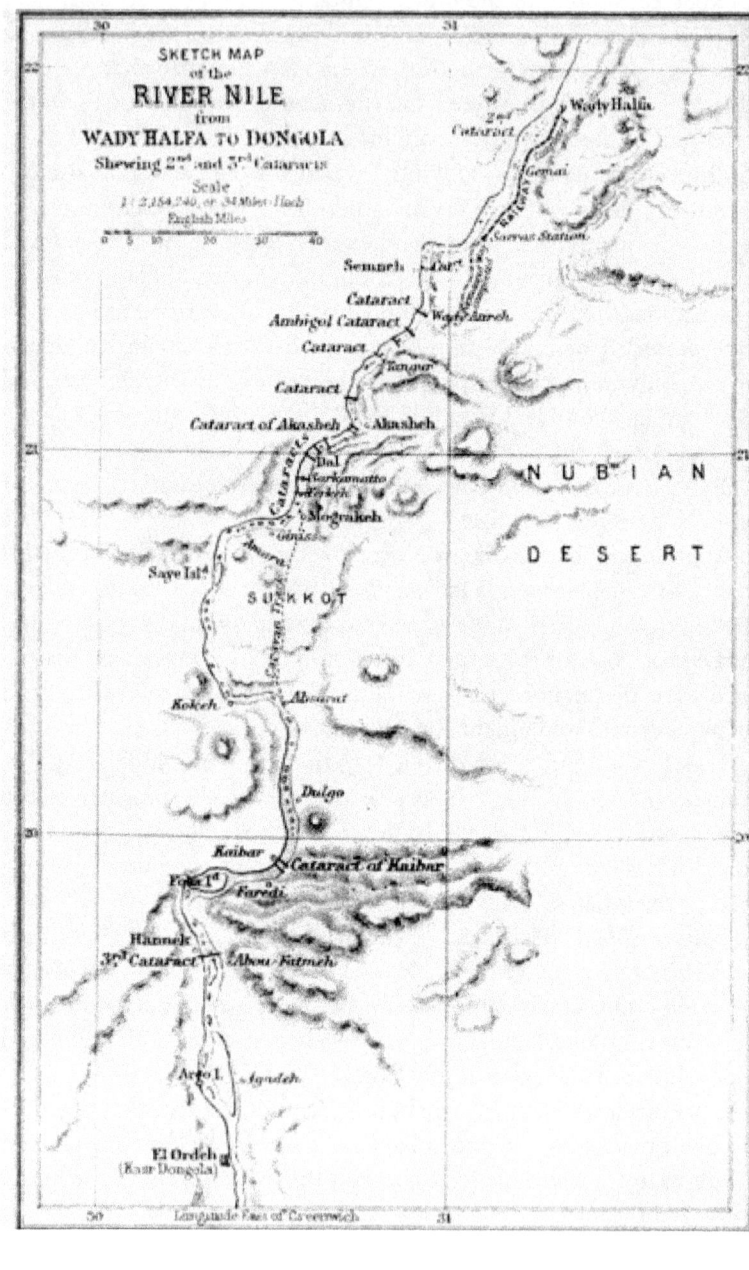

laden boats of the expedition.

The usual geological formation of the districts in which the cataracts of the Nile occur, and extending from Silsilis, below Assouan, to Khartoum, includes the Upper and Lower Nubian Sandstones. In certain localities these are traversed by bands of volcanic rocks.

The Nile makes its way evenly and easily through the soft sandstones, but is interrupted in its course when these harder igneous rocks cross its channel, as they do where the cataracts occur.

As the river falls, the rapids thus formed become in many places wild and desolate archipelagos, flanked by a series of rocky and precipitous cliffs, which there form its banks. In fact, from Hannek to Wady-Halfa, it may, without much inaccuracy, be described as a mighty mountain torrent, strewn with rocks and seething with whirlpools and rushing currents. The general sombre and gloomy appearance of this *Batn-el-Hágar*, or 'Belly of stone,' as it is colloquially called, is such as to give one the idea of utter desolation. This is enhanced by the colour of the rocks laid bare in the bed of the stream. These were usually jet black, and so polished by the action of the water as to look as if they had been black-leaded. For the most part also the only verdure visible was here and there a few dwarf acacia or mimosa trees, or tufts of coarse grass. In some places, as will be noticed farther on, nature strives to hide the prevailing desolateness by fringes of palms along the banks, as she sets the oases in the sandy desert. The only sound breaking the dreary silence was the ceaseless roar of rushing waters, or the harsh occasional cry of a dusky, ill-omened-looking bird.

The first of these rapids with which the expedition had to contend were those forming the second cataract. These began a few miles above Wady-Halfa, and extended twelve or thirteen miles up the river, in a succession of broken water, caused by numerous palm-fringed islets and black slippery rocks, with which the Nile is here thickly studded. The larger rocks were in mid-channel, and as the water flowed past them they formed whirlpools, eddies, and rapid currents. In some places—specially in the second cataract—these rocks exhibited when broken a compact grain with *laminae* of *mica* irregularly interspersed, and were generally greenish in colour inside. Under the black polish was a layer of red oxide—which fancy might look upon as the rich tint of a Northern Nubian's skin.

One of the greatest obstacles to the passage of this cataract was the *Bab-el-Kebir*, or 'Big gate.' This gate, or, properly, rocky channel between a large basin above and a smaller one below, was about 300 feet long by 70 wide, and had sufficient water in it, six weeks before I saw it, to float such large steamers as the *Nassif-el-Kheir* and *Ghiza*. It had now, however, dwindled down to a stream so shallow that it would not have floated a biscuit-box, and so narrow that I could stand astraddle over it.

Lord Wolseley saw it at its best on October 25, and telegraphed to London that he had witnessed Colonel Butler and Commander Hammill, R.N., tracking up the first four whalers, and that 'it was the only serious difficulty we know of on the Nile.'[2] At present, as no boats could be tracked through it, or through any of the adjacent channels, a portage had to be established here. It was originally 2,480 yards long, but when I visited it, on November 23, owing to the great fall of the river it had to be extended nearly two hundred yards.

I then ascertained from Colonel Smith, in command of the Egyptian battalion, sent to work this portage, that in twenty-three days 409 whalers had been taken over it. On that day ten boats had been taken across in two hours and a half.

The systematic manner in which the work was done was very remarkable, I saw boat No. 505 undergoing the process when I arrived. The soldiers received it on the shore at the lower end of the portage and emptied it of its tackle, oars, masts, and sails, which were loaded on mules and donkeys. Thus denuded, it was drawn up the bank to the level above, turned bottom upwards, and two masts placed underneath it at each end. By these the boat, weighing 1,100 lbs., was lifted and borne rapidly to the upper end of the portage by eleven relays of the Egyptian soldiers, each relay comprising thirty men. It was then lowered, turned right side up, and, with the tackle replaced, was slidden down the bank into the stream, without a scratch or bruise, and then taken four miles up the river to Gemai, ready for its journey up the Nile.

These Egyptian soldiers were not allowed to take part in the fighting operations of the expedition, but here they were cheerfully and effectively aiding those who were to be thus privileged. In such a climate neither our soldiers nor sailors could have long carried on the work they were doing at this portage without suffering under it. Useful also as were the Dongolese labourers, yet from want of discipline they could not be relied upon. Although the work in which the latter were employed was less continuous and less arduous than was that on this portage, they declared it to be beyond their strength, and deserted

---

2. Blue Book, Egypt, No. 1, 1885, p. 30.

in large numbers.

In the rocks at the bottom of the channel a great hole had been drilled for blasting, and evidently some attempt had thus been made to widen and deepen it. This, I heard, had been the work of Sir Samuel Baker—but I am not certain of this. It is interesting here to notice that in one of his letters General Gordon, writing to the late Mr. Jansen in February 1877, asks him not to forget the 'rock-borers,' for they 'might remedy, even if they did not cure, the falls and rapids.' The blasting here may have been done by them, for its object was to widen the passage as well as deepen it.

Some sanguine people at home seem also to have entertained this idea, and a quantity of gun-cotton was sent out by the authorities to be used on the rocks on the cataracts, so as to clear a channel for the whalers. Anyone who had had a right conception of these cataracts would never have dreamed of such an expedient, for it would have taken many months to accomplish any useful work of that nature.

In fact but very little was known of the second and third cataracts, and less of the others all the way up to Berber. The information afforded by the very useful map supplied by the Intelligence Department merely indicated that here, there, or elsewhere, rapids, rocks, and swift currents would be encountered, but the changes in these, at different stages of water in the river, were only summarily mentioned.

It was, therefore, to a certain extent misleading, and conducive to optimist views as to the progress of the whalers. General Gordon, at the time his letters were written, also seems to have had but little information about the cataracts, and when he speaks of them it is evidently as they are at high Nile. Hence his anxiety to have a line of steamers on the open reaches of the Nile between Wady-Halfa and Berber, in order to afford facilities for the examination of the river.[3] It will be noticed, however, that while be speaks of tramways drawn by steel wire along the cataracts, he still clings to the hope of being eventually able to complete his projected railway. The stress he lays on the latter seems to indicate his want of absolute faith in the success of any engineering efforts to improve satisfactorily the navigation through the cataracts by any mechanical or engineering expedients whatsoever.

Space prevents an extended comparison between the difficulties encountered by the Red River expedition and that of the Nile. A perusal, however, of the descriptions of the former, published at the

3. See Appendix C, Gordon's letter, Nov. 17, 1877.

time,[4] and of Major Dixon's journal in the Appendix, will force the admission that in the difficulties it had to overcome the latter was the greater feat of the two.

In the former case, for example, there were long stretches of unbroken and slack water, or favourable strong currents. However difficult were its portages, they did not involve very serious delays. The Canadian waters, also unlike those of the muddy Nile, were so clear that dangerous rocks and shoals could always be seen soon enough to be avoided. While the Red River expedition traversed 200 miles in ten days, Major Dixon and his company of Royal Irish were twenty-eight days between Sarras and Abu-Falmeh, a distance of 172 miles. The Red River expedition, it must also be remembered, enjoyed the great advantage of having the constant and able supervision all along its route of its able commander. As General Lindsay, then commanding the troops in Canada, said in his final despatch about it:—

> The mainspring of the whole movement was the commander. Colonel Wolseley, who has shown great professional ability. He has the faculty of organisation and resource in difficulty.'

From what I learned personally in passing up the Nile, and on good authority from others, I have no hesitation in expressing the opinion that, could Lord Wolseley have been in three places at the same time in the line of advance from Assouan upwards in November, matters might have turned out more advantageously for the expedition. But it lacked at different points along its line on critical occasions the decision and skill of that master mind which had the art of filling the men under his command with the same spirit that actuated himself, and which made him perfectly at home in all circumstances, however trying and unexpected. In an article in *Blackwood* on the Red River expedition, he writes:

> We treated our men not as machines, but as reasonable beings, having all feelings in common with ourselves; and they responded to our appeals as British soldiers ever will when under men in whom they have unbounded confidence.

But here I must guard myself against the suspicion of sympathy with the unjustifiable views expressed by a colleague in one of our magazines, as to the causes which contributed during the progress of

---

4. See *Blackwood's Magazine*, January 1871, and a lecture by the late Capt. Huyshe in the *Journal of the United Service*, vol. xv., No. 62.

the expedition to its eventual failure.

In making the above observation relative to the difference between the model expedition and that of the Nile—so far as superintendence was concerned, I had in my mind not officers who had reported against the river route, but some of those who were most enthusiastically in favour of it. These officers found the work they had entered upon so enthusiastically more difficult than they had anticipated. There is no use now referring to this matter in detail. Every wheel moved—but sometimes the wrong way, and so we lost precious time. Give men time and they may accomplish great things. The late date at which the expedition was started must therefore be taken into account as covering whatever faults may have occurred in its execution. Only think of a line of communications extending inland 1,500 miles from the sea! What was it then, after all, but a forlorn hope heroically undertaken by its able chief, and, despite the physical and all the other drawbacks, nearly successful?

Chapter 6

Gordon's Plans for Opening River to Khartoum

The railway here, which played so important a part in the advance of the expedition, formed part of a line projected in 1865 from Assouan to Khartoum.

It was begun in 1873, after survey by Mr. Fowler, but suspended in 1877 from financial reasons, after fifty-five miles of permanent way south of Wady-Halfa had been completed, on thirty-three miles of which rails were then laid.

General Gordon was well aware of the fact, that not the least of the causes which have led to the disorders in the Sudan has been that Egyptian policy which aimed at forcing its trade down the Nile, instead of allowing it to find its natural outlet at Suakim.

Although these were doubtless General Gordon's views about a Sudan railway, he also proposed to utilise the Nile when navigable for small steamers, and to lay tramways along the intervening spaces where its navigation was interrupted by the cataracts, as stated in his characteristic letters to the late Mr. Jansen, published, by the kind permission of his sisters, in our Appendix.[1]

The impression produced upon the writer by the undeveloped agricultural resources of Dongola and the wretched administration of its affairs was that even a better mode of communication with it than that proposed by General Gordon was most desirable, in the form of a railway, if not all the way from Wady-Halfa to Dongola, or at any rate to Hannek.

But all this apart, so far as the expedition was concerned, the thirty-three miles of completed railway from Wady-Halfa to Sarras was

1. See Appendix B.

of immense value as a means of sending both stores and men past a great portion of the second cataract. Before leaving London it was announced that a detachment of Egyptian troops had been sent here to lay the rails on the completed permanent way for a distance of twenty miles beyond Sarras, and that this work would be completed in six weeks, or by the beginning of November. Had this work been accomplished, it would have saved at least a fortnight's time in the advance of the expedition, for it would have enabled both stores and many of the whalers to be passed quickly beyond the Semneh and Ambigol cataracts.

Although Lord Wolseley must have known these advantages that would thus have been gained, it was stated, upon authority which warrants its repetition here, that on his arrival at Wady-Halfa in October he stopped the work of this extension, giving as his reason that the expedition was not of such importance as to require the construction of a railway. But as it might be needed later on, he ordered that everyone should 'stand by' and be ready to continue the work, and that in three weeks' time he would decide what should be done. When the three weeks had expired, it was reported that instructions had been given to construct a branch up the Wady-Attireh to the Nile, thus avoiding the Semneh cataract. At any rate, the Egyptian soldiers employed in laying the rails were taken off the work, and employed, with others of them, in the portage of the whalers, at the Big-gate of the second cataract and as garrisons at the stations up the Nile.

This indecision puzzled me at the time, and, although I have pushed my enquiries for information on the subject in every direction, I have only been able to extract evasive answers from those best qualified to speak on the subject. The internal evidence supplied by Lord Wolseley's published instructions and some of his own despatches leads, however, to the conclusion that his movements were largely restrained by Her Majesty's Government, either from economical considerations, or in order to keep them within the hard-and-fast lines of their Sudan policy.

Another view taken of the abandonment of this commenced railway extension project was as follows:—Lord Wolseley, from the facility with which a few whalers were drawn up the Bab-el-Kebir, evidently underrating the difficulties of the cataracts, came to the conclusion that he could do without that extension. It was, therefore, assumed that he placed his whole reliance on whaler transport. Of the two views the former one appears to be the more credible. At any rate, if the extension of the railway had been completed the facilities for quick transport would, no doubt, have been welcomed, when General Gordon's letter of November 4 was received on the 14th of that month. In this he said, as will be remembered, that he could hold out for forty days— but that after that it would be difficult.

The headquarters staff were very reticent at first about Gordon's critical position, and seemed inclined to think that if General Gordon could hold out for six weeks he could do so for six months. Lord Wolseley did not seem, however, to take this optimist view of the case, for immediately on receipt of this letter he came rapidly down the river from Dongola to Wady-Halfa, arriving there at midnight on the 17th. Spending the next day in consultation with Generals Buller and Sir Evelyn Wood, he returned in the evening to Dongola as rapidly as he had come down from it.

From a subsequent conversation with General Sir Redvers Buller I gathered that some uncertainty hung over the future of the expedition, for that no decision had as yet been arrived at with respect to an advance beyond the former place. Referring to Lord Wolseley's published despatch of November 22, 1884, a confirmation of this will be found. Lord Hartington had asked him how the information in Gordon's letter of November 4 affected his plans, and in reply he telegraphed as follows:—

> News from Gordon makes no change in my plans, but it seems to indicate the almost impossibility of his relief without fighting'

Her Majesty's Government up till the middle of September, as already noticed, had not decided to send any portion of the force under his command beyond Dongola. It is not unreasonable, therefore, to suppose that now they gave Lord Wolseley authority to do so. Hitherto their vain hope was that the very report of a British force coming up the Nile would frighten the *Mahdi*. General Gordon's news of November 4 was a contradiction of this; and when Lord Wolseley learned that 20,000 Arabs were round Khartoum, with a warrior's instinct he tells them it is almost impossible to relieve Gordon without fighting.

The extremities of Gordon's position could not now be denied or gainsaid; and at this eleventh hour, when their indecision had made the expedition for his relief not much more than a forlorn hope, no doubt they felt compelled to give its gallant commander fuller liberty of action.

The original small boat plan of the expedition was most tenaciously adhered to, even in face of the emergency which had now evidently arisen. This may be fairly traced to the overweening confidence in General Gordon himself, and his ability to hold out until the expedition could reach him. When discussing the matter with one of the headquarters staff I was told that 'if Gordon says he can hold out for six weeks, he can do so for six months.' My interpretation of the word 'difficult' was, however, 'desperate.' They seemed also to have entirely ignored General Gordon's letter of July, in which he distinctly stated he could hold out four months—that is, to November 13.

They also knew at Dongola and London that Gordon, in his dire extremity, when he found that his personal appeals for aid had remained unanswered, had sent Colonel Stewart to repeat them. And now that his messenger had perished on the way, what then would become of Gordon himself if we could not speedily rescue him?

In the last week in November the military authorities practically admitted the difficulties which had arisen to retard the upward movement of troops and stores by the boats, by not only reducing the number of men in each whaler from twelve to nine, but by ordering that nine boats were in future to carry the cargoes of stores heretofore assigned to seven of them. Then I was also informed that as soon as the necessary sidings were completed, the seven miles of hitherto unused railway extension beyond Sarras was to be utilised for the transport of stores to Ambigol, camels being employed between it and the railway terminus.

The following synopsis of the actual position and prospects of the force at the moment shows what might possibly have been done to reach Khartoum earlier than we did.

Only 130 tons of Nile boats' or whalers' stores had yet to come up to Wady-Halfa, and a large quantity of commissariat supplies had been sent up the river in various ways to Dal, Hannek, and Dongola. The whole expeditionary force could now be moved forward. The Black Watch had sailed up in the whalers from Assouan in nine days. This was encouraging, but on the other hand the Staffordshire regiment, which left Gemai on the 6th of the month, were only now making their way through the cataract of Tanjur, that is, had accomplished somewhere about forty-four miles in about a fortnight. As the other regiments of the expedition were so long a way behind the Staffordshire, no advance beyond Dongola was expected until the end of December. The Royal Sussex regiment and a large detachment of the

Mounted Infantry were already there.

On the 13th three sections of the Guards camel corps had left Wady-Halfa for Dongola, and on the 21st four more had started for the same destination. Up till the 22nd of the month about 1,500 infantry and cavalry (19th Hussars) had gone up the river. Of the Guards camel regiment, the Royal Marines were still at Wady-Halfa waiting for camels, and also six sections, or 306 rank and file of the Heavy Camel regiment, and on the 21st 146 rank and file of the Light Camel regiment had arrived. There were thus 2,571 rank and file between Wady-Halfa and Dongola, on December i. The three first sections of the Guards camel corps arrived at Dongola on November 27, and were sent on to join the Mounted Infantry at Handak, where General Stewart then was.

If my information is correct, there had now been accumulated at Hannek rations for at least 1,000 men for forty-two days. There was also on November 28 so large a quantity of supplies at Debbeh that Lord Wolseley despatched thither 200 men of the Royal Sussex to protect them. Colonel Kitchener had telegraphed in August that several thousand baggage camels could be obtained there at the same prices as at Korosko. He had also reported from Dongola that native craft capable of transporting 4,000 men were available on that reach of the Nile. In view of these facilities for pushing on to Khartoum a force in advance of the main body of the expedition, it is difficult to understand why this was not done. Had Lord Wolseley deemed such a movement practicable, no doubt he would have risked it, as he already had his military reputation in undertaking the command of the expedition to rescue friend Charley Gordon. The whole incident, however, tells with thrilling force against the government, who did not promptly accept the proposition in July, by which he proposed to get a force up to Dongola by the middle of October.

Next to Wady-Halfa in importance, so far as the whalers were concerned, came Gemai, sixteen miles up the river, pleasantly situated at the head of the second cataract. As the bank of the river here rose cliff-like about thirty feet from the river's edge, facility of access to the shore was secured by flights of steps cut in the compact alluvium of which it was formed. Its top was beautified by a grove of *dom* palms. Between them and the railway line—about 150 yards distant—was a level space occupied by the commissariat *depôt* and the camp of detachments of troops stationed here for the protection of the place.

Coming from the train, the first object that attracted one's attention was the tops of a forest of masts rising above the bank. Looking down from its edge, there lay along the shore scores of Her Majesty's Nile boat fleet, ready waiting for their crews to proceed up the river to Dongola, Korti, and perhaps to Berber and Khartoum. At the lower end a number of boats were drawn up on the beach to have the damage they had received coming up the cataract repaired. This dockyard had been for some time under the special charge of the Royal Engineers. They were, however, outdone by some of my fellow-countrymen—the Canadians—as Colonel Grove, the commandant of the station, informed me.

Several boats condemned by the Engineers were shown to one of their number, who undertook to repair them, and with the aid of a few of his steady comrades had them afloat in a few hours. This poor fellow, named Armstrong, subsequently fell a victim to enteric fever.

The whalers, on their arrival at Wady-Halfa, were taken up to the foot of the second cataract by the sailors of the so-called Naval Brigade—sometimes under sail, but generally towed up by a steam-launch. They were drawn up the cataract and carried over the portage at the Big-gate, as already described, by the Egyptian troops. Some assistance was afforded in this work below the gate by the sailors and Canadians, but General Sir Evelyn Wood told me that the former had shown the most aptness for such work. I had often remarked the ability manifested by young officers for such work, the philosophy of which had not been taught at any military college, so far as I know. Here Lieutenant Peel did excellent service, and it was rather amusing to see a cavalry officer working these small boats up this torrent-bed.

Early on the morning of November 18 the headquarters of the Duke of Cornwall's Light Infantry left Wady-Halfa for Gemai, there to embark in whalers for Dongola.

Going out by a later train, I arrived just in time to see the last half-dozen boats started on their journey up the river. This is how it was done, and what happened. As each boat received its complement of men, and all were seated with oars out ready, a sailor pushed the craft stem first into the stream with a boat-hook. Then ensued an amusing scene. Many of the crew seemed never to have had an oar in their hands before, and it required some shouting ere they were got fairly under way. Some would insist on pulling when they were told to back water, and *vice versâ*. However awkward many such boats' crews were in starting, I noticed further up the river that they had even learned to feather their oars.

On November 18 a squadron of the 19th Hussars, under the command of Major and Colonel French, left Wady-Halfa for Dongola, after being inspected by General Wood. Dressed in grey they would hardly, have been recognised as British Hussars; but, nevertheless, they presented a very soldierly appearance, and seemed in capital spirits. The horses they bestrode looked at first sight too small for their riders, and hardly strong enough to carry the eighteen-stone weight of man and kit. They were, however, hardy, compact animals, and did their work better than our larger English horses could have done. My own horse was of the same breed, and even after a double march across the desert, on my return to Korti he finished up with a canter of over a mile and a half across the plain between the camp and the edge of the desert, and apparently as fresh as when he had left it six weeks previously.

On the previous Sunday morning I had seen the troop paraded on bare backs before going down to the river to water, and amusing were the criticisms made by the men about the size and qualities of their steeds. One stalwart Hussar laughingly said, 'I believe I could put my legs round my fellow!' and so he did.

They were ordered to proceed to Dongola by the river route on account of watering their horses, and its 245 miles was ordered to be covered in sixteen marches. The extra luggage and rations of the detachments were carried on camels.

It is but faint praise to say that no force of the expedition did more useful service than the 19th Hussars. From their much loved and honoured Colonel Barrow, now, alas! lost to the service of his country, down to the humblest trooper, the regiment manifested on all occasions the greatest efficiency. They were British cavalry in their right place—on horseback—and as such acquitted themselves as British cavalry ever has done.

No part of the expeditionary force made themselves more comfortable under existing circumstances at Wady-Halfa than did the detachment of Royal Marines forming part of the Guards' camel regiment. When they landed here on the 20th and 21st from the barge on which they came up from Assouan, what with their pipe-clayed sun helmets and their polished boots, they looked as trim as when I saw them inspected by the First Lord of the Admiralty at the Egyptian capital. Much of this trimness must of course be referred to the strict, if not rigid, discipline maintained by the officers. It was, however, also largely due to the habit of theirs of being quite at home when most abroad, as they certainly were on this occasion.

When under canvas on this dusty plain the same order and regularity was observed. During one of my daily strolls through the camp I noticed a tent labelled 'Rose Cottage.' The whole surroundings were so foreign to a flower garden as to make the designation suggestive of something quite out of the common so far as its occupants were concerned. It suggested a poetical tendency, and such, in fact, I found was the case. One of the marines, Sergeant Eagle, was a poet! He had written some verses on the present position of this detachment of Marines in the camel corps, of which his comrades seemed very proud. Falling in with their humour, I accepted an invitation for sunset to hear it sung. Seated round the tent, accompanied by a banjo, they sang the song of which I here give the first verse and chorus:—

> *When years ago I listed, lads,*
> *To serve our gracious Queen,*
> *The sergeant made me understand*
> *I was a Royal Marine.*
> *He said sometimes they served in ships,*
> *And sometimes served on shore,*
> *But never said I should wear spurs*
> *And be in the camel corps.*
>
> *I've rode in a ship, I've rode in a boat,*
> *I've rode in a railway train,*
> *I've rode in a coach, and I've rode a moke.*
> *And hope to ride one again;*
> *But I'm riding now an animal*
> *A marine never rode before,*
> *Rigg'd up in spurs and pantaloons*
> *As one of the camel corps.*

The allusion to spurs was specially emphasised, as this part of their equipment excited peculiar interest among the men. 'Surely,' I asked, 'you have not been supplied with spurs for camel-riding?' 'Yes, indeed, sir, we have,' was the answer; 'we were served out with them at Cairo, and wore them when Lord Northbrook reviewed us.' The spurs found their way back to the Ordnance Department at Wady-Halfa, but the men carried away with them the kind words of Lord Northbrook on that occasion, and his hearty recognition of their deeds and sufferings at Kassassin and Suakim, whence the detachment had been brought to join this expedition.

My last evening at Wady-Halfa, December 1, was spent in a stroll along the bank of the river in the beautiful moonlight. The Royal West Kent had come up in a steamer during the day, and its band was discoursing sweet music The first battalion of the Royal Irish regiment had also arrived, and were welcomed as a valuable addition to the forces being assembled there for the expedition.

Meeting three of its non-commissioned officers, I entered into conversation with them about the work which lay before them. During the day they had evidently watched with interest the ferrying over from the left bank of a detachment of the camel corps which had ridden up from Assouan on their new steeds, for the awkward manner in which this detachment handled their camels was severely criticised. 'Sure, sir,' said one of them, 'they took the loads off the beasts and had to reload them when they got over—a thing we never did when crossing several rivers in India with camels heavily laden, nor in our campaign in Afghanistan.' They were bronzed, clad in khaki, used to camels or anything, and impatient to get to the front.

If a dash across the Bayuda desert should become necessary, they were certainly the kind of troops fitted for such an expedition. With some surprise I therefore learned subsequently that the Royal Irish had been ordered to proceed up the Nile in the whalers; but it was no surprise to hear also that its colonel had uttered this protest against the order: 'Do they think I am the colonel of a lot of sailors? My men are soldiers, and why don't they let me therefore march them up?' And he could have kept his word, for he marched his men from Korti to Metammeh in the February following, 176 miles, in eleven days. But the order to come up to Korti by the whalers was, of course, imperative; but, as might have been expected, this regiment made the best time up the river, and landed their stores with less loss and in better condition than did any other of the boat corps.

Chapter 7
Departure of Marines and Artillery, &c., for Korti

Early on the morning of December 2 the Marines, under the command of Major Poe, and Major Hunter with a battery, 1 Battalion, Southern Division of Artillery, and a detachment of Hussar regiments, forming part of the Light Camel Regiment, under Colonel McCalmont, left Sarras shortly after sunrise for Gemai, *en route* for the front. Glad to move on, I started my men, horse and camels, laden with stores and what little baggage I carried, after them, following myself three hours later by train, and reaching our common destination an hour earlier than the troops.

My men bivouacked under a clump of palms on the bank of the river just below the marines, and near the camp of the Canadians. Thanks to the kind hospitality of their officers, and a shake-down in Dr. Neilson's tent, this first night of my march to the front was spent under the most favourable circumstances.

The Abbé Bouchard, Chaplain to the Voyageurs, was, like his race, an intelligent French Canadian. He had been a missionary at Khartoum, and he enlivened our conversation with information as to the condition of things in a part of the Sudan upon which our attention was now so earnestly fixed. Colonel Kennedy, as well as the doctor and the other officers of the Voyageurs, expressed their strong indignation at certain statements which had appeared in a London paper about them, in a letter from its correspondent at Gemai, dated the day before their arrival there.

His statement was that the Canadians, when coming up the river, were armed with either a bottle of rum or a revolver, or both. He also charged them with disorderly conduct. When taken to task for these statements by the late Colonel Kennedy and Dr. Neilson, his only excuse was that 'he had heard so,' and yet upon mere hearsay evidence this gentleman wrote to an influential London journal that which was utterly untrue respecting a body of men who had come from their distant western home to serve the Queen and country on the Nile. I was assured by those officers that the eight or ten revolvers possessed by the 360 Canadian Voyageurs when they landed at Alexandria were soon afterwards taken from them, and that with few exceptions the men were teetotallers. I am sorry to say that this military correspondent was of a class too often employed by British journals—on the score of economy rather than that of efficiency.

These men, from their tone and bearing, whenever I came in contact with them led me to conclude that they not only imagined they could excel all others in writing for the papers, but that they could themselves run the 'expeditionary machine' better even than the commander-in-chief himself.

Next morning the column marched from Gemai, sixteen miles distant, at seven o'clock, and shortly after I started my caravan, following myself by the train which passed there at 10 a.m.

The Light Camelry detachment made the journey in five hours and a half, but the marines and artillery did not put in an appearance until two hours later, having lost their way in the desert. This is quite easily done, for the road, or rather track, leading for the most part along the railway, diverges from it in several places in order to round the rocky hills. It was on one of these occasions that the marines went an hour astray, and consumed another hour straying back again.

The column as it marched past the Sarras railway station, where I was waiting for it, presented a novel and interesting sight First came Colonel McCalmont (Baby McCalmont, as he was called) and his detachment of the Light Camel Regiment. Then followed the battery of seven-pounder screw-guns, with wheels on one camel and gun on another, followed by the ammunition on others, and rendered rather picturesque by its gaily turbaned Aden camel-drivers.

The gallant marines, with their spiked helmets, brought up the rear, and with them came my 'caravan.' For convenience, I bivouacked a short distance from the station, and near a detachment of an Egyptian mounted battery, now, however, on transport duty, and bound to Kaibar with stores. As for myself, I enjoyed the hospitality of the commissariat, who kindly lodged me in one of their vacant tents. It was fortunate that I had thus secured shelter, for at 9 p.m. we had a gale of wind which made matters very uncomfortable.

The surface of the cultivated soil around the camp, owing to its dryness, was ankle deep in dust, and across the river, the direction from which the wind blew, were the yellow sands of the desert. Consequently, when the wind rose the air became charged with both kinds of these particles, carrying them everywhere. The officers and men, sheltered only under *tentes d'abri*, spent a wretched night and presented a pitiable sight in the morning. Although subsequently, throughout the expedition, our force often suffered from this infliction, common to the region, no one ever seemed to get used to it.

I was glad to meet here Captain —— of the ——, who had been my fellow-traveller from Cairo to Assouan, and who was now bound for Dal to join his regiment, then on its way up the river in the 'whalers.' So we arranged to travel together thus far. Even though prepared to brave the excessive heat of a December day, we could not get off before 2.30 p.m. on account of the guide promised to him by the Transport Department not having earlier put in an appearance. Only two of these valuable persons were available, and Colonel McCalmont had secured the other for his detachment. The marines and artillery, being left without one, agreed to march when we did, although they had arranged to do so an hour and a half later.

Personally I was independent of a guide, for one of my men said he had worked on the railway station between Sarras and Ambigol, and could take me through. Still, having learned to doubt the Levantine race to which he belonged, in case of accident I was glad to have this official guide along with us. It was decided to march on until sunset and halt until the full moon rose at 7.25 p.m., and then to make a night march of it to Ambigol.

Starting punctually at the hour named, I rode on past the bivouacs of the artillery, marines, and light camelry. I was shortly followed by the Egyptian detachment under Major Carter, but the two former were late in getting under way. So I moved on gently over the hot, dusty plain through which our road lay, halting occasionally for the column to come up. Soon after it began its march it halted longer than usual, and I therefore suspected something had gone wrong. An Egyptian officer came trotting out to me with a message from Majors Carter and Poe to say that our official guide had turned out a fraud, for he now declared he did not know the road to Ambigol at all, but did, however, that to Semneh. As the latter was not our destination, he was ordered to the right about, and I was asked, with their compliments, if

I would wait and lead the column, to which, with much satisfaction, I agreed, and, halting until they came up, on we marched again.

Our road beyond Sarras, for seven miles, followed the railway track on which the rails had been recently laid. Soon after leaving our bivouac it turned sharply to the left by a narrow cutting through the rocks, quite impassable for animals laden as were ours. Leading further on, my man took us over a rocky hill which soon descended into a long narrow plain, where we again struck the railway. We traversed this plain until within six miles of Ambigol, near a heavy but uncompleted rock-cutting, beyond which no work had been done on the road. Up to that point, however, the route presented no engineering difficulties greater than those encountered by railways over the Western prairies.

Sometimes we rode on one side of the railway and sometimes on the other; and when we had passed the portion upon which the rails had not been laid we rode on the embankment itself, only having to leave it here and there when a place was reached which had either been washed away by a mountain torrent or which had been left to be bridged over a torrent bed. Engineers were working at the rail end of the road from Sarras, making sidings required to facilitate the transport of stores by rail and thence by camels to Ambigol.

Lieutenant Vidal, R.E., was in charge of this detachment. It was cheering, after our hot ride through this dreary desert route, to come again in sight of European civilisation, though only in the form of soldiers' tents. Riding up to them Lieutenant Vidal invited Major Hunter, Captain Wilson, of the Canadian Artillery, and myself to what would in England be called afternoon tea; but, alas! without the fair hands to dispense it to which we were accustomed.

Immediately after sunset we halted, as arranged, until the moon rose, and decided to have a grand repast. Unfortunately, we had forgotten our candles, and so, after fumbling about some time in the darkness that could be felt, our elaborately arranged bill of fare had to be reduced to tea, oxtail soup, 'bully' beef, biscuits, and, last of all, a tin of jam. After all, we did not do so badly under the circumstances, and, sitting together in a circle on the ground and chatting over our pipes, waited for the advance to sound.

The moon at last put in her appearance, and soon the quiet that had reigned for the last two hours was broken by the groanings of the camels as they were being got on their legs again for the march.

Continuing up the valley, the road was a capital one until we reached the end of the railway embankment, between eleven and twelve o'clock, when it became stony and much broken.

We had now been on the tramp for nine hours, and part of the time under the intense heat of a tropical sun. It was, therefore, excusable that some of us should show signs of drowsy weariness.

One commanding officer declared he could not keep his eyes open, and, riding up to the front, said, 'Well, it's no use struggling any longer; I must have a nap. My detachment will not be up for half an hour, and if I can get that amount of sleep it will be a relief; so here goes.' Drawing on one side, I saw him trying to get his camel to stay down after he had made it kneel; but whether he succeeded I know not, for I was borne along with the moving column, as tired and sleepy as this gallant officer. As we rode along I fell into a half-dreamy state, which made those riding in advance appear like gigantic figures of the 'Gog' and 'Magog' order. The men on their camels looked like enormous women clad in old-fashioned, short-waisted dresses: the rider being the head, the saddle the body, and the moving legs of the camel the flowing skirt. I am quite sure that several times two of our five senses had 'shut up shop.'

All at once we were startled by the appearance of a bright light right ahead. What could it be? It looked like an electric light, such as I had seen flashing from the foretop of the *Minotaur* off Ramleh in 1882. Then it became more subdued. It was a lantern! No; it was a fire. Then it turned greenish, suggesting the head signal-lights on some of the Metropolitan locomotives. After all our puzzling it turned out to be nothing but the moon's rays reflected from the bright tin lining of a biscuit-box which had been emptied and left on the roadside by some detachment which had preceded us.

Soon afterwards camp fires were seen off the road ahead, and figures coming from them towards us. Upon being challenged, they answered that they were conductors of a commissariat convoy brought to a standstill here, because their 'niggers,' that is, native labourers, had struck work. Major Poe interviewed the recalcitrants, and frightened, probably by his scarlet tunic, they resumed their duties, and this while we were passing by the spot like the inexorable stream of time.

The road now led over a shoulder between two rocky hills, through which the railway cutting of which we had heard so much had been commenced. It was difficult in the dim moonlight to estimate the work done, but it appeared to be considerable.

Our ride now became perilous, for on one side was the dark abyss of the rock-cutting and on the other a wall of rock, with only a narrow ledge between them. Even the moonlight failed us, owing to the shade of the ridge on our left. I trembled for the heavily laden and top-heavy artillery camels, for one false step, and over they must go into the rocky pit on our right. So nervous did I become from the dangerous character of the path, that I dismounted, and led my horse over it, and then down through another, crooked and uneven, but of no great length. It was so narrow at the point where it ended in a sandy plain that a loaded camel could with difficulty pass through it. One of the artillery camels here dropped down dead from exhaustion.

It was now 2 a.m., and we were all dreadfully tired. After riding a short distance over the sandy plain the roar of the Ambigol Cataract sounded from the near distance as delightful music. Some of the sleepy commanding officers began to be impatient, for, at first, the cataract appeared from the sound to be nearer than it was. One or two of them rode on ahead, then to the right, and came back in their disappointment, and began to blow up my man for leading them astray, and said many naughty things. They declared he did not know the way, and that I should never trust him again.

This I thought rather a poor reward for having led so far and so well a column of Her Majesty's troops in a moonlight night march. They wound up by declining to follow him any further. 'Do as you like,' I said; 'I'll follow him,' and I did, and they were glad to follow us, for at 3 a.m. he led us to the best camping-ground at Ambigol. I was soon stretched on my camp bed, and forgot all the fatigues of the march in a sound sleep, from which the blazing sun awakened me at 8 a.m. The ingrates had, however, the decency to apologise to me next day, and I forgave them, for we were all tired enough to be very cross with each other.

The marines and artillery did not march until next morning at three o'clock. First came the saddling and loading of the camels, and their wretchedly unmusical groaning. Then followed the mounting—in many cases a difficult task. First the camel is made to kneel, and then, lest the animal should rise when his rider attempts to mount, a rapid spring into the saddle is required to avoid a fall. Some camels have so inveterate a habit of thus rising that one man must stand on his bended leg before the other can mount him. Many scenes of this kind took place that morning among the Jollies, and many a struggle for mastery between these strange brutes and their riders before the division could march. One man's helmet fell off and was crushed by the foot of his camel, and I had to hand up their head-gear to several others who had become similarly dispossessed of them.

As next day was the Sabbath, I resolved to rest on it, and start off again on Monday. I am sorry to say, by way of parenthesis here, that, excepting at some of the principal stations, all days of the week were regarded alike. This I am thoroughly convinced is a mistake, for, besides the Divine command, it has been found beyond doubt that neither man nor beast can be worked continuously with safety or profit. In 1849, for example, when the great rush took place to California across the plains, it was found that both the men and their animals who rested one day in seven reached the end of the journey sooner and in better condition than those who travelled on Sunday and Saturday alike.

The cataract of Ambigol appeared at first sight to be a formidable, if not an insurmountable, obstacle to navigation. The Canadians, however, after first inspecting it, were reported to have 'guessed they had come up worse bits already.' The river here tumbles over a succession of dangerous rocks, and at the same time turns sharply round a rocky corner; as the number of wrecks showed, it had proved fatal to many a *nugger*,[1] but still a way up the cataract for boats had been found close inshore on the right bank. Nevertheless, when the main descent was reached, the water poured down a slope at a most alarming angle to anyone sitting in a boat ascending it.

The Canadian in the leading boat of the Engineers' flotilla of whalers, when this point was reached, I am told, wished to know, 'Who was running this show? For himself,' he said, 'he could swim, but was not sure whether the soldiers in the stern could,' So he recommended that a large portion of the cargo should be disembarked for the sake of safety to all concerned. The difficulty then presented by this cataract had now considerably increased, and the progress of the boats up it had become very much slower.

An officer in command of a detachment of the Essex regiment in eight whalers told me, on his arrival at the landing above the cataract, that in passing through it he had lost one boat and severely damaged two others.

Subsequently I went down to the rocky point on the right bank in order to watch another detachment working its way through the rapids. Hitherto the channel used had been on this side of the river, but through the falling of the water it was now a raging torrent, and

---

1. The natives told me that 10 *per cent*, of their boats had been thus lost.

wholly impracticable for boats of any kind. The whalers now used the channel on the other side, close to the left bank. Even this was so difficult that it took the crews of these eight boats two hours to make three hundred yards of headway against the rapid current, and twenty-four hours to pass up through a mile and a half of it. In order to accomplish this the cargoes of the boats had to be landed and conveyed to the smooth water above by camels. All this was terribly hard work for men unaccustomed to it, and made more so by the fierce rays of a tropical sun.

On November 3 they were aided by a number of Dongolese labourers, without whom they declared that their whalers could not have been hauled up the cataract. The cargoes had to be taken out of them and carried to the upper end of it by Egyptian soldiers. Now these engineers, as a part of their education at Chatham, had been thoroughly trained in rowing and managing boats, and, therefore, if they then found this work on the cataracts so difficult, how much more so must it have been to our common soldiers, many of whom had never handled an oar until they embarked in the whalers at Gemai! [2]

Appended is the letter of an officer and the interesting journal of Major Dixon, of the Royal Irish, which graphically though concisely illustrate the difficulties with which they and the other infantry regiments had to contend in coming up the cataracts in the whalers. Many of these difficulties, as will be noticed, were caused by the unsuitable materials of which the whalers were constructed and the faulty manner in which a number of them were put together. Had they, for instance, been planked with pine in place of with common white spruce, fewer holes would have been punched in them by the rocks with which they came so often in contact. The only explanation General Butler could offer on this point was that the chief constructor at the Admiralty had told him that a sufficient quantity of pine for the boats could not be obtained in the country when they were ordered.

In some cases unsound wood was employed for timbers, for I found that the stern of a whaler, lying on the rocks at Ambigol with her bow torn open, had been made out of elm too rotten to hold the blunt copper nails, about an inch long, by which the planks had been fastened to it!

Surely an additional supply of pine could have been speedily obtained from Norwegian or neighbouring European ports.

---
2. See Appendix C.

Then again, many of the whalers were also faulty in their construction owing to the manner in which they had been fitted with the iron straps with which, according to contract, each boat was to have been strengthened. These straps ought to have been extended in every instance from the top of the cutwater, down it, and along the keel, and then up the stern-post. In a number of the boats this strap was—as it ought to be—in one piece, and properly attached to the boat by long screws. But in many others it was in three pieces, one along the keel and the others over the cutwater and down the stern-post, to which they were respectively attached by screws so small as to be easily torn off or displaced by a moderately strong collision with rocks. In fine, there was so marked a difference in these and other respects in the construction of these boats as to suggest the want of oversight on the part of those whose duty it was to see that they were not merely in appearance, but in reality, according to contract.

In confirmation of these remarks the reader is referred to Major Dixon's journal, where in one case he reports the iron along the keel of one of his boats to have been fastened on with small nails. In another case he speaks rather amusingly of putting three patches of tin on a whaler, which, with the nine put on her by previous occupants, made twelve. It is also to be noticed in several places in his journal how much the flotilla was delayed by the time required for these repairs.

So far as the model and construction of the whalers were concerned, there were differences of opinion. Some of the Canadians complained of their being dangerously difficult of management in the rapids on account of their keels. The few accidents, however, which were thus caused hardly bore out this objection. On the other hand, without keels the boats could not have so effectually used the sails with which they were fitted, and by the use of which in smooth water and against a stiffish current they could average four miles an hour, and with larger sails they could have done better than that. Possibly larger sails would have been dangerous, owing to the inexperience not only of the soldier crews, but also of the Canadian Voyageurs, who in many instances which came under my own observation showed very great clumsiness in handling them.

One of these instances occurred at Sarkamatto, when two squadrons of whalers were coming up the river full sail before a stiff northerly breeze. The leading squadron ran full speed ashore, nearly pitching a man overboard. As the other approached I shouted to the leading boat to let go their sheet ropes, which they did, and came easily ashore.

The Canadians in charge no doubt wondered who I was, but nevertheless received kindly a few words of advice about sailing up a river, based on experience acquired in my early days on their own grand St Lawrence.

Passing down to the cataracts I visited the hospital tent, which was full of patients, chiefly suffering from enteric fever. In the physician in charge I met Dr. Stewart, who had been my fellow-passenger from Assiout to Assouan. He told me that one stalwart Irish doctor, who had come up with me from Assouan to Halfa, had succumbed to the climate and returned to Cairo.

My tent was pitched on the bank a short distance from the landing-place, and on the road thence to the commandant's tent above the rocky point. Of course I had some callers, and amongst them another of my fellow-passengers from Assiout. This young officer was a most intelligent fellow, but rather bumptious, and this led to a collision with a boat-load of Canadian Voyageurs with whom he had come some distance down the river to Ambigol. He was boiling over with indignation at their disobedience to his orders. 'Why,' said he, 'I ordered them to land at such a place, and they refused to do so. I am going to report them to the commandant.' I showed him a better way, but he would not walk in it.

On his return, however, he was quite calmed down, and said no more about my fellow-countrymen. I can very well understand how the latter would refuse to obey orders in the tone in which doubtless he would give them. In fact Lord Wolseley, with his knowledge of Canadian human nature and his own kind consideration for everybody, had issued an order placing the Canadian Voyageurs in a position independent of officers, for while in charge of boats none of the latter were allowed to interfere with them at all.

On Sunday evening, strolling down to the commissariat *depôt*, I met Colonel Burnaby, who had just arrived from Wady-Halfa with Colonel Blundell. He said that they had been appointed inspectors on the river between the points above in order to hurry on the boats. I was not very much surprised at this, for we had previously heard of his arrival at Cairo, and it was certain that by some means or other he would find his way up the Nile. He said that unless he had been able to get this appointment it would have been impossible for him to do so, for otherwise he could not have obtained supplies. In fact, in order to gain his end he had even endeavoured to secure a position as press correspondent. This incident is mentioned because it throws light on a serious matter. There were a number of officers from different regiments who had in some way or other obtained appointments in the expedition, who were not only utterly useless themselves, but were often in the way of others whose services were invaluable. I never could credit Lord Wolseley with their selection, but put it down to court or some other influence.

CHAPTER 8

Off Again After Wolseley

In order to lighten my camels' loads I managed to send part of my stores on ahead to Sarkamatto, and two hours before sunrise on Tuesday morning we left Ambigol for Akasheh, our next halting-place. The day before my man was instructed to make certain of the road to it, and assured me when we started that we were all right. In a short time the road we were following became impassable for camels, and, judging by the stars that we were considerably out of our course, we retraced our steps, and started off again by another route. My man amusingly blamed the moonlight for his blunder. Shortly after noon, instead of Akasheh, our last road landed us at Tanjur. The picturesqueness of the station here and its beautiful Nile landscape, however, compensated for this blunder number two.

During the afternoon several squadrons of whalers having cleared the rapids below passed up the river under sail. With my glass I watched others still labouring in the whirl of waters which here interrupts the navigation of the Nile.

On November 18 we heard at Wady-Halfa of the slow progress of the Staffordshire regiment up these rapids, caused by the attempt of its colonel to bring one wing up through them at a time. This plan worked badly, for any delay to one boat kept all the others back. From these circumstances an order was issued directing that the regiment was to push on in companies moving independently of each other, and this was the plan acted upon subsequently by all the regiments coming up in the whalers. The results proved the wisdom of this order, not only by the delay and congestion it prevented by the smaller number of boats passing up through some of the narrow channels at one time, but also by the emulation it excited among the different companies, and the consequent acceleration of the general progress of the expedition up the cataracts.

A number of Egyptian geese frequented the river hereabout, and were often easily shot. Captain Lloyd, the commandant at Tanjur, had that day bagged a very fine one.

We had halted under the branches of a large *sondt* tree some little distance from the station. The spot was very sandy, and, dreading a repetition of my experience of such a locality at Sarras, I secured furnished lodgings for the night in the tent of an officer who was absent. After a month's hard and narrow beds, it was pleasant to lie down on a soft mattress broad enough to allow of bending one's knees.

We started early next morning, and after one of the most enjoyable rides, so far as wild scenery and balmy air were concerned, we reached Akasheh at an early hour, and bivouacked for the night.

Leaving early next morning, we jogged on as usual, all alone, until we overtook a detachment of the Light Camelry regiment bound for Mograkeh. Their company was unfortunately so pleasant away out in the wilderness that we went two or three miles beyond Sarkamatto before the error was discovered.

Retracing our steps, we reached the latter two hours before sunset, and were accommodated for the night in one of the large Egyptian tents kept vacant for stragglers such as we were. It was near the river and fully exposed to the north wind. The defectiveness of its pegs let in the cold blast all round. Near it was the hospital, and about three hundred yards off, and fortunately to the leeward, was the native village, in which smallpox was epidemic. My fellow-traveller who missed the crocodile below Wady-Halfa was the commissariat officer here, and had duly received my boxes of stores and honourably handed them over to me. I mean the last part of that sentence to be emphatic, for his conduct was a contrast to that of some other officers of that department with whom I had had a similar transaction.

Mr. John Cook and his son had come down from Dongola in a small *dahabeyeh*, and were waiting at Sarkamatto for camel transport down the river. He kindly invited Captain Man and myself to dinner on board of his *bijou* craft, and a capital dinner we had, although our dining-saloon was rather cramped.

Conversing about the Nile between Dongola and Berber, Mr. Cook mentioned to us that his *reis*, or pilot captain, was one of the oldest of his profession on that part of the river, and recommended me to interview him on the subject. This I did next day through my dragoman, and elicited the opinion that the voyage between Dongola and Berber could not be accomplished at low Nile under three months. Of course the old fellow meant native craft, over which our whalers had great advantages for such navigation.

During the day several squadrons of whalers put in for rations here, and two boats leaking badly were hauled up for repairs.

After another wretchedly cold night in our dilapidated Egyptian tent, we started off again up the river after breakfast. The road was fairly good, but the day was so close and hot as to make travelling wearisome. Probably these drawbacks to comfort would have been lessened if want of sleep had not reduced our powers of endurance.

Mograkeh was reached early in the afternoon and quarters secured in the house of a villager behind which we had halted, and whose front door was guarded by a crocodile's head, of which he seemed very proud. The old fellow actually turned all his women out to accommodate us, although he might safely have let these Sudanese beauties remain, so far as we were concerned. It was, however, a happy thought, for with the women we got rid of a numerous tribe of youngsters, including not a few babies, and so had a quiet night of it. This was something, for the next had to be passed in the open desert between Mograkeh and Absarat

Our patriarchal host readily accepted a dollar (4*s*. 2*d*.) in the morning for the accommodation he had afforded us. While loading up the camels some of the ladies returned, and as they passed into the house they looked daggers at us. Poor old fellow! he must have had trouble with his household that day, for from all appearances a domestic eruption was imminent

At 7 a.m. we started for Absarat by the short cut across the desert, instead of by the more pleasant one along the river, which, as the map shows, curves west from Mograkeh, and after a short sweep to the south re-curves east to Absarat. Between these two points the distance is roughly estimated at thirty-five miles, but I think it is nearer forty miles.

Our road led first up a *wady*, which was now evidently a torrent-bed, but which from its general appearance may have been formerly the channel of a river. It was on an average about a quarter of a mile wide, and bounded on each side by rocky hills of the same extraordinary burnt appearance that had characterised the rocks above Wady-Halfa, and in fact for some distance below it. They were either of a very dark brown or of a shining jet-black colour. Sometimes, as in the case of magnesian limestone, this weathering only extended to a depth of the sixteenth of an inch, and in schistose rocks to a mere skin, but in some others to an inch or more.

From the fragments of which they were composed, and their forms, many of the hills resembled gigantic heaps of anthracite coal. Geologically and ethnologically—so far as colour went at any rate—things were pretty well harmonised in the Sudan, for as its rocks, so its inhabitants were—some brown and others black as polished ebony.

The travelling up this *wady* for some hours was as heavy as its surroundings were gloomy, for the road led through light yellow sand, or heavy sandy gravel divided here and there by strips strewn over with small stones.

The road, so called, was simply eight to twelve or fourteen narrow well-beaten paths running parallel to each other, with here and there between them a tuft of grass, or decorated by small yellow and lilac flowers, not wasting their sweetness on the desert air exactly, for they did something towards relieving the dreariness of the journey. By-and-by the bottom of the *wady* became dotted over with *sondt* and mimosa trees and patches of *savas* grass of a light bluish-green colour.

After a gradual ascent for six hours a rocky ledge was reached, over which the road dipped into what was probably the basin of an ancient lake. Judging from the graceful outlines of the hills which surrounded its shores, and the islands which rose from its bosom, it must have been a beautiful sheet of water. Riding halfway across it, we halted and bivouacked for the night near a bed of light bluish-grey gravel, the stones of which were well worn by water.

It was well we had come provided with both wood and water, for neither was to be had hereabouts. So barren and desolate was the spot that my old dragoman, in reply to an inquiry I made about snakes, said I need not be afraid, as there were none about here, for there was nothing for them to feed on. Dined as usual on tinned soup, bully, beef, tea and biscuits, and then prepared for sleeping. This required some care, for a cold northerly wind was blowing, and we had no protection from its keen blast. Placing my portable table, covered with a waterproof sheet well anchored by stones, at the head of my bed, and, of course, to windward of it, I lay down and fell asleep, satisfied I had checkmated old Boreas, but I was mistaken. During the night the wind freshened, and at 1 a.m., awakened by the cold, I found my table overturned, and had to set it up again and repair other damages. Long before sunrise we were all up, and as it was still bitterly cold, I had a run across the plain and back again to warm up for breakfast

While the camels were being loaded a flock of vultures put in an appearance and squatted near us on a gravel swell, with the evident expectation of a feast after our departure. My old dragoman had evidently also spent an uncomfortable night, for he was out of temper with everything. His grumbling at last found final expression in the declaration: 'I do believe, sir, that God Almighty made dis country on purpose to put de people in he doesn't want.' This cleared our domestic atmosphere, for it provoked such a laugh from me that it had to be translated for the benefit of my camel-man, and then off we moved again.

Our road on leaving the level plain soon began to ascend the broken and stony ridge which formed the southern rim of the basin in which we had bivouacked. When its crest was reached, the Nile, with its groves of palms and blue water, came again in sight. This was most refreshing after the barren wilderness through which for several days we had pursued our weary way. Descending to the plain which separated us from the river, we met a pair of natives on their way through the wilderness we had just left. First came an untidy looking Sudanese, comfortably seated on a donkey, and, following on foot, his wife, carrying on her head and under her arm the baggage of the pair. This included a roll of the invariable palm-leaf mats on which these people sleep.

We saw a number of such illustrations of Sudanese gallantry subsequently, when, with few exceptions, the lady travelled on 'shanks's mare,' while the gentleman rode the family donkey.

From the foot of the hill we had now descended to the river the country appeared to be a dead level, and consequently the palm groves on its banks appeared much nearer than they actually were. The road to them was also lengthened doubtless by the oppressive heat of the day and our great weariness, and our halt at Absarat was therefore looked forward to with satisfaction.

The plain we had thus ridden over, in common with several others in the valley of the Nile above Assouan, was both topographically and geologically interesting, and therefore claims a passing notice. All the indications went to prove that at a not very distant date they had been periodically inundated by the river, and also cultivated. It can hardly be questioned that the first cataract, originally at Silsilis, was transferred to Assouan by the wearing or giving way of the sandstone rocks at the former point. A little south of some mounds on the east bank, opposite Philae, are masses of old alluvium, deposited there by the river before its level was lowered by the changed condition of the rocks at Silsilis.

Its general level is 80 feet higher than the inundations of modern times, and the highest masses of this old alluvium deposit are 10 feet higher still. The irregularity of these masses and the sudden depression in them indicate a probability that the giving way of the rocks at Silsilis took place while the river was high. From the point where this deposit occurs it is also evident that the bed of the river at one period ran straight on over the plain between Assouan and the ridge of mountains which bound it on the east Upward from Philae to Wady-Halfa, this old alluvium deposit may be easily traced on the river-bank, and always high above the reach of present inundations. It is probable, therefore, that some change less violent perhaps than that which is supposed to have taken place at Silsilis may have occurred at one of the series of rock interruptions either at Ambigol, Dal, or Kaibar, but most probably at Dal.

Taking the height above the sea as given in the map of the Nile from Wady-Halfa to Khartoum, issued by the Intelligence Department, the difference of level in a distance of 126 miles between Dal and Kaibar is but 60 feet Now the present level of this plain near Absanat is not many feet above that of the Nile inundations. Consequently the change in the rocky bars across it at Dal need not necessarily have been very serious to prevent it now, as it may have been formerly, from being periodically overflown. The same remarks apply to the plain from Abu-Fatmeh upwards on the east bank for 25 miles, if not for a greater distance.

The distance to Faredi, the next military station above Absanat, is about twenty-eight miles—'about,' because such was the distance on the road itineraries supplied to the troops by the military authorities; but I thought in this and several other instances they were longer than therein stated. This distance was in excess of a fair day's work for camels by at least six miles.

Starting just before sunrise as usual, we reached Dulgo, halfway, about 11 o'clock, and halted for luncheon. This was the first native village of any importance we had come to since leaving Wady-Halfa. The people showed themselves very friendly, and ready to supply us with eggs and milk, and fodder for the camels. The male portion of the villagers thronged round me, old and young, down to the merest toddler, but the women kept at a distance, indulging, however, in an occasional peep at the stranger. It was a treat after our long ride through a desolate region to meet again with signs of home life, and while my men were preparing lunch I indulged in a good romp with the youngsters, much to their amusement and my own. Their laughter was most refreshing, for it had a home ring about it Although there were some mud houses in the village, the people generally lived in straw huts. At the lower end of the village was a large ruin extending to the river, but whether of a church or an old fort it is difficult to say. The probability, however, is that it was the latter, although some parts of its architecture inclined towards the former.

The road from Dulgo led over a level tract of land, apparently as easily irrigated as that under cultivation. The absence of a market and the consequent lack of incentive lead to its lying waste.

We soon passed on our left the lofty table-topped Jebel Barbour, which rose in solitary and isolated grandeur from the plain by which it was surrounded. There were a number of such mountains here and there over this desert region; sometimes they appeared to have a volcanic origin, and at other times to have been bodily raised up by some subterranean force to their present elevation. Sometimes again their sides bore the marks of water, and imagination pictures the water of the Nile having once covered their flat summits now so high above the level of the river.

Within an hour of sunset I ascertained we were at least six miles from Faredi, or a good two hours' march. As there is no twilight in this region, it was therefore always necessary to look out for a suitable halting-place for the night before the thick darkness came on. The object always was to bivouac near a village, in order to secure a supply of milk and other luxuries of the kind, and also near the river, on account of water. As at Dulgo, so everywhere going up the Nile, we found the villagers very friendly, and showing so many 'touches of nature' as to awaken a feeling of human kinship. On our return down the river in April, and especially above Dongola, they showed a remarkable coolness towards us, often verging on the rude and insolent.

The sun had just set when we reached the village of El Davneh, nearly opposite Kaibar, and a short distance below the cataract there, and early next morning rode into Faredi, the station for the Kaibar rapids.

This station was very prettily situated on the right bank of the Nile, where the river bends sharply to the west. The bank here was high and fringed with palms along its western curve. Towards the north-west the view extended ten miles down the river, with a background of mountains and hills of blue and purple hues. Nowhere in the world are these distant tints more delicate and beautiful. Mr. Villiers, of the *Graphic*, in his artistic enthusiasm, often expressed to me his admiration of them. Nature had thus compensated in the distance of her pictures for the desolateness of her foregrounds.

The middle foreground of this landscape was filled in by the long stretch of the Nile north-westwards—bluish a little distance off, and then fading away into a silvery streak. The banks on both sides were fringed by groves of palms and bunches of mimosa, brilliantly green in the sunlight, through the contrast afforded by the golden sand and light-coloured soil beneath and around them.

After my arrival a detachment of the Light Camel regiment, under Colonel Stanley Clarke, came in and bivouacked on the cultivated soil below the village, at the bend of the river. They spent a most uncomfortable night under their *tentes d'abri*, for they felt the full force of the north wind, and were well sanded and dusted in consequence.

I had halted further up the right bank, and pitched my tent under a grove of palms, safe both from sand and dust At the lower end of this grove the station commandant had pitched his, and near it was the commissariat *depôt*, on the edge of the high bank. Below this was snugly moored Lieutenant Inglefield's steam-pinnace, which I had seen off up the river some weeks before from Assouan. He was doing duty in the 'reach' between Faredi and Abu-Fatmeh, using wood for fuel. And hard work was this for his crew, for first they had to get it and then saw and chop it up for use. Nevertheless, I found the 'jolly tars' enjoying the kind of amphibious life they were thus leading, for they sawed and chopped their logs and tossed up their pancakes in their frying-pans in the best possible humour.

Above this grove of palms, at a rocky point, crocodiles were generally to be seen basking themselves in the afternoon's sun. Lieutenant Inglefield told me he had occasionally a shot at them. It appeared, however, that he never hit them in a vulnerable place, for the results of his sport were *nil*.

Returning to my bivouac one evening after dining with the commandant, I had to pass the commissariat *depôt*, and answered the challenge of the Egyptian sentinel on guard over it in the usual way. Although he must have known me by my dress and from having seen me moving about the camp during the day, he brought his rifle down to the 'ready,' and marched me off to the commissariat-sergeant to give an account of myself. I always mistrusted these Egyptian soldiers when on such duty, and so this one came much nearer being made ready for a mummy than he was aware, for the moment he began to handle seriously his Remington I loosened the handle of my 'Colt,' and cocked it. The commandant next day offered to have his sentry *courbashed* in order to appease my wrath, but I had none to appease, and begged him off. It was rather a joke, after all, for it often appeared to me that this fellah soldier, like most of his comrades, was only an opportunist, and wished on this occasion to show the *Inglese* how bravely and even fiercely he could discharge any duty imposed upon him. It was a dangerous practice, however, and several times previously, and once later on, I had been served the same way by these soldiers.

At Faredi I met Colonel Butler on his way up the river, as enthusiastic as ever about the 'whalers', as certainly he had a right to be. As a proof of their usefulness and success as a means of transport, he told me that seventy of them had already passed Debbeh. So far so good; but there was another aspect of the case. It was now December 14, the day after which Gordon had plainly told us in his letter of November 4, it would be difficult for him to hold out. These seventy boats had taken forty days to reach Debbeh, and at this rate of progress one naturally asked, Can the expedition be expected to reach Khartoum before it has fallen? Those who had designed its plan and were working it out with an earnestness worthy of its object hoped to do so. But could they? I had my misgivings; but it would have been ungenerous to tell the gallant colonel so, and I therefore kept my thoughts to myself. Had Lord Granville or Mr. Gladstone been near me at the time, and been disposed to listen, I should not have hesitated unburdening my mind to them.

Learning from Colonel Butler that the commander-in-chief had shifted his headquarters from Dongola to Korti, and judging that therefore some important movement was imminent, I started early next morning for Abu-Fatmeh.

Our road after leaving the village of Faredi led over land from which the crops had been gathered, and then along the bank of the river, to where we had a view of it for some distance upwards. In the early morning light, and from the strong wind blowing against its current, it looked refreshingly blue. To enhance this feeling, the green of its fringe of palms appeared darker than it would have been later in the day. Life was also given to the landscape by the appearance of Lieutenant Inglefield's pinnace, on its way to Hannek with Colonel Butler. She was steaming and under full sail with the St. George's ensign flying, man-of-war fashion, from her mizen peak.

The road now left the river to follow the chord of the arc made by the considerable curve it makes between Faredi and Abu-Fatmeh. The first thing we stumbled on was another of the many dead camels we had passed on the way, and on which a flock of vultures were having a feast, in company with a number of those untidy and repulsive-looking birds, the turkey buzzard. Although for the greater part of the day the road was rough and stony, we covered its twenty-one miles in seven hours.

It led us across a new geological region, comprising traps and schistose rocks with interstratifications of various coloured slates. One band of the latter was a very reddish brown and another greenish, both carrying quartz. From the latter circumstance and their general appearance they certainly would warrant a search hereabouts for copper and its associated minerals.

At the end of this wilderness we rode through a gravel plain strewn with gigantic granite boulders of fantastic forms, one of which at a distance resembled the Sphinx. This plain sloped down to a dead level, which extended to Abu-Fatmeh, some eight miles distant. So level was it that the commandant deemed it prudent, in the absence of landmarks and the ill-defined track, to maintain a beacon light for the benefit of belated travellers.

The camping-ground here was very sandy, and virulent small-pox prevailed at the dirty native village, from contact with which a Canadian had died a day or two previously; and so, after a night's rest and the replenishment of my supplies, I was glad to leave it.

On a hill below the station there was an old fort in which the detachment of Egyptian troops was stationed.

Major Morris, R.A., the courteous station commandant, occupied a straw hut with an entrance to it almost as low as that to an Esquimaux ice-house. He seemed, however, as comfortably happy as if lodged in his London club. The approaches were so well defended against loafers by a *chevaux de frise* of thorny branches as to render access to the major in the dark rather troublesome, as I found to my cost It was my misfortune not to have met here another major who had come to be regarded as the astronomer royal of the expedition from his persistent efforts to fix the longitude of the stations. His celebrity, however, grew more out of his numerous failures than from his successes in these efforts.

In order to attain his object, as is usual in such cases, he sought to compare the moment at which the star or planet he was observing crossed the meridian with that at Cairo whose longitude was known. This could only be done, of course, by the cooperation of the telegraph operators. It generally happened that when the star he observed had reached the right spot overhead some block occurred on the line, and the observation thus missed fire. In one instance the blame of failure was laid upon the respected superintendents of the Egyptian Military Telegraph Department, for at the supreme moment of his astronomical observation one of them unluckily took hurried possession of the line for the despatch of an official message to the other. By his absence I also missed the opportunity of thanking him for the comfortable night's rest I had enjoyed in his well-appointed tent at Tanjur.

Strolling down to the landing-place below the old castle I found a detachment of the —— regiment which had just arrived in whalers from Dal. They had now completed a second trip thence to Abu-Fatmeh with stores, under a recent order by which all troops, when they arrived here, discharged the cargoes they brought up on their first trip, and went down the river to the former place to bring up another. The sergeant in command and his men were in a most desponding mood, grumbling as only Tommy Atkins can occasionally.

They complained, amongst many things, of being out of 'baccy' and having to smoke tea as a substitute. Then they had not had enough to eat, and no white lead with which to patch up their boats, and so forth. They were not a fair specimen, however, of the spirit which actuated the boat corps, and some of their complaints were most unreasonable— as, for example, in the case of tobacco. It was their own fault being out of it, for there was a plentiful supply of it at Faredi commissariat *depôt*.

The sergeant and his detachment had, however, come up the Kaibar rapid, as was usual, by the channel near the left bank, while the commissariat *depôt* was on the right bank. As all boats were supplied with an itinerary showing where commissary *depôts*, &c., were, it was therefore owing either to this non-commissioned officer's stupidity or neglect that any such deficiency in his stores had not been replenished The sergeant at the commissary *depôt* at Faredi had plenty of tobacco, and declared that it was at present a drug in the market, for he had had no demand for it. Unfortunately, there was not a plug of it here at Abu-Fatmeh. Mentioning the matter to Major Morris he told me that he had sent to Faredi for a supply.

This was but one of the many instances of the kind consideration, even in little matters, of the commandants at these stations, as well as other officers of the expedition, including, I need hardly say, the commander-in-chief himself, for the comfort of the troops.

Chapter 9
Abu-Falmeh to Dongola

Shortly after my arrival at Abu-Fatmeh Major Carmichael, of the 5th Lancers, who so unfortunately lost his life in the square at Abu-Klea, came in with a contingent of the camel corps, comprising detachments from the Royal Dragoons, the 5th Lancers, and the 20th and 21st Hussars.

It marched shortly after I had started, but caught up to me, owing to the trouble and consequent delay I had in getting one of my camels along. My man would persist in arranging the loads in such a manner as to oscillate, see-saw fashion, across their backs, thus causing much unnecessary chafing. This camel in particular, when badly loaded, uttered a peculiar groan, indicating pain, and as if asking relief from it. Then it was 'Halt! off with the load, and reload in better form.'

Ordeh, or new Dongola, the next military station, was thirty miles from Abu-Fatmeh. This necessitated two marches under ordinary circumstances, but I had to make three of it.

After leaving Abu-Fatmeh the road for two hours was rather heavy, as it led along the base of a range of low sand-hills between it and the cultivated lands and the river on which the villages were built. On our left, a mile or so off, were a number of hamlets surrounded by cultivated land and trees, irrigated from wells supplied by infiltration from the Nile.

The road gradually drew off from the sand-hills, and led over hard ground, besprinkled with pebbles of quartz and flint, variously coloured white, red, yellow, and orange. As bloodstones, cornelians, amethysts, and agates were often found amongst them, I kept a good look-out as I rode along, often dismounting and letting my horse follow me—as the kind animal would, like a pet dog. I succeeded in finding only a few, though very pretty, specimens of cornelian and moss agates. Sometimes the pebbles lay very thickly, just as if there had been a shower of them. It was a puzzle to me for some time where they came from. I found out at last, as will be seen in the description given further on of the rock formation at Jakdul. Besides the pebbles, there were also strewn in some places pieces of pottery ware, much of which appeared to be more ancient than that now used by the natives.

This plain, on the western edge of which we were riding, extended away in an almost unbroken level to the horizon on our left. It looked as if at one time it had been a lake, in which, from their loom in the prevailing mirage, the distant isolated hills and purple-coloured mountains appeared as islands.

About four hours from Abu-Fatmeh there are two large fort-like ruins, which, owing to their distance from the road and to want of time, I could not inspect. The natives whom I questioned about them said they were '*minzerman ketír*,' i.e., very ancient. They were evidently built of mud, which, in the Sudan, either from the quantity of silica or some other substance it contains, becomes as hard as concrete. The more eastern of the two appeared to be the larger.

We rode on ahead of Carmichael's column, and at noon drew off the road to the Nile for luncheon. Soon after it followed our example, and halted near us. It was a pretty spot, opposite an island near the village of Bergad. The slope of the sand-hills towards the cultivated ground was covered with herbage and a few low trees, which afforded a pleasant shade. Below us was the level cultivated soil, extending from the grassy bank on which we were to the now almost dried-up channel of the river, and so dotted over with trees and bushes as to resemble a somewhat neglected park.

Major Carmichael and the other officers with him joined me, and we feasted on a tin of preserved mutton and sardines. How lighthearted we were! and chatted amongst other things about the stars. The major called my attention to the southern cross and the false cross, now visible, laughingly remarking that he considered the former a fraud, because one of its stars was out of square with the others. I recalled our conversation then during our night march from Abu-Klea, when these constellations glittered and sparkled before us, and remembered sadly that several of those who had joined in that conversation had only a few hours previously met a soldier's death. How gloomy was the place where we buried them, and how bright were these southern constellations! Still to us stars were they now themselves in the brighter galaxy of British heroes!

At sunset we bivouacked on the Nile, near a small village, opposite the lower end of Argo Island, from which, as usual, was obtained an abundant supply of milk and eggs. Carmichael's detachment had bivouacked a short distance beyond us, as I judged by the sound of his bugles.

Before sunrise the people came with more supplies. These were usually brought to us by the males; but now several little girls put in an appearance, carrying calabashes of milk. They wore only a short kilt made of a fringe of twine and a string of beads. Such sparkling black eyes had these dusky maidens, and such well-formed features! Their mamas, only a little more attired, and some of them wearing strings of large yellow beads, came just outside of their houses to have a peep at us as we moved off, and would, I believe, have come nearer but for the jealousy of their spouses.

We had a tiresome day of it, between the heat and the slowness with which the camels travelled. My big Bishareen had badly chafed the cushion between his forelegs, upon which camels rest that part of their body when kneeling. He groaned piteously and began to travel unwillingly. Twice he stopped altogether, and as usual dropped down on his knees. At last we had to transfer part of his load to one of his mates before we could get him to go on.

My stirrup on the sunny side became so heated that I had to wrap it round with a piece of cotton cloth, and a tin box in my pocket holding lozenges became so hot that it could only be handled with difficulty. And this was the middle of December.

By an easy method I had learned to time our rate of progress. A camel on the average steps thirty-seven inches each step; therefore, by counting the number of his paces to the minute, a pretty accurate calculation can be made of the hourly run of the 'ship of the desert' Thus two miles and a half per hour requires a camel to make seventy-one paces to the minute. I found we were going not quite fifty, or less than two miles an hour. It was impossible therefore at this rate to reach Dongola that day, so an hour before sunset I gave up the attempt and turning off the road halted for the night at the village of Akadeh, opposite Argo Island. It was found with some difficulty, as the narrow road to it led through a forest of tall, luxuriant *dhura*, the stalks of which were from eight to ten feet high.

At last we met one of the villagers, who conducted us to the building set apart for strangers, and the headman, a *sheik*, being absent, his deputy did all he could to make us comfortable.

Like *khans* everywhere in the East, it consisted of one room devoid of furniture; the entrance to which was by a low door. Holes in the mud wall high up from the floor served as unglazed windows. This was not unusual, for, from the time I left Wady-Halfa until I returned again, excepting at one house in Dongola, I did not see a single pane of glass. In the front of the *khan* a yard was divided off by a low mud wall. Not liking the confinement of the room, I decided to sleep outside, and now followed an amusing scene. The first things always taken off the camels were my portable bed, table, and chair. A number of the villagers clustered round watching these preliminary operations with great interest. The setting up of the table did not excite much curiosity, but the opening out of the chair was followed by a burst of admiration in the common salutation, '*kweis Inglese*.' For half an hour or more that chair had to be opened and folded up again. The news of the novelty spread, and others came to witness the operation, when the opening and folding up had to be gone through again.

Then the portable bed, contained in a canvas case 36 inches long and 12 x 9 square, came under their notice. What wonder was now in store for them! The bed was at last opened and placed in position for sleeping on amid exclamations of still greater surprise than the chair had excited. Twice had we to unfold and then fold it up again before they were satisfied. Every part of it was minutely examined; the canvas and tacks, fastenings, its legs, all came in for a share of close inspection. My *dragoman* at last caught the excitement, and exclaimed, 'Now, sir, you can take the place of the *Mahdi* after working such miracles. Dress up like a *sheik* and let me be your interpreter, and they'll all bow down and pray to you.' This I tacitly declined, and as dinner 'was announced,' I brought the amusing scene to a close by an exhibition of my air pillow. Quietly blowing it out, and leaving the valve open, I invited some of the people to inspect it. A slight squeeze and the consequent jet of air in their faces afforded some fun until it was emptied.

With some difficulty the enclosure between the low mud walls was cleared of the curious throng of chattering natives. But we did not get rid of them entirely, for they stationed themselves outside the enclosure and watched the '*Inglese*' feeding. One has to get used to this kind of staring in the East. A white man and his paraphernalia are as great a curiosity to these people as a Bedouin riding through a London thoroughfare on his camel would be to us. I do not think, however, that the former in some parts of the great city would fare as well as I always did with these kind but untutored children of the Sudan.

Of course you could trust them up to a certain point. Beyond that it was not safe, for they are, as a rule, and with few exceptions, from the highest to the lowest, liars by nature. My old dragoman, after having been humbugged by some of them on one occasion, thus expressed himself: 'Well, sir, I do tink dese people believe God Almighty tell lies and de debble tells de truth, and dey lie because dey tink dat please God.' However pleasant and kind they may therefore appear, one has always to be painfully suspicious of these Eastern people.

In fact the closing incident of this evening is a case in point. When preparing for the night's rest one of the villagers, noticing that the room was not to be occupied by me, asked permission to do so. He fortunately mentioned that he might have to go in and out during the night, and hoped that would not disturb us. This was rather suspicious. In order to get rid of the fellow and to appear civil at the same time, I declined to agree to it, for as we were in the habit of firing at anyone prowling near us at night, he might therefore be accidentally shot. He took the hint and found a safer lodging elsewhere.

Up again before sunrise, awakened by the twittering of the flocks of birds overhead and around us, and the cooing of the doves. More milk and eggs were brought by the villagers, and after a hasty breakfast off we were again. The road for some distance led away from the Nile over a loose sandy district, which made the early part of the day's ride rather dreary. About noon, however, we came in sight of the river again, and rode near its bank. It was now a broader stream than anywhere we had noticed it to be above Wady-Halfa.[1] How all the water passing through this broad channel ever got to the sea by the very much narrower channels below was a puzzle to some people we met. These hydrostatic philosophers judged, *a priori* of course, that this could only be accounted for on the hypothesis of subterranean channels, of which, however, no proof exists. The depth as well as the breadth of the stream here, as well as below, and the force of the currents in both places, afford, however, the basis of a more correct calculation on which to solve the apparent difficulty.

We passed on the way many native cemeteries, in which each grave was marked by a row of white, red, or yellow quartz pebbles, and covered over by them in convex form. Red earthenware vessels

---

1. On the upward journey we had not seen the river near Saye Island, as we avoided the bend of the Nile there by crossing the Mograkeh desert. There, however, as we noticed on our return voyage, the channel is very wide.

or pots of various shapes were placed on them. These, my man said, were those last used by the deceased and placed there in memory of them. These cemeteries were almost invariably located on the edge of the desert abutting on the cultivated land, which added considerably to the dreariness of their appearance. The site seemed generally to have been chosen with a view to secure them from being covered by the drifting sand. In none of them did I notice tombstones. There were, however, many tombs of either holy or celebrated men, generally near villages. These had a sugarloaf-shaped roof, and not domed as in Lower Egypt. Some of them were twenty to twenty-five feet in height and built of Nile mud.

The opposite shore presented a most refreshing appearance, strongly in contrast with the dreary sandy desert along which we were riding, as it was fringed with stately palms and numerous trees, with their bright emerald foliage, backed by the darker verdure of *dhura* fields. The long-looked-for El-Ordeh or Kasr-Dongola, as Dongola is variously called, at last came in sight on the opposite side of the river. With its dark grey mud buildings, some of which were in a very dilapidated condition, its appearance was anything but attractive.

Carmichael's detachment, which had arrived on the previous evening, was encamped on a very sandy spot, and exposed to the full force of the strong north wind which was then blowing. The poor fellows looked wretchedly uncomfortable in the consequent sandstorm as I rode through them to bivouac near the commissariat tent higher up the river.

A long flat island extended between us and Dongola, dividing the river into two channels. The only means of transport across were unwieldy *nuggars* wholly dependent on their sails, and, from the direction from which the wind was blowing, crossing was a very difficult and tedious operation. So I decided to wait where we were until next day, hoping by that time the gale would blow itself out. The marines, artillery, and part of the camel corps with whom I had travelled up from Sarras, had reached Handak, forty miles up the river, having continued their march up the right bank instead of being ferried across at Dongola. As there was a block at the ferry there, owing to the numbers collected and want of wind, I decided to take the left bank. My man very foolishly, in pitching my tent, placed the door to windward, and when I returned from a visit to Carmichael I found it inflated to its full capacity, and in danger of being carried off like a balloon.

Too tired to alter it, and anxious for a shelter from the drifting sand,

I tied up the door and made everything otherwise as tight to windward as I could, and, Esquimaux fashion, crept in under the canvas to leeward. It was difficult to keep a fire alight in the wind, and almost as difficult to protect our breakfast while cooking from being peppered with the drifting sand and the other objectionable pulverised substances mixed with it. Riding in such a climate without proper rest was not likely to induce a hearty appetite, and the sense of taste, as well as the stomach, resented food charged with such gritty matter. My men, from want of proper attention, made a mess of cooking our prize. Fresh meat was not to be obtained every day, but on this morning some had been served out to us.

After the first mouthful I had to have my share washed to free it from the gritty sand with which it had become impregnated before it could be comfortably masticated. This certainly was not the kind of comfort to which I looked forward when I reached Dongola during our weary march of over two hundred miles through a desert region.

The wind lulled next morning, and I managed to get over to the town to arrange for ferrying my camels and horse over to the left bank. Captain Leach, of the Remount Department, kindly permitted my animals to be brought back in one of the *nuggars* employed in taking over camels to replace those lost or invalided by Carmichael's detachment While conversing with the captain a verbal message was brought to him that General Sir Redvers Buller's baggage from Wady-Halfa had reached the opposite bank on forty camels! Whew! Forty camels for one general's baggage, and that general had refused a press correspondent permission to purchase two baggage-nets from the Ordnance Department at Halfa, because 'we are short of them'! I returned to the right bank in one of the *nuggars* taking the camels over to Carmichael, and we landed below the steep sandy bank just below my bivouac. Its narrow foreshore here made loading and unloading rather troublesome.

Then the water was so shallow that the *nuggar* had to lie off some ten feet The puzzle now was how to get the animals into this vessel, for it had a freeboard of nearly three feet and its depth of hold was over four. The luggage was easily shipped, but not so the camels. At first I thought it could not be done, although I knew it must be. It turned out to be another Jumbo-shipping affair on a smaller scale. Some soldiers who had come down to water their camels kindly extended a helping hand, and so after a struggle they got the fore-feet of my big Bishareen camel over the side, and, by tugging at his halter and pushing from behind, started him, and with a spring he drew over his hind-legs. There was less difficulty with the remaining camels, for their objections to rough handling seemed to yield to their desire to follow their comrades.

The next difficulty was to get the horse on board. Had a clear jump been practicable, this could easily have been managed. When he was brought up to the side of the boat, the poor brute seemed quite nonplussed. He pranced about in the water alongside of it, pricked up his ears, snorted, looked earnestly at me and then at his comrades, as if to say, 'I am really anxious to get over. I know I ought, but I am not used to this kind of jumping. You know at Cairo I have cleared five feet four; but how can I get into that hole without help?' Fortunately four men of the 'Royals,' who had come down to water their camels, kindly came to the rescue, and lifting 'Saladin's' fore-feet over the side of the *nuggar*, he sprang into the boat all right.

On reaching the other side, the animals were easily landed, and loading up we rode to a square beyond the Mudireyeh and soon secured an empty house for our temporary quarters. It was not much of a house, after all, for it consisted of but one large room, lighted by a few holes high up on the walls and by the low door through which it was entered. The walls and floor were of mud, and extending across one end of it there was a divan of the same material. As we were now in the region of white ants, stones were scattered about on the floor on which to place the luggage in order to preserve it from their destructive attacks. The door was low and fastened by a wooden lock of curious construction, which was opened by a curved piece of wood with several iron pegs about a quarter of an inch long on its inner face. There was a certain position in which this novel key had to be inserted sideways into the lock and a knack in pressing it against the bolt—or a wooden bar rather—before the latter could be drawn back. One day I missed this knack, and as my men were absent I had to invoke the aid of a passing native in order to gain admission to my domicile.

This house of one room and a small kitchen built apart from it was separated from the street by a high mud wall enclosing a courtyard about twelve feet by fifty. The horse was tethered in this enclosure and the three camels left outside. The camel-man took up his quarters with the latter, sleeping on a divan of dried mud along the wall outside the gate.

The first thing needed was fodder for our five or six days' journey to Korti. Green stuff, I learned, could be had on the way, but *dhura* and barley were scarce until Debbeh was reached, as the military authorities were large purchasers. Of these grains I had some difficulty, therefore, in obtaining an adequate supply, and only succeeded by purchasing it in small quantities. One of my men was inclined to remain here, and it took a good deal of coaxing and threatening intermixed, and a loss of twenty-four hours, before I succeeded in keeping him with me.

Dongola I found to be a comparatively insignificant town, built on the edge of a fertile plain, extending back from the river some two or three miles. The land of the plain is very productive, and under a better system of cultivation could be made to yield much finer crops than it now does.

The population, composed of the representatives of the various races of the Sudan, numbers from five to six thousand. Some of its buildings, such as the Government house, courts of justice, barracks, and prison, and also several private houses of the better class, are rather pretentious in their appearance. Generally, however, they were small, and invariably constructed of Nile mud. The streets, as usual in Eastern towns, were narrow, dusty, and in many cases filthy. The town has an air of greater importance given to it than it deserves by a wall, or rather line, of earthworks enclosing it on its land side, and of such an extent as would require at least ten thousand troops to defend it. The principal bazaar comprised about twenty shops, with very limited stocks of inferior goods. Manchester cottons, prints, towels, Swiss muslins, homespun cotton sheets and cloths, home-made twines and ropes, German knickknacks and hardware—these with cloves, henna, and other Eastern toilet articles, made up the bulk of the merchandise exposed for sale.

Outside there was also an open market, where eggs, milk, bread, vegetables of all kinds, and fresh meat could be bought. Going one morning to this market to forage for fresh meat, in the first butcher's shop I entered there was none to suit me. Looking round, I saw at a little distance a quantity of what I thought, from its fresh redness and fatness, must be prime beef. On closer inspection something about it struck me as unnatural; and' on further examination I found it to be dead camel! My appetite was very good that morning, but not sufficiently so to induce me to patronise that butcher; so I went back to the other one for my supply, and took what I could get.

Tired of drinking out of metal teacups, I pounced upon a delft one, exposed amongst a small stock of bowls of the same material in a china shop in the bazaar. It resembles a small pudding-basin, is about a quarter of an inch thick, with two bunches of three dark blue flowers on opposite sides, and united by sprays of green, with a 'true lover's' knot in dark pink between them. It is now on the desk before me as I write, and no china collector could value a piece of delft more than I prize this bowl-cup, for it reached London safe and sound after our desert marches and two battles. Somebody at my elbow tells me that my sentiment is wasted on a bit of the commonest delftware which could be picked up any day at a street stall in London!

The last time I dined with the mess of the Intelligence Department at Dongola it had gone in for a supply of the larger bowls which I had seen at the same shop, and it was amusing to see the interest their possession excited, and to hear the strong opinions expressed about their usefulness as 'porridge bowls'—that is, for porridge made of ground *dhura*.

Earthenware amongst the natives was confined to the simplest forms of rude crockery, such as pans used for milk, pots, and peculiarly shaped water-jars. I managed to bring home safely two of the latter all the way from El-Gubat. Our empty glass bottles found either a ready market among the natives or were accepted by them as valuable gifts.

All the way up the Nile, as soon as a detachment left its halting-place, a crowd of men, women, and children swarmed over it to pick up what had been left, and seemed to value specially the empty meat tins.

The camp was admirably placed above the town on the bank of a river, but at the time of my arrival was comparatively deserted, a detachment of the Sussex regiment and a few details of other regiments being its sole occupants.

My first visit was necessarily to the Commissariat Department, where I was soon served out with six days' rations for myself and men. Below this was the headquarters of General Earle, who added to my anxiety to reach Korti by informing me that he intended leaving Dongola in two or three days to join Lord Wolseley, and that I had better hurry on, for important movements were impending. This was my last interview with that brave and noble soldier, and the kind tones of his voice on that occasion, and his pleasant smile as he answered my parting salute from the steam-launch when subsequently he left Korti for Merawi, are still sadly fresh in my memory.

I did not pay my respects to the *mudir*, for I had but little respect either for him or his deputy, the *vakeel*, on account of certain well-founded rumours which had reached me about both of them. In fact, if only half the stories current about their treatment of the natives employed through them by our military authorities were true, they were a precious pair. One report, for instance, stated that they were in the habit of levying such a heavy tribute on the wages of the native labourers they supplied for the purposes of the expedition that only a moiety of the large sums which were paid through their hands ever reached these poor fellows.

In some instances the latter were cheated out of the whole of their earnings; and in acting as intermediaries for the supply of camels for transport purposes, and, in fact, in everything they undertook to procure for us from the inhabitants, the same kind of robbery was practised by them. The *vakeel*, in fact, boasted that he had made ten thousand pounds out of such transactions.

Unfortunately we were implicated in their nefarious proceedings. This was undoubtedly wrong, and, as wrong always is, it was most impolitic. If, for instance, the loyalty and friendship of the *mudir* had to be bought, we should have paid the price out of our own pockets, instead of letting him take his reward by robbing the men who worked for us and supplied us with necessaries. The proper course to pursue was to have temporarily assumed the administration of affairs in the province of Dongola. If this had been done, supplies of all kinds would have been more abundantly brought in to us by the natives, who now withheld them because they feared being robbed by the *mudir* and his satellites.

All this was bad enough, but there were some things in the government of the province of Dongola even worse than this. The *bashi-bazouks* in the service of the *mudir* tyrannised over the hard-working and peaceably disposed tillers of the soil. For example, a band of these armed ruffians would go to a bazaar or cattle market, select whatever sheep or cattle they fancied, oblige their owners to drive them to their quarters, and then silence their demands for payment with threats of the *courbash*.

When grain, or anything was needed, these brigands would go coolly to a village and carry it off without payment. Even the women of the villages were not safe from them, for it was their constant practice to seize any girl or woman they fancied and carry them off to their quarters. When tired of their victims they would then; either sell them to their officers or let their husbands or friends ransom them.

Who can wonder at a rebellion against Egyptian authority in the Sudan when it tolerates such abominable oppressions as these? So far as I could learn, the condition of things in the Mudireyeh of Dongola was worse than ever it had been in Turkish Armenia, and quite as bad as the reported atrocities in Bulgaria which so roused and horrified the civilised world in 1876.

CHAPTER 10

Departure from Dongola

After this vexatious delay of several days I was able to move on again early on the morning of December 23rd.

Immediately after leaving Dongola we passed several large villages, the houses of which were so closely built together and so high as to give them at a little distance the appearance of forts. Such, in one sense, they were intended to be, in order to secure protection to their inhabitants from the raids of the desert tribes, to which they were frequently exposed.

We passed through Sorto about noon, where a typical Sudanese bazaar of cattle, grain, and other merchandise, home and foreign, was being held on the shore. All operations were suspended as we rode through the motley throng, to whom we were evidently objects of great interest.

Our road generally lay outside the cultivated land and along it on the drier and more healthy soil of the desert, on which, for that reason, most of the villages were built. Some, however, were placed near the river, behind a thick forest of the thorny *sondt*, or mimosa, which rose up like a bulwark between them and the desert About sunset, having judged (as the sailors say) that we had run our distance, and were off the village of Tekhameh, lying behind such a thicket as I have just mentioned, we threaded our way through the thorny intervening maze 'in the gloaming' and halted. Our quarters for the night were very comfortable, and the supplies of eggs and milk plentiful, but no fowls were to be had at any price.

We started early next morning for Handak, at least sixteen miles distant. It was Christmas Day, but to be spent without any of its associations or cherished home festivities. There was nothing even in the weather to remind a Briton of the festival, for not a cloud was to be seen, and it was hotter than many of the hottest days in our island's summer. This heat, however, on account of its dryness, was not in itself so hard to bear as was the continued and intense glare of light to which we were exposed. We halted for luncheon under the grateful shade of a patriarchal mimosa, whose branches extended many feet from its trunk, and which seemed to be a favourite halting-place, for the marks of many fires were to be seen under it. There was also a plot raised a few inches above the level of the adjacent ground and marked round by stones, which was evidently intended as a place of prayer for the Mussulmans who frequented it.

Before reaching this spot a well-dressed young Sudanese, riding on a donkey, overtook us. He carried in his hand the well-bleached shoulder-blade of a camel on which was written a sentence from the *Koran*. This he told us in passing he was going to place at the corner of a field he was sowing with barley, in order to insure the blessing of a good harvest. Here was an illustration of the traditional perpetuation of a practice twelve hundred years old at least, for Mahomet wrote the *Koran 'on palm leaves and shoulder-blades of mutton; and the pages without order or connection were cast into a domestic chest in the custody of one of his wives.'* [1] Here we had now one of his followers using that of a camel. In school-houses in the Sierra Nevada the shoulder-blades of horses are used by the pupils instead of slates. It is probable that when the Moors were driven out of Spain they left behind them the practice of using these bones for writing upon, as well as specimens of their peculiar form of arch.

After leaving our resting-place we met another party of Sudanese, riding donkeys, two of them, the blackest of the lot, carrying nankeen-coloured French sun umbrellas. They were quite jolly and very much amused when I seized a sunshade from one of them and pretended to ride off with it. The owner trotted after me, and the rest laughed heartily at us. It was so comical to see these *blackamoors* using such a protection from the sun, not only on account of their complexion, but from their universal habit of going about bare-headed. Another instance of this was that of a dark brown, stoutly built native 'lady' in the bazaar at Korti, sporting one of these nankeen-coloured sun-shades, and holding it over her with as much pride as our fair ones display their crimson ones at home.

The Sudan donkeys on which these men were riding are very swift of foot and generally very handsome-looking animals. Lord Charles

---

1. *The Decline and Fall of the Roman Empire,* vol. ix.

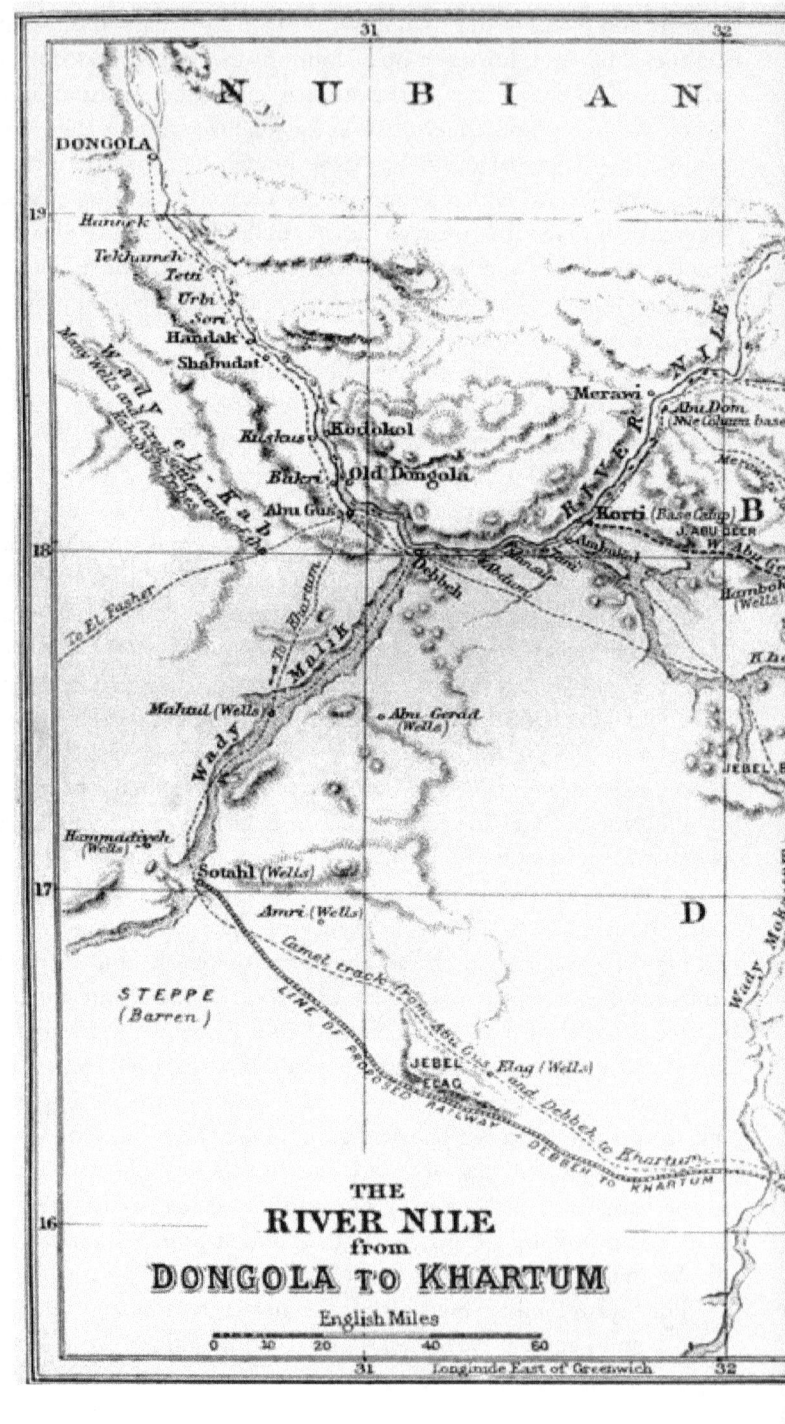

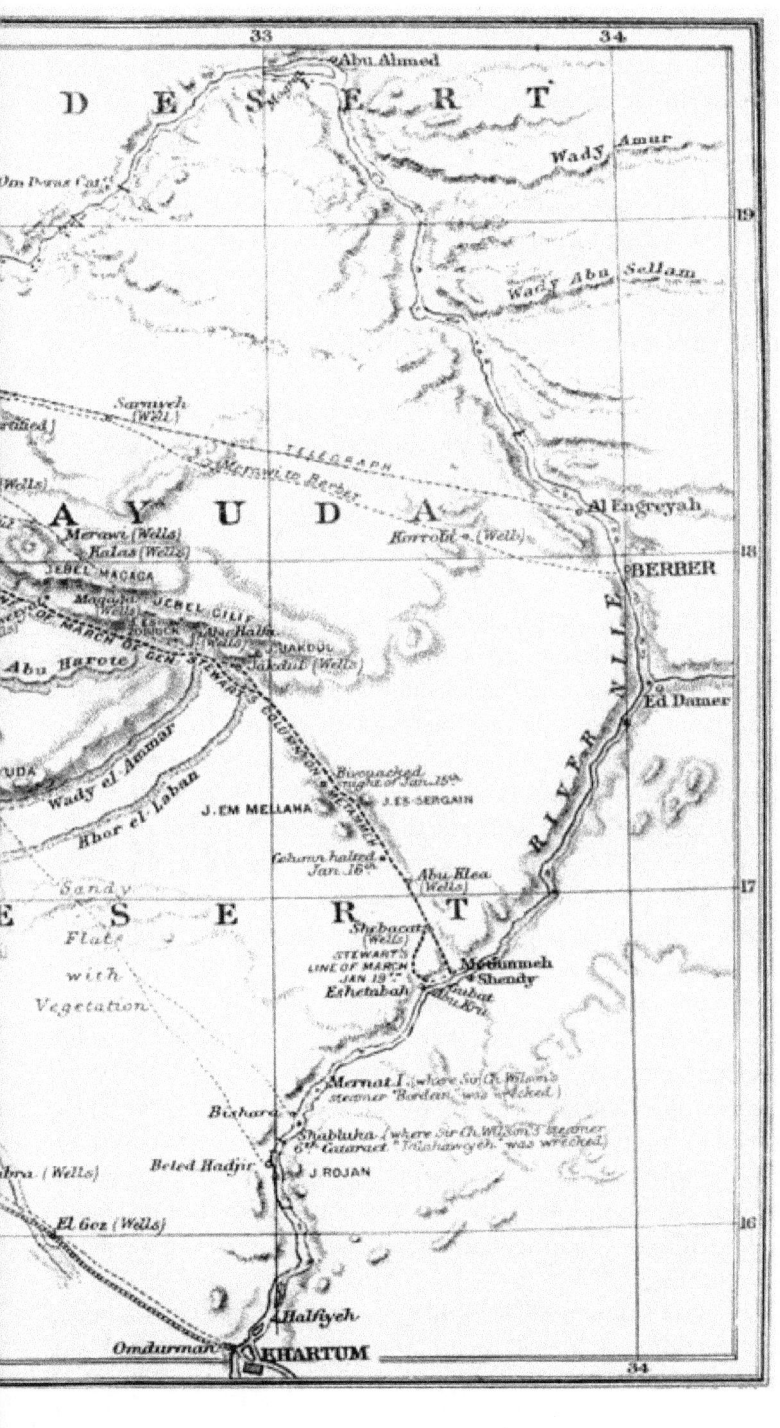

Beresford had one of the prettiest animals of this kind. He named him 'Waterford' because the animal had tumbled him off his back as many times as he had been rejected as a candidate for Parliamentary honours by that Irish constituency. Poor 'Waterford' fell, I believe, in the square at Abu-Klea.

The road began to lead nearer the villages on the Nile, and this suggested foraging for our Christmas dinner; so halting at once, I was fortunate enough to secure a pair of fowls. Plum-pudding had, however, to be given up, for we had no plums. My old dragoman, in order to save time, began plucking our substitutes for turkey as he rode along on his camel.

The plain was thickly strewn over with pebbles, some of which were agates, and others beautifully rounded and oval-shaped crystals.

For about twelve miles above Dongola on the Handak road, the alluvial plain gradually narrows, and at the latter place the sandstone hills come down to the right bank of the river, and continue to do so for some distance. On the left bank, up which we were travelling between a range of low sandhills, there was a level stretch to the river, low enough to be overflowed at high Nile. Much of the soil cultivated seemed to have been reclaimed from this apparent desert plain, which despite its dry appearance was pretty often covered over with trees sustained by the moisture of the earth beneath them. Beyond this low range of hills on our right was the extensive Wady-el-Kab with its many wells and the fixed settlement of the Kabbabish tribe. The appearance of this immediate region would indicate that in not very ancient times it was periodically flooded by the river, and that, with but little expense, a large part of it could now be irrigated and brought again under cultivation.

Early in the afternoon we came in sight of Handak, which, from its elevated position and substantial buildings, presented rather an imposing appearance. Instead of going round the town as is usual, I rode through it. The buildings were of stone, and one and two stories high. The main street was broad and, as might have been expected from thfe site of the town, rocky. On passing through the gate at the upper end, we found a number of well-dressed people who, from their manner, in directing us to the camp at Shabatut, seemed unwilling that we should remain in the place.

The camp was two miles further up the river, and as it was but an hour to sunset, we hurried on and soon reached the cultivated land. Whether it was owing to the contrast between the verdant prospect which now greeted us and the comparatively barren district through which we had for some time been travelling in the hot sun, I cannot say, but the luxuriance of its vegetation seemed to exceed anything I had noticed since leaving Assiout

On our left and between us and the river were fields of ripening *dhura* and maize, rich in their tropical verdure and luxuriance. On our right scores of slaves were busily engaged in preparing the land for the barley crop sown at this season. They were superintended by their masters, who in flowing robes of the purest white and white turbans moved about amongst them. The agricultural scene thus presented was most picturesquely Oriental in character.

Several aqueducts leading from the water-wheels on the Nile crossed the road. These were built up with earth often three feet above its level. When any leakage occurred from these aqueducts, it rendered the ground, on both sides of them, so soft and treacherous that great care had to be taken in crossing them. One of my camels now unfortunately missed the beaten path and sank into one of the quagmires with one of his hind legs, tumbled over, and lay helplessly groaning under his heavy load. I thought it was all over with him, but when we had pulled his leg out of the hole, he got up and went on again as if nothing had happened.

The camp at Shabatut was admirably situated about three miles from Handak, on the bank of the river, under a group of *dom* palms, and in order to prevent too close contact with the natives these were prohibited entering it, specially the women, and for trading purposes with them bazaars were arranged outside at convenient distances, and kept under military supervision. In the case of the camp here, this was, from all I learned of the immorality of its inhabitants, most imperative.

It was so dark when we reached the camp that it was with some difficulty that I found a place for bivouacking, and thus ended our Christmas ride.

After dining off one of the pair of fowls we had picked up in the morning, I adjourned to Carmichael's mess, and was just in time for plum-pudding. Complimenting them on the enterprise which had secured such a seasonable treat, the officer who had evidently been acting as 'chef' for the day, said in reply, 'It was awfully difficult to get anything to make a plum-pudding here. The flour came from the commissariat, and the eggs we bought from the natives. The raisins we got at Dongola, but had to make up the quantity with figs, as we had to look after our men also. The raisins we subsidised with dates. It took me half an hour this morning to mix it.'

Our readers will readily understand that imagination had to be called vividly into exercise before the compound before us could be regarded as the veritable article.

One of the soldiers told me subsequently that he had met with a sad accident with the plum-pudding he had undertaken to cook for his mess. Having no pudding bag, a sock was substituted. Unfortunately all the ingredients leaked out into the pot through an unobserved hole in its toe!

Such a Christmas Day as this was to us all only occurs once in a lifetime, and to many not at all. The oddities of the occasion, however, compensated for the absence of the home traditional enjoyments of the festival. There we were, far, far away from fatherland, in a comparative wilderness, depending under Providence for safety on our strong arms; and yet, borne up by a sense of patriotism and duty, all seemed as happy as happy could be. For the moment the hardships of the journey so far, and those yet to come, as well as the dangers of the future, seemed all forgotten. Major Carmichael told me that before dinner he had asked one of his men, who had originally been a member of a travelling circus, how he stood the expedition, and if it was not harder work than he had been used to, and so forth. The man replied, 'Law, no, sir, 'taint half so bad as the work I've been accustomed to!'

The men sat in a circle round a roaring fire of the logs and branches of defunct mimosa and palm trees, chatting merrily and singing songs they had learned and loved in fatherland.

At the end of an avenue between the palms on our left was the mess-table of what, borrowing a military phrase, might be termed 'details' of officers from various non-combatant departments of the expedition —such as the commissariat and transport corps and Telegraph Engineers. Amongst them were Colonel (now General) Webber, our energetic telegraph chief, and Major Sandwith, who did such good service in the Egyptian campaign of 1882. The most remarkable figure, however, in the group, owing to his Moorish costume, was that erratic but companionable Englishman, Mr. Curtis—better known as Abd-el-Kadir, a name he had adopted after the great Algerian chief. His light-blue *kaftan*, white turban, and sun-bronzed face looked through the vista of palm branches most picturesquely Oriental.

Before the festivities of the evening were ended, wearied out by my hard ride in the heat, I laid me down to sleep, but did not become unconscious of my strange surroundings until the men round the camp fire had wound up their Christmas sing-song on the banks of the Nile with 'Auld Lang Syne,' 'Rule Britannia,' and the 'National Anthem.' Alas! it was the last Christmas for not a few of the singers, for three weeks later many of them fell in the square at Abu-Klea.

About sunrise Carmichael's detachment marched for Abu-Gus, the next station, which was nearly forty miles distant, and I followed an hour and a half later. The day was very hot, and the road in many places heavy on account of the drifted sand. Owing to a fresh breeze the air was so full of the latter that I had to protect my eyes with 'goggles.' These were blue, but through them the shadows of my men and camels appeared a bright crimson!

The mean maximum temperature of this region in the shade is given in the map of the Intelligence Department From December to January it is 94° to 104° Fahrenheit, and the minimum at night is 31° to 50°. On the 26th it must have been 98°. Just think of plodding on between two such fires as we had on this occasion—the burning sun and the heated sand! It was weary work for both man and beast, and our progress was consequently very slow.

Towards noon, however, matters somewhat improved, for the road now led over a hard gravel soil. Between us and the river was a high drift of yellow sand, beyond which waved, at no great distance, the line of dark green palms along its banks.

At one o'clock we reached Bakri and halted here for a rest and luncheon. It was a small but very populous village, and our arrival had evidently created quite a sensation, for the men, women, and children of the place crowded round us. Soon they began to show a strong inclination for trading, and produced such quantities of eggs, milk, and home-made bread as to bring down prices considerably. They even wanted to sell us donkeys, trotting out a whole troop for our inspection, when one of the dusky-skinned riders was pitched off his long-eared steed. This untoward circumstance enabled me to get rid of their owners' importunity by pleading the well-known, and now proved, vicious habits of the Bakri donkeys.

So interested had these people become in our party—especially in myself—that we had great difficulty in keeping them at a comfortable distance. They squatted around my man during his culinary operations, in which, simple as they were, the natives seemed to take a curious interest During mealtime they watched all my motions but when informed that such attentions were not agreeable to the *pasha*, they invariably and good-naturedly withdrew.

After luncheon I walked down to the river through fields of *dhura* and beans, and saw several birds of beautiful plumage, one of which, as large as a thrush, was entirely of a bright emerald green.

At 3 p.m. we were off again and travelled on long after sunset, aided by the bright moonlight, hoping to reach and bivouac at Kus-Kus, within eight or nine miles of Abu-Gus. Both men and camels, as well as myself, became so weary that we lost the main road and found ourselves wandering about among sandhills. Happily we stumbled upon a couple of houses, and a woman from one of them sent her son to put us on the road again. A little further on a clump of palms on the bank of the river came in sight, and I decided to bivouac there for the night. Carmichael's detachment was not far ahead of us, for I heard his men sounding the 'last post,' and learned from the inhabitants of the adjacent village that the '*Asaker Inglese* had passed there about sunset.'

The strong north wind still continued and made the night bitterly cold. The people of the neighbouring hamlet were not as friendly disposed towards us as the natives generally were, and charged us double prices for everything we bought. One more communicative than the rest told me that crocodiles were plentiful about here, and that they occasionally gobbled up a man or woman.

When we halted, my attention was attracted by a man who had also just arrived from somewhere, and who had taken up his quarters a short distance from us. The first thing he did was to light a fire, and when it had burnt up brightly to extinguish it. This looked like signalling some one. He was short of stature, dressed in white, and wore a turban of extra size. His whole appearance and cat-like movements recalled in fancy the Marabout in the *Talisman*, who attempted Richard's life in his tent. The man was evidently not at home hereabouts, and like travellers in this region was well armed. Once he came stealthily near to our bivouac and then as stealthily withdrew. This movement rendering me suspicious, I watched him for some time under cover of a bush. Twice during the night I peeped out of my tent after him. The first time he was there, still sitting up, but the second time, near daybreak, he was nowhere to be seen. Next day I learned at Abu-Gus that the *Mahdi* had sent a number of his emissaries into this neighbourhood, and so perhaps this disturber of my rest was one of them.

The orders were that after leaving Shabatut all detachments on the march to Korti should do so in battle array. This was a necessary military precaution, for from that place the troops were now supposed to be in a more or less hostile country. It was also a useful drill for the camel corps; and as a military display it served to impress the natives and the spies of the *Mahdi* with exaggerated ideas about the strength of our army, for it made its numbers appear tenfold greater than they were. The stereotyped expression of the natives, when we referred to the subject, was: '*Ketír! Ketír asaker Inglese!*' (Many, many are the English soldiers!) One man declared to me that we were as numerous as the sands of the desert.

We started next morning an hour after sunrise. This was later than usual on account of our disturbed night's rest. Our next halting-place was Abu-Gus, which was reached about noon. The camp here was below the town on the cultivated ground alongside of the river. There was no shade whatever, not even the usual fringe of palms along the bank. I was therefore compelled to bivouac in the open, where old Boreas, still piping away, made our situation rather uncomfortably cold.

The village, which lay below the loose sandhills which divide the cultivated land on the river from the desert, comprised a few well-built and comfortable-looking houses. There were natives and camels moving about, giving the place a lively aspect. The camels were for the most part of a light cream colour, often marked by patches of fawn.

Abu-Gus is about 268 miles in a direct line from Khartoum; it is the Nile terminus of the road from Darfur, and consequently, in a normal condition of the times, an important commercial centre. At the moment, however, I had more interest in our commissariat *depôt* at Abu-Gus than in the place itself, for we were short of biscuits, and the stock here had run very low. After some diplomacy, however, I secured a supply sufficient to last us till we reached Debbeh, our next halting-place.

We moved out of camp early next morning, shortly after Carmichael's detachment had started. There were two roads to Debbeh from Abu-Gus, one by the river, and the other across the desert. The former was heavy on account of the sand drifts to which it was exposed, and following the curve of the Nile longer than the latter which led over harder ground, so we decided to take the short cut across the desert. The first thing was to find the beginning of it, among the loose sand dunes and scrub above the village, where the river road and another from Khartoum converged. For some time we were fairly bewildered. At last my camel man was certain he had found the road, and on we confidently went for nearly an hour. After clearing the loose yellow sand, we struck hard gravel, then came to round-topped gravel hills, that looked as if they had been formed by the action of tremendous floods of water. They were strewn over with quantities of other pebbles, curiously worn, one of which, from its peculiarity, I pocketed and brought home. It resembles a petrified oyster or clam.

The track now became less distinctly marked, and began to divide up and lead in several directions. This made me suspicious, and looking round I noticed the sun did not shine from the point it naturally would on travellers bound to Debbeh. So we halted, and riding up to the top of one of the gravel hills to reconnoitre, I discovered that we had actually been steering for Khartoum, for instead of travelling in a direction parallel with the Nile, we had followed one at right angles with it.

The annoyance felt at this blunder from the delay it caused, and the extra travelling to my heavily laden camels, was forgotten for the moment in the extensive and beautiful landscape which now opened out to me as I looked back towards the Nile. There along its banks was that ever welcome dark green line of palms which marked the course of the river, and which distance had softened by a blue haze. Behind it rose in graceful outlines golden and purple coloured hills and mountains. The middle distance of the picture was filled up by the light-coloured soil of the desert, relieved by groups and bands of bright green trees and shrubs. As the former came up into the foreground they became a forest, which spreading up between and around the hills near us made even their rocky barrenness look beautiful by contrast.

Another object of more importance in our embarrassed position now attracted my attention as I scanned the desert plain below us in a north-westerly direction. This was the commissariat convoy, which, when we left Abu-Gus, was preparing for its march up the river. Here then we had a point to steer for which would obviate the necessity of retracing our steps in order to regain the missed road. So moving along the hypotenuse of the triangle, one side of which had already been traced in our erratic journey to where we halted, we soon struck the caravan track, and in three hours afterwards reached our destination.

Before arriving at Debbeh, we rode through quite a forest of osiers,[2] interspersed with acacias and mimosas in rich leaf. Many goats

---

2. *Asclepias gigantea*.

were browsing on these, standing up on their hind legs close to the prickly trees in order to feed on the more tender leaves. Camels also of the beautiful colour I had noticed at Abu-Gus were grazing round amongst the bushes and on the thorny branches, of which they are very fond.

Chapter 11

Gordon's Critical Position

The camp here, as usual, occupied the cultivated ground along the river bank from which the corps had been recently gathered; and, as usual, it was dusty and as shadeless as was that at Abu-Gus. Between it and the fort were fields of *dhura* and other crops, and on the edge near the Nile was an uninhabited mud house, of which I took possession for the night It was not much of a habitation, after all, for it had no roof, and neither windows nor a door. In order to make things comfortable, I placed my bed under the windward wall, closed up the hole in the other where the door once was with sacking, bolting it inside when I retired for the night with heavy stones, and also blocked up a hole in another of the walls leading out to the back premises of some adjacent native huts. With all its imperfections, it was better than my tent, for it would not delay us in starting in the morning by having to strike it, as we should have had to do if the other had been pitched as usual. Once during the night my door was blown in by a stormy gust of wind, but I soon repaired damages.

A road led past this green spot along the river bank to the cosily placed camp of the detachment of the Royal Sussex, the pioneer regiment of the expedition, which had been sent up here to garrison the place. At its lower end was the commissariat *depôt*, plentifully supplied with tea, biscuits, and fresh beef. Immediately below the camp was the landing-place, where soon after we had settled down the steamer *Nassif-el-Kheir* came in from Korti, bringing news which indicated that the toilsome preliminary phase of the expedition was past and that we were now about to enter on its real work.

The Staffordshire regiment, we were told, had left Korti in boats for Abu-Dôm, opposite Merawi, accompanied by a detachment of the 19th Hussars, along the left bank of the river. A column composed of the Camel Corps was being rapidly prepared for a dash across the desert to seize and hold Metammeh. This last piece of news started Major Carmichael and his detachment at sunset, although he had proposed to rest at Debbeh until next day. Want of fodder alone prevented my going on with him. This delayed me until next day, when by honest manoeuvring I secured a supply from the agent of the *mudir* at the fort.

This fort occupied a commanding position on the high bank of the river, and was quite defensible against a savage foe unprovided with artillery. It was now held by a detachment of the *mudir's bashi-bazouk* scoundrels, who were, as already hinted, the terror and plague of the peaceable and industriously inclined inhabitants of Dongola. You could read villainy in their very faces. They spoke Turkish and took kindly to my men, as they could converse with them in this language. Through my *dragoman* they told me some wonderful stories about their fight with the *dervish* force in June 1884, of whom they said they had killed four thousand. On Gordon's principle of estimating such statements I divided the latter by seven, taking the quotient as outside the number killed on the occasion. There was something terribly repulsive in the tone of these fellows, for they gloated in their butchery, and seemed to roll the word 'killed' as a sweet morsel under their tongues.

On its land side the fort had a natural glacis leading up to it, and over which the rebels in June had attempted to storm the place. When the Sussex regiment first came to Debbeh, this glacis was bestrewn with the skulls and bones of the slain. Some attempts had evidently been made to bury the dead, but not effectually, for when I rode over this part of the battlefield in December many human remains were visible, having been scratched out of their shallow graves by dogs, which in one place were gnawing and quarrelling over the dead Arabs' bones.

Across the river from Debbeh nothing was to be seen but dunes of moving yellow sand, only relieved here and there by narrow strips of verdure. From every direction, excepting from the north, the winds are always hot and oppressive. Its insignificant village is now included within the mud walls of the fort, and the only decent building in it was one of stone, occupied at the time as the military telegraph station. The natives of both sexes, specially the women, were miserable and dirty specimens of humanity.

Both above and below the village, however, on the left bank there was a considerable extent of cultivated land, with many comfortable houses on its borders.

The Wady Malik here comes down to the Nile, but for five or six miles it is so filled up with sand as to be scarcely recognisable. Colonel Colston says that through the plains beyond this drifted sand 'a good teamster could without difficulty drive a six-mule wagon from Debbeh to Obeiyad, and *that the route to Khartoum is still more practicable.*'

Captain Brocklehurst, with a large convoy of camels and grain, &c., for Korti, arrived at Debbeh the day before I had, and intended proceeding at 5 p.m. (December 29). There were vague rumours of danger between Debbeh and Korti either from robber bands or from small parties of the enemy; and therefore, as a precautionary measure, I departed from my usual habit, and decided to go on with this convoy. At the hour named we were loaded up ready for the march, but something or other delayed the convoy. As my camels were restless, I rode slowly ahead, hoping soon to be overtaken by it It was now after sunset and as usual dark, for the moon did not rise until an hour later.

It is always difficult at night to distinguish the camel track, as the drifting sand obliterates it. The telegraph line was, however, a safe guide, therefore I gave my men orders to follow it. We halted several times for the convoy, but as it did not appear we went on again. About ten o'clock the track was entirely missing, and the telegraph posts out of sight As the line of palms was, however, visible, the general direction was easily followed, but as we were off the beaten track travelling became very heavy. For half an hour we floundered about in the soft sand searching for the road, but could not find it even in the now bright moonlight. I did the scouting on my horse, and at last fortunately sighted a village behind the sandhills (or dunes) on our left. Nobody was to be seen, and it was some time before we could get anyone to hear our shouting.

At last one of the inhabitants made his appearance, and offered to show us the road. There seemed to be no immediate end to our troubles, for when he was leading us through a burying-place down went the hind legs of my camel into the ground. It was the same fellow who had sunk into the softened earth near Shabatut, but now he had gone down into a grave. I thought he was done for this time, for he sank into the ground with such a plaintive groan; but we managed, after taking off his load, to extract that part of him which had thus disappeared. Kindness in adversity seemed to have been lost upon this camel, for no sooner had my man got him upright again than the brute snapped at his arm. As this was his besetting sin when I bought him, we had to muzzle him, and therefore he could not do the harm he now so maliciously intended.

On we went in the bright moonlight until the quiet desolateness by which we were surrounded was suddenly broken by the reports of several rifle shots on our right, accompanied by confused shouting. What could this mean? Had Captain Brocklehurst's convoy been attacked? Leaving my camels I cantered off in the direction of the sounds we had heard, and, riding up the top of a hill near me, listened and heard more shots, and then a good Anglo-Saxon 'Confound it, why don't you close up!' Then came some language as strong as any that had ever broken the silence of a desert on a moonlight night, and I judged that the convoy had straggled, and that Captain Brocklehurst and his officers were trying to get it together again. Ridiculous as this alarm may now appear, unprotected as we were, it was, at the time, a decidedly uncomfortable experience. Although now reassured myself, I could not quiet my men, so we rode behind a sandhill, out of the top of which jutted a fort-like looking rock, and bivouacked below it on the yellow sand until daylight.

Climbing the rocky crest of the sandy hill on which we had bivouacked, I had another fine view of the country. Ahead I recognised the Jebel-Ambukol, and a little to the south of it the long and table-topped Jebelel-Kord. How I watched these mountains during our hot day's ride, and how very slowly we seemed to get up to them, for in the clear atmosphere they at first appeared so near. It was long after sunset before we passed Tani, five miles below Ambukol, and after 8 p.m. before we reached the latter place. Myself, men, and animals were quite done up after this weary ride of forty-one miles from Debbeh. Eighteen hours out of the past twenty-four I had been in the saddle, and therefore welcomed our well-earned halt. As all the indications were in favour of a cold night, our first search was for a sheltered spot on which to bivouac.

The people of Ambukol had however either retired for the night, or were inhospitably inclined, for they did not respond to the shouting of my men. At last an armed *bashi-bazouk* on picket duty put in an appearance, with the bright barrel of his Remington glistening most uncomfortably in the moonlight. The Turkish of my men, in explaining matters, secured his friendship, and on his invitation we rode down to the stockade where his detachment was encamped. Several sentries challenged us as we neared the place, and every time they did so I expected to hear the crack of a rifle and the whiz of a bullet, but our guide answered promptly, and we passed on in safety. He was of short stature, and as he walked alongside of us recounted with much volubility the story of the battle of June at Debbeh, and the number of dervishes whom he and his comrades had killed on that occasion. He made it five thousand, and it was not politic under the circumstances to express a doubt on the subject.

The commandant, a veritable Circassian in appearance and manner, received me very kindly, and insisted that I should take up my quarters in his own straw hut Soon my portable bed, table, and chair were brought in and opened out, and excited as much curiosity as they had done on previous occasions.

My meal, simple as it was, was watched with some interest, especially the coffee made out of tinned coffee and milk. The commandant seemed to enjoy it, for after the first cup he asked for another, and then another. The only news he could give me was that an English force had left Korti that day for Shendy. This was rather a damper after my hard struggle up from Dongola in order to be in time to join any such forward movement.

My camels and horse were well taken care of by the orders of this Circassian officer, and sheltered from the cold north wind I enjoyed a much needed and comfortable night's rest. My tired men were also well taken care of.

Before reaching Ambukol our road had led through a tract of country which, though now desolate, bore evidence of having been once under cultivation. Even the *dom* palms on the banks of the river along it were withering away from neglect. During the afternoon we passed the remains of several dilapidated villages, ruined by the miserable oppressions to which their inhabitants had been subjected, and latterly by the raids of the *Mahdi*'s dervishes. A large area of land between Dongola and Ambukol thus lying waste could through an improved system of irrigation, and under a civilised government, be brought into profitable cultivation, yielding large crops of cotton and the various cereals of the country. With this valuable area of land, cut: off as it is from the southern portion of the Sudan by a wide stretch of desert, the province of Dongola is too valuable an acquisition to Egypt to be abandoned to the barbarians. In fact, on strategical grounds Egypt is not safe without occupying it, and our Government ought to give earnest heed to Lord Wolseley's opinion on this subject

While at breakfast in the commandant's tent I was much amused at the offhand and patriarchal manner in which he dealt out justice between several plaintiffs and defendants who brought their cases of dispute before him for settlement He squatted on a mat, and they squatted round him. Everything passed off quietly, and his decisions had a common sense and justice about them that would have been welcomed by many suitors in British courts.

We rode on to Korti, four miles distant, about ten o'clock, and I at once reported my arrival to Colonel Swaine, military secretary to Lord Wolseley, and was directed by him to that part of the camp assigned to representatives of the press. Happily I had a tent with me, else I should have been as houseless as were my colleagues, for Colonel Swaine adhered rigidly to what had been laid down as the limits of War Office courtesy towards the representatives of the British press with this expedition, and which excluded not only a passage in any of the boats, whalers, or *nuggars* to correspondents, but food for camels and horses, and even tents. It was satisfactory to find, on our return from El Gubat, that these limits were so extended by the late Colonel Primrose that a whole line of bell tents were placed at our disposal.

The site of the camp at Korti was chosen by General Stewart, and did great credit both to his taste and judgment It was one of the most cheerful and picturesque of spots. Along its front was a grove of tall acacias and graceful *dom* palms, which afforded an agreeable shade to a large portion of the troops whose tents were pitched beneath them, as well as to the hospital tents. Between this grove and the edge of the bank a broad path was left, not only facilitating locomotion from one part of the camp to the other, but also affording a pleasant promenade in the cool of the afternoon and evening. Headquarters occupied an open space at the lower end, thickly walled in on its three sides by acacias and palms, with a fringe only of them on its river front. Carpeted with green and surrounded with what to our European eyes were 'exotics,' it resembled a beautifully decorated hall for special occasions at home.

At the lower end was the commander-in-chief's marquee, and cosily pitched under the waving branches of the palms, on both sides, extending to the river, were the tents of his staff. Alongside of it was a tall mast from the top of which during the day floated that flag which now on the Nile, as it had the world over, '*braved the battle and the breeze.*' At night this mast resolved itself in imagination into a railway semaphore pole, showing the danger signal, for in place of the flag it carried a red light

Above the general's quarters and in close proximity were the Commandant's tent and those of the intelligence and headquarters of the transport and other departments. Then came in upward succession, in rows of tents at right angles with the river, the camp of the Mounted Infantry, Light and Heavy Camel regiments, 19th Hussars, artillery, infantry regiments, hospitals, Sussex regiment, and commissariat and ordnance departments. Along the shores were moored scores of the whalers, proving by their presence here that all the 'cocksure' predictions of their failure *per se* as a means of transport up the cataracts had been fallacious. They had been a little longer on their way than had been anticipated, yet here they were. It was estimated that the total loss from drowning did not exceed eighteen men, and that the average loss of boats was not more than three per regiment, but I cannot vouch for its correctness.

Immediately in rear of the general's tent was the straw hut used as the Headquarters mess-room. There was just room enough in it for a table comfortably accommodating a dozen or fifteen guests. No one who was a partaker of the hospitality of that straw hut will ever forget it or its kindly and distinguished host.

The river at Korti is very broad and its water much clearer than it was further north, so clear that at a pinch it could be used without filtering. The opposite bank was covered with green crops and fringed with trees; with a long flat mountain in the background with its numerous foot hills of graceful outline. During the day, the purple-bluish and golden tints and the bright green along the river's edge made the outlook from the promenade along the bank beautifully picturesque. But as the sun declined towards evening the aerial golden tints changed into carmine and then crimson, defying all description.

The camels and horses were picketed in rear of the camp, where the cultivated ground denuded of its crops was dry and dusty; when the wind blew in the wrong direction for comfort, it raised clouds of this finely pulverised soil, which discounted considerably the beauties I have just described.

Had not the water wheels on the high river bank been utilised for the purpose, watering such a multitude of animals as we had would have been a tedious and troublesome operation. Every day at fixed hours these *sakeeyeh*, as the natives call them, were set in motion and sent streams of water through the aqueducts leading inland from them across the camp, serving as watering troughs for the animals.

No iron is used in the construction of these machines, which in their design are probably as old as the time of Pharaoh. As they were never lubricated, anyone can imagine what a continuous groaning, squeaking, crunching, wood-breaking noise they made when in motion. They were very numerous on both sides of the river about Korti, and at night, when the camp was still, their sounds, blended and rendered harmonious by distance, often reminded me of the chiming of church bells in our distant island home. Often in the still hour of night, when on my way down the river in a *nuggar*, the groaning, grinding noise of these wooden machines was tempered by the plaintive but not unmusical airs sung by the slave boys who drove the oxen that kept them in motion. They were a vulnerable part in the body politic of these regions, for their destruction by an enemy was a most serious affair for the growing crops. Gordon, as we have read, used to avail himself of this weak spot in the side of his enemies above and below Khartoum, and destroyed many of these *sakeeyeh* from his steamers.

All the music and poetry, however, of those from Korti down to Dongola was taken out of them by the subsequent withdrawal of our troops from the Sudan; for the poor people to whom in good faith at the time our protection had been promised when we first came among them, fearing the vengeance of the dervishes on account of their friendliness to us, tore their *sakeeyehs* to pieces and fled down the river floating on their wheels.

During the short time spent at Korti the troops from below kept coming on daily, chiefly in the whalers. The boatmen were like the beggars in Molloy's song, '*ragged and tanned*,' but made fit to go anywhere or do anything men could do, through their three hundred odd miles of rowing, carrying, and towing in a beautiful climate, though often just a trifle too hot for such work. No men, in fact, could be in more perfect physical training. They were all strong, for the weak ones had been weeded out on the way up, and left behind. An Aldershot martinet would often have been startled from his propriety by their tattered clothing, but the man was to be pitied who would dare to cross bayonets with them.

Returning from this digression from my narrative, I found on my arrival at Korti that after all my anxiety to be up in time for the first direct effort to open communications with beleaguered Gordon, I had missed it, for General Stewart had marched the day previously (December 30) to Jakdul. His force on this occasion numbered 1,100 officers and men and 1,800 camels, and comprised the following:— Guards Camel regiment, 381; officers and men, Mounted Infantry,

31; detachment Heavy Camel regiment, 90, with 239 camels; Light Camel regiment, 90, with 250 camels; Royal Engineers, 29, with 40 camels; artillery (without guns) 20, with 16 camels; commissariat, 20, with 200 natives and 500 camels; 19th Hussars, 45 (mounted); medical staff, 4 officers, 15 men, 30 natives, with 90 camels, including a section of movable hospital tents, a section of the Bearers company with litters and 750 gallons of water. Each man carried with him on his camel 7 gallons of water, 7 days' rations, and 150 rounds of ammunition; the reserve ammunition being 40,000 rounds. The Guards and Marines were to be left at Jakdul and the remainder of the force to return to Korti, bringing back with it all the camels, including those of the former. A detachment was also to be left at Hambok, halfway, with a view of increasing, if possible, the water supply at the wells there.

The detachments of the Heavy and Light Camel regiments and of the artillery were to act merely as a transport corps, and the 60,000 rations taken by it were to be left at Jakdul.

As Lord Wolseley described it in his telegram to Lord Hartington, December 29, General Stewart had been sent 'to establish a post at Jakdul wells, halfway to Shendy, and return to Korti,' but with secret orders to go on to Metammeh, if he found an insufficient supply of water there.

Major Carmichael had, therefore, uselessly hurried up from Debbeh in order to take an active part in this movement, for as he told me, when I first met him after my arrival at Korti, 'General Stewart being short of transport had annexed two-thirds of the camels of the Heavy Camel regiment, leaving the officers and men behind.' Even their riding saddles, as well as their camels, had been taken for the transport of stores. 'And you know,' he said, 'how little can be carried on them!'

Two days before Stewart marched, 550 rank and file of the 2nd battalion South Staffordshire left in fifty-five whalers for Hamdab, where a camp was to be established as the rendezvous of the Nile column. Thirty-seven days' rations only were taken by the regiment, and as this could only be about a third of the cargo which the boats brought up to Korti, it was expected that they would make much more rapid progress against the current than had hitherto been the case in coming up the cataracts. A detachment of the 19th Hussars followed on the left bank. There are good reasons for believing that General Earle's orders were first to punish Colonel Stewart's and Mr. Power's murderers, and then to proceed up the river to Abu-Hamed, and to open up thence the road back to Korosko, where the stores were being collected to be forwarded across the desert. Having done this. General Earle was ordered to push on to Berber. Commissariat and other stores were being accumulated at Korosko for transport by camel across the desert to Abu-Hamed, when the latter was reached by the Nile column.

The only useful work done by this force was the punishment of the Monnasir tribe for their treacherous murder of Colonel Stewart and his companions, and probably also in diverting to some extent the attention of the enemy in the region through which it passed from General Stewart's movement across the Bayuda Desert. In fact, this was all the 'crack' regiments composing it contributed towards the great end of the expedition. So far as any direct effort to rescue Gordon was concerned, two-thirds of the Nile column might have safely been left behind.

The cry of punishing Stewart's murderers was so vehement on my arrival at Wady-Halfa as to appear to me to excite quite as much enthusiasm as the rescue of Gordon. It did then occur to me, and the impression is as strong now, that it would have been better to have concentrated all our efforts to save the living. That secured, we could then have avenged the dead.

At the moment of my arrival at Korti there was considerable excitement in the camp with respect to Lord Wolseley's plans. So far as my colleagues were concerned, I found them very much divided in opinion on the subject, as is evidenced by the forecasts of the expedition they then telegraphed to their papers. The policy as to correspondents laid down in the *Soldier's Pocket Book* had evidently been most successfully acted upon in their cases.

In one case, for example, it was telegraphed to London on December 26, that:

> The general issued a memorandum today directing all the troops to hold themselves in readiness to move forward to Meroe (Merawi) immediately, the infantry first, the South Staffordshire leading the way; the camel corps and cavalry to follow.

In another case, a message was despatched on the 28th, stating that:

> The cavalry portion of the camel corps have for the present been dismounted, as their camels will be employed to carry stores to Merawi.

The most ludicrous illustration of the obfuscation thus produced is shown in the following telegram wired to a London paper on the latter date:—

This morning the Guards' camel corps, with them the Royal Marines and Mounted Infantry, a bearer company, a section of the field hospital, altogether 900 strong, will, according to the arrangements, set out from Korti to *march alongside of the South Staffordshire whalers* to the new camp; General Stewart and staff, and not General Buller, will go with this force.'

On Monday, the 29th, Mr. Pigott, Reuter's agent, seems to have been able to grasp the situation, and with a decision and courage which do him credit, he accompanied General Stewart next day as the sole representative of the press on this ever-to-be remembered march to occupy Jakdul.

Lord Wolseley had despatched letters to Gordon dated September 20 and October 26, probably informing him of the expedition and asking for information as to his position. On December 31, the day after General Stewart had marched to occupy Jakdul, a messenger who had succeeded in reaching Khartoum with copies of both, returned to Korti with Gordon's reply. All that Colonel Swaine felt at liberty to make known to my colleagues and myself was the contents of the tiny letter 'Khartoum all right,' and the fact that Gordon had disabled one of the *Mahdi*'s guns. As the letter did not contain the latter statement, it occurred to more than one of us that there was some other news kept back, as eventually proved to be the case.

We tried interviewing the messenger, but got very little out of him. All he would tell us was that Gordon was well, but that he spent his nights in a ceaseless watch, visiting the outposts and keeping his sentries on the alert, and slept during the day. The messenger said he was cheerful, and well supplied with tobacco. This was all we could get out of the fellow, for besides his imposed reticence, he was closely watched —at least we were, lest we should become too well informed. The tiny letter, the disabled gun, and the cloud on Colonel Swaine's usually bright face haunted me all the way to Metammeh, for something serious was suggested by the three.

We learned afterwards, as our readers did, that the verbal message fully confirmed Gordon's letter of November 4, and that after the forty days from its date had expired he was in a desperate position. It is important to recall that verbal message here.

It began by stating that Khartoum was besieged on three sides, and that fighting went on all day, and that the enemy could not take the place except by starving out the garrison. But that portion of it marked 'secret and confidential' was as follows:—

> Our troops at Khartoum are suffering from lack of provisions. Food, we still have a little, some grain and biscuit. We want you to come quickly. You should come by Metammeh or Berber, make by these two roads, do not leave Berber in your rear. Keep enemy in your front, and when you have taken Berber, send me word from Berber.

This message had urgency, but Gordon's ability to hold out for some days was fairly suggested by what he says about Berber, and sending him a message after it was captured. Under the circumstances of the hour there was therefore yet a fair chance of being able to reach and save him.

Some anxiety was naturally felt about General Stewart and his expedition to Jakdul, as no news had been received from him, and owing to various native rumours of his having had a fight. On the morning of the 4th Lord Cochrane (Earl of Dundonald) accompanied by Lieut. Hine of the Mounted Infantry and two other officers, came in with despatches from him. Lord Cochrane presented himself at the 'Straw Hut,' just as we had finished dining. Lord Wolseley instantly left the table, asking where Buller was, leaving us in a state of joyous excitement, for it was now known that Sir Herbert had successfully carried out his instructions and that there was now good hope of opening up speedy communication with Gordon.

Lord Cochrane stated that Stewart's column, which had left Korti at 3 p.m. on Wednesday, December 30, had arrived at Jakdul on Friday morning about 7 o'clock, and found the wells unoccupied by the enemy. From prisoners captured it was also ascertained that the road was clear to Metammeh, which was only occupied by a small force of the *Mahdi's* troops. The water at the wells was reported to be abundant and good, the desert road well supplied with fuel, and easy travelling. General Stewart had left the Guards' regiment at Jakdul, and a detachment of the Mounted Infantry and a few Engineers at Hambok wells, to increase the water supply; and, Lord Cochrane said, was on his way back to Korti with the transport camels and would be in next day (January 5).

This march of nearly two hundred miles told terribly on the camels, although the men stood it splendidly, not a single case of sickness or breaking down having occurred.

The troops were now coming up with a rush. The leading boats of the Black Watch arrived on New Year's Day, and the first detachment of the Naval Brigade with a Gardner arrived on the afternoon of the 5th. The camp was all alive and ready for any work, however arduous and daring.

Amongst the later arrivals was good-natured Colonel Butler, who had come up the river in his boat manned by *kroomen*. I was amused at his incidentally mentioning his being out of soap and having to use sand as a substitute. But such inconveniences had not lessened his enthusiasm about the whalers. He was quite confident that the journey from Korti to Khartoum would not take more than forty days. This coincided with General Buller's opinion, but not with that given to me at Sarkamatto by Mr. Cook's *reis*, nor with the subsequent experience of the Nile column. Had the expedition been six weeks earlier, possibly the Colonel's estimate would have been very nearly verified.

Looking back to the few days spent at Korti, and a longer time on my return from Metammeh, a crowd of interesting events and incidents are recalled, but which from want of space are passed over here with regret. To a civilian, unacquainted with camp life, the regularity and order which prevailed would be to him a striking illustration of how the drill and the principles of military science come into practical operation. We hear at home of our soldiers and are proud of them, but no one who has not been with them when in the field can rightly estimate their true value.

The last and most ominous extension of the camp at Korti took place two days before we marched for Metarameh, in the pitching of the hospital tents. Their size and number prognosticated disease, wounds, and deaths as the natural sequence of 'horrid war.' As later experience showed, and the statistics given in a previous chapter too sadly indicate, these necessary and humane preparations were not in excess of the requirements of our force.

Chapter 12

Lord Wolseley's Adieu

Early in the morning of January 7, I learnt that orders had been issued for the despatch of a convoy of stores to Jakdul. Colonel Stanley Clarke, who was to escort it with 10 officers and 106 men of the Light Camel Regiment, kindly invited me to accompany him. Stewart's column was to march next day for Metammeh, and, in order to secure a day's rest at Jakdul before his arrival, I therefore decided to go on ahead of it that far with this convoy. It was ordered to march at 1 p.m., then its departure was postponed until 3 p.m., but it did not actually get away until 5 o'clock. And hereby hangs a sad tale. Amongst the reasons given for this delay were the shortness of camel drivers, and the longer time it consequently took to load the camels than had been anticipated. A walk round that part of the camp where the preparations for the despatch of the convoy were being made was anything but assuring. 'Confusion worse confounded' seemed to prevail, and from all I saw and heard, I could not but feel painfully convinced that this contemplated dash across the desert had never been thought out as a possible contingency in the expedition, as it certainly should have been.

The problem was an easy one to solve: it was simply this, if a dash across the 170 miles of desert between Korti and Metammeh is found eventually to be necessary, how many riding and how many pack camels will be required for so many men and so many tons of stores? and how can these camels be most readily equipped for such a service?

In the scramble and hurry I witnessed in getting the convoy ready, it was painfully evident to me then, and more so now, when I look back upon all that subsequently occurred, either that this forethought in planning the expedition had not been duly exercised, or, as appears to me to be the more likely, that if it had been the details decided upon had been most inefficiently carried out Some of the prime necessities for such a dash across the desert as this was to be, were wanting when it had to be undertaken. For example, we had plenty of riding saddles made for the expedition at the arsenal at Cairo, although much less cumbersome and much better ones could have been manufactured in England, and in less time.

The question of packsaddles, however, and their lashings became a very serious one when the troops reached Korti. Attempts were made to increase the small supply in hand by purchase from the natives, and even by manufacturing them ourselves on the spot. The deficiency in rope lashings had to be made good by native manufacture. Nor were the saddles, either bought or manufactured, very suitable for the transport of British stores, contained in wooden and tin cases, as the sore backs of the pack camels plainly showed, as well as the scores of their dead carcases scattered along the line of our march.

At 2 p.m. I struck my tent, and by 3 o'clock my three camels were loaded and ready for the march. Tent and all extras were left behind, and in their place fodder was carried for the animals. Certain minor arrangements, including the despatch of telegrams, detained me for a short time after we were loaded up, and so I ordered my man to meet me with the camels at a point he well knew on the other side of the camp, but when I rode out after him, neither camels nor man were to be seen at the appointed rendezvous. In some anxiety I cantered about the camp, hoping to find my lost property, but in vain, and then, almost in despair, I rode out to the village of Korti, where I saw part of the convoy had assembled. It was only, however, my friend Surgeon Allin, who, with his usual energy and promptness, had got his part of the convoy ready for the march two hours before anyone else. So I cantered back, feeling most uncomfortable from a suspicion that the fellow had, in some way, given me the slip.

At last, on the very spot where I had first searched for him half an hour previously, there I found him trying to look as innocent as a lamb, but I could plainly see by his face that he had been up to some mischief. What it was I had not then time to find out, but, upon my return to Korti in February, I missed a small box of stores, and I rather suspect that during the time of his invisibility he had conveyed them to the booth of a Greek suttler, with whom I subsequently found he had been on rather surreptitious terms of intimacy. Off we rode at last to the village of Korti, and up on to the edge of the desert below which it is situated, to wait for the convoy. Shortly before 5 o'clock Lord Wolseley and his staff rode up to where I had halted, wearing behind his usual cheerful mien a look of great anxiety. Soon Colonel Clarke rode up to the general, who advised him to form up on the plateau where we were, rather than down in the hollow, with the caution, 'Else you will get into confusion.'

Just before leaving, Lord Wolseley wished me a good time of it, and, in return, I expressed the hope that we might soon see him at the front. A quarter of an hour only before sunset the head of the column marched up on to the desert plateau, and when its rear had passed over the crest of the hill it halted, and bivouacked in marching order to wait until the moon rose. As she was then in her last quarter, this would not be until about midnight.

The next thing was dinner, or a substitute for it, and as I had halted near Colonel Clarke, I joined his mess, contributing my quota to our first meal in the desert. We sat on the sand round a lantern, and our menu was a simple one, comprising only 'bully beef' and other preserved meats and biscuits. Tea was out of the question, as there was no wood with which to make a fire, and so we had regretfully to content ourselves with Nile water, either pure and simple or fortified by a drain of Captain ——'s Lorne whisky. It was tantalising, under the circumstances, to look back at the lights of the camp and to hear the sound of the mess dinner bugles, and natural out here in the desert to hanker after the fleshpots of the Egypt still in sight, but out of reach. Intentions to return were uttered by some, but stem duty forbade.

The chattering of the Aden camel drivers and the groaning of the tied-down and unladen camels gradually subsided. Smoothing a place on the soft yellow sand, I wrapped myself in my plaid, and soon fell asleep. From exposure to a draught at night while on the *dahabiyeh* at Assouan, my left leg had become painfully stiff with rheumatism. When I awoke I found that the warmth of my bed had entirely removed the discomfort, and I was thankful for the relief. The advance was sounded at 1.30 a.m., and off we went by the light of the moon and to the unearthly groaning of a thousand camels. Soon, however, the halt was sounded, in order to close up the rear of the column which, to use a nautical phrase, had 'drifted considerably astern.' Everybody seemed pretty tired. I certainly was, and dismounting lay down on the hard gravel, and with my water-bottle as a pillow, and holding the reins of my horse, fell fast asleep, but was quickly roused by the noise Lieut. Stuart Wortley, who had halted near me, made in falling from his tall camel, saddle and all, and just in time for the advance.

After frequent halts in order that our straggling column might close up, or to relieve an already exhausted or dying camel of its load, morning at last began to dawn, with Venus as its star glittering like a diamond in the rich roseate hues which in this region always precede daylight

At 9 a.m. we halted for breakfast, and then marched on again with our usual numerous halts. I rode in front with the advance guard in order to escape the noisy confusion of the column, and also to get a better view of the region through which we were passing.

This so-called Bayuda Desert is wholly unlike the rocky and sterile deserts of the north, on account of its abundant signs of vegetation and water.

It comprises a number of extensive plains, divided by low rocky hills black or brownish in colour. These plains are sparsely covered with trees and a coarse tall grass. In many places both trees and grasses were very abundant, the former being the ordinary acacias and mimosa of the country.

Situated just within the region of tropical rains, this desert has a wet season from May to August, with an average rainfall of fifteen days' duration. From the appearance of its torrent-beds it was evident that the rainfall was very great. These channels led down to the more depressed parts of the plains over which the water flows, but within twenty-four hours after its fall it sinks through the sandy gravelly soil until it reaches a substratum of clay. It was from such subterranean reservoirs that the wells of Hambok, El Howeiyat, and others of the same class, were supplied. During the rainy season the soil of these plains can be profitably cultivated owing to the rains and the moisture derived from these stores of water beneath their surface.

Several nomadic tribes inhabit this region, of which the Hassanieh are the most numerous, although numbering only about one thousand souls. They subsist chiefly by keeping flocks of sheep and goats, and by breeding camels. Like Bedouins everywhere they wander from spot to spot in order to find herbage, always, however, keeping sufficiently near the wells to water their flocks. They also raise small crops of beans and lentils, and trap the gazelles. Flocks of these beautiful animals frequently came within shooting distance of us, but it was not often safe to leave a marching column to go in pursuit of them. Occasionally, however, I heard the crack of the rifle of some ardent sportsman behind me as we moved along, but the results were not very great. The droppings of the gazelles were plentiful and gave off a strong odour of musk.

The convoy had evidently not kept very well together, for it was not till some time after the front had halted that the rear came up. My man with the camels had orders to keep as near as possible during the march, and if by any mischance he had drifted to the rear, not to halt until riding back from my usual position at the front I met him.

We halted on this occasion in a thicket of mimosa and brushwood off the main track, and I had to ride back some distance before I found my fellow. He was so far astern that I halted for breakfast where I met him, as time would not permit riding nearer to the head of the convoy, but upon which I kept as sharp a look-out as I could while we halted. After breakfast I thought I heard the advance sounded. My attention was for the moment distracted by the coming up to where we had halted of a lot of stragglers and the consequent confusion that ensued. Unfortunately I allowed myself to be persuaded that I had been mistaken, for when I looked again the front of the convoy had disappeared, and full of anxiety I immediately started after it. First we had to get back to the caravan road from which we had diverged. This I found to be a puzzling matter, for between us and it lay a pathless tangled wilderness of trees and scrub, cut up by a number of parallel ditches. Camel marks were plentiful on the soft sand of the latter, but they were very irregular in their direction, and therefore difficult to follow.

We rode on for twenty minutes until we were brought to a standstill by a tract of hard gravel with hardly the trace of a track over it I then rode up a gravel knoll on our right to look out for the convoy, but it was invisible. Happily our late halting ground was recognisable in the distance, so I despatched my man on the horse back to it to begin the journey anew, for personally I had become somewhat obfuscated. My position was not a very comfortable one, for here was I bewildered and alone, with my three camels, with the risk of being deserted by my not very trustworthy Greek, or attacked during his absence by wandering Arabs. It was a relief, therefore, when half an hour afterwards the fellow returned with the news that he had found the road not a hundred yards to my right. It was now evident that on leaving our halting-place I had erred in not crossing instead of following the line of ditches to which I have referred. The incident shows how easy it was to get lost in this desert, and reminds me of the case of Captain Gordon, who accompanied the expedition as a press correspondent, and whose disappearance in the Bayuda desert has never yet been accounted for. He was last seen somewhere in this vicinity under the following circumstances, as communicated to me by Lieut. Douglas.

Gordon had left Korti on January 9, with the intention of accompanying a supplementary convoy despatched after General Stewart under Colonel Burnaby's command, as he thought the latter I believe had started ahead of him. On January 13, four days afterwards, Lieut. Douglas, who was then surveying for a line of heliograph signal stations to Jakdul, had halted eight miles west of El Howeiyat wells, and one of his men, after firing at some game, heard what he supposed to be the echo of his shot Firing again and hearing another echo, he saw in the distance the smoke from a rifle. Fearing it might have been fired by a foe, he at once fell back on his party. Shortly afterwards. Captain Gordon came up with his Greek servant and two camels, but so thoroughly exhausted that he could hardly speak.

He told Lieutenant Douglas that he had been without water for two days. His eyes glared with excitement During the evening he said he had a great deal on his mind, for he had volunteered to carry despatches to General Stewart, and then he rambled on about having lost his sword. Such an adventure, he said, as he had had only occurred once in a man's lifetime, and he must write it down. During nearly the whole of the night, Lieut. Douglas informed me Gordon's light was burning. Early in the morning, Douglas rode on with him some distance, when Gordon spoke about the landmarks in connection with finding his way. In reply he was told to keep his eye more on the broad well-marked track so recently made by our thousands of camels. After parting with Douglas he was never heard of again, and it was supposed that he had either perished of thirst in the desert or been killed by wandering Arabs.

It has recently been reported that a European has reached Berber, and there is yet a hope, faint as it may be, that the poor fellow is still alive. The adventures subsequently of several of my colleagues further illustrate how easily one may leave the beaten track through this wilderness, and how difficult it is, when lost, to find it again. Two of them, on their way from Jakdul to Korti, travelling without a guide, were found by an officer carrying despatches to the front, utterly lost, though only some hundred yards off the main track. Their misadventure had to me a ludicrous aspect, for I had travelled with them from El Gubat to Jakdul, and the night before we marched for the latter place, after we had gone to bed under a mimosa tree, the question of how to find the road to Korti was discussed. One of them was quite sure of being able to direct his steps by a certain star.

Unfortunately, the star was not visible when he and his companion lost their way. The desert roads, as already remarked, were simply a series of hard beaten paths, but only clearly discernible when they crossed a hard gravel soil. Occasionally belts of soft sand were traversed, when to the unpractised eye the tracks were difficult to follow. Besides the main track, there were often others similarly marked crossing or diverging from it in a most perplexing manner. Happily for those acquainted with the general direction, it was sufficient to have a compass, or to observe the landmarks in the shape of stones put up on spots where the ground rose in swells or on the higher adjacent hills.

It was about noon when we got back to the track. My man as well as myself, rendered nervous by our recent adventure, were naturally anxious to catch up with the column, lest a similar accident might again occur. He rode one of the camels, leading the other two, tied one to the other by their rope halters. The rear camel, which had travelled so bravely thus far from Wady-Halfa, began to lag behind. He seemed either unable or indisposed to keep pace with his comrades, and they were consequently held back by him. This added to the anxiety of the moment, and so, unwillingly, when his halter became taut, I had to apply the *courbash* to him.

In passing Hambok wells the road led through a tract thickly covered with beautifully verdant trees and bunches of *savas* grass of a light sea-greenish colour. The landscape was thus quite in contrast with what might have been expected in a so-called desert, and as it lacked but little of that trimness which marks cultivation, it seemed as if it had been laid out by a landscape gardener. To keep up this delusion we soon passed through a part which, from the shape and size of the trees and their regular distances from each other, resembled an orchard. Amongst these we caught sight of some figures on camels, which proved to be the rear guard of the convoy. Their first salute was, 'Well, you have had a narrow escape of being shot, for supposing you to be some of the enemy's scouts, we were just about to draw a bead on you!' This we found subsequently was half a joke; but in our nervous anxious state it was not even then a pleasant salute.

Riding on ahead, and still keeping slack the halter of my lagging camel by the occasional application of the *courbash*, we overtook the detachment of mounted infantry left at Hambok wells by Stewart on his first march to Jakdul. Colonel Featherstone, who was in command, told me that their efforts to increase the supply of water there had comparatively failed, and that they were going on with us to El Howeiyat. Soon we had proof that many of the heavily laden and half-fed camels were succumbing, for several were passed which had fallen under their loads, and which neither thrashing nor coaxing could induce to rise. Over twenty so far had died; and no wonder! The poor brutes were only allowed about one half their daily quantity of *dhura*, and this was their third day without water.

On emerging from the parklike tract through which we had passed, the road led up a broad, gentle slope, and, curving to the right across our front, brought the long straggling column of the convoy again into view. That long grey line, brightened here and there by scarlet uniforms, was in the fading sunlight an interesting and picturesque sight—at any rate, so it appeared to me after my recent adventure.

The head of the column had dismounted when we arrived at the wells, and the ten Hussar scouts, with Sergeant Alcock, began watering their horses, and anticipating the rush to the wells when the convoy halted. I promptly replenished all but one of my water-skins. The hurry and scurry which ensued as our thirsty men came in crowded round these deep pits dug in the gravelly soil—for such really were the openings from which water was here obtained—was a sight not easily to be forgotten.

The supply from the largest well was first drawn upon. Here a lance-corporal, representing the Royal Engineers, had taken up his position, armed with a pump on three legs, attached to which was a length of *gutta-percha* hose. After the pump was placed in position more than one bucketful of water had to be poured into it before it would draw. When at last it was thus coaxed into working order, many hands were held out with canteens and other vessels to be filled with the precious fluid.

The first well or pit into which the hose was dropped was soon emptied, and then the pump had to be moved to another, and then another, until it had gone round to all the pits and drained. them. Operations had then to be suspended until nine p.m., when it was expected that they would be refilled, for the source of the water supply here was by percolation from the stratum of soil in which these pits had been sunk, and not from springs.

The force then began to be supplied by detachments, that of the

21st Hussars, under Captain Richardson, being first on the list. He had promised to fill my empty water-skin for me, and in the thick darkness I made my way to the wells by the light of my lantern. The captain could not keep his alight, as it lacked one of its glasses, and mine was borrowed for the occasion. At the side of the pit at which these operations were resumed our Royal Engineer lance-corporal with his three-legged pump reappeared, preparing for action. Down at last went one end of the suction hose into the pit, but not having been properly attached to the nozzle of the pump, down it went altogether, and once again after it had been fished up.

The abashed and despairing look of that corporal after this second catastrophe is still fresh in my memory, and the more than forcible epithets applied to his pump by the weary, thirsty men round it still ring in my ears. It was no joke to have come so full of hope to El Howeiyat, after our thirsty march, to be thus tantalised.

At last the pump had to be abandoned, and men were sent to the bottom of the pit to fill the iron tanks by hand. Leaving my water-skin with one of the men to be filled, I returned to my bivouac to rest, but had it sent back to me empty long before daylight. Returning at daybreak to the wells, I found them still the centre of anxious interest Although we were ordered to march at 6 a.m., it was 8 o'clock before all the detachments had secured a supply of water.

That, after only a two days' march from the Nile, the convoy should have run so short of water, was not either creditable or encouraging. Besides the personal supply taken by the men in their leather bottles and water-skins, we carried a number of iron water tanks; two of these constituted a camel's load, and would therefore contain about thirty-seven to forty gallons. At El Howeiyat when we halted, I noticed that a number of them were so battered by careless handling, that their contents had either in a great measure, or wholly, leaked out. Had they been shielded by a wooden case, this accident would not have happened.

There were good reasons for believing that a supply of water could easily have been obtained at several points on our route, and especially at the Wady-Aboo-Geer, through part of which our second day's march from Korti had led. The appearance of much of the ground there, as well as the abundant vegetation which covers it, fully justifies Mr. Fowler's statement that water is to be procured by sinking wells along this route. In many places the soil was so damp that I was afraid of my horse sinking into it. It therefore seemed a great oversight not to have made the same provision for procuring water on this expedition as that which formed so interesting a feature in the outfit of the Abyssinian. On that occasion it proved, if I remember rightly, to be superfluous, but in this instance such a provision would have been invaluable.

When mounted and waiting for the advance to be sounded, our two Sudanese guides from Korti came to me complaining piteously that they had not been supplied with water. The word for water in Arabic, '*moyeh*,' has a melancholy sound about it, and on this occasion it was made more pathetic by the deplorable tone of these men, emphasised by their holding up to me, with significant eloquence, their empty water-skins. The oversight, for such it was, was soon however remedied. While we were in this state of 'suspended locomotion,' the head of the convoy was startled by the braying uproar of a pair of donkeys, one of which was in hot pursuit of the other, which at his very best pace was trying to escape from him.

Round and round several clumps of bushes the pair went at full speed, until the pursuer, turning too sharply round one clump not previously circumnavigated, tumbled over a pair of camels which were kneeling behind it. The latter showed their resentment at this rude intrusion by groaning at their loudest pitch. This closed the amusing incident, for in the collision the saddle of the pursuing donkey becoming loosened and trailing by its girth, anchored him, and he was easily secured by his owner. This was a short, bandy-legged soldier of the Mounted Infantry, I believe, who met us when riding up the slope to the wells on the previous afternoon. He was then leading this very donkey with its saddle trailing behind him, and asking everyone he met if they had found a 'gold spur.' This excited some merriment along the line, for gold spurs and a donkey, combined with the scene out here in the Bayuda desert, made an incongruously ludicrous medley of things.

The last of our force supplied with water was the detachment of Egyptian troops sent with us as camel drivers. They presented a pitiably forlorn and exhausted appearance. In fact, they were utterly devoid of that soldierly endurance which so characterised our fellows under the trying circumstances of this march. It was sickening to see them wandering about early in the morning with empty milk tins begging for '*moyeh*.'

At length the advance was sounded and off we went, soon regaining the caravan road about fourteen miles beyond the point where we had diverged from it for El Howeiyat on the previous afternoon. We passed on our right the volcanic-shaped Jebel-el-Messalima, and at the 710 kilometre[1] two hours later we rode through a narrow pass between hills of blackened rocks.

The pass opened out into what may be termed the southern slope of the Jebel-Jiliff range, in the torrent gorges of which are situated the Magaga, Jakdul, and other wells, or rather rock cisterns, which during the rainy seasons are filled with water. Our road crossed a number of the beds of torrents flowing southwards, and which are always dry excepting in the rainy season, when from their appearance an abundance of water flows through them. Between these occurred several belts of sand and sandy loam covered with scrub, and bunches of the sea-green-coloured *savas* grass.

In crossing one of these belts, near a torrent bed, our ever-watchful scouts reported the discovery on our right, near the road, of a suspicious-looking straw hut. Inside was a roughly constructed divan, and several broken earthen vessels; and it bore marks of very recent occupation. As little fear was entertained of the convoy being attacked, the discovery of this hut, concealed though it was amongst a clump of trees and low brushwood, caused only a passing sensation, and relieved somewhat the monotony of the march.

Clearing these sandy belts with their scrub, an extensive landscape opened out on our right, bounded by a range of low gravelly hills about eight miles distant; the middle ground of the picture was filled up by extensive bands of mimosa trees of the brightest green, running parallel with our road. The whole scene had beauty of its own, enhanced by contrast with the dreariness of its surroundings. The wilderness through which we had been riding had all at once blossomed on us 'like the rose.'

On our left we now passed a supply of water which would have relieved our thirsty convoy had we known of it. The place was designated 'Wells' on the Intelligence Department map, but seemed to have been entirely overlooked until these water-reservoirs were explored by the wide-awake Royal Irish on their march to Jakdul early in February, and subsequently by the writer on his return to Korti with the convoy of sick and wounded under charge of Surgeon Harding and

---

1. The sketch map of the Intelligence Department of the country between Ambukol and Shendy here quoted, based on Mr. Fowler's surveys for the Sudan railway, had the distances between these points marked on it in sections of ten kilometres, that at Ambukol being 610th.

escorted by Major Wyndham and a detachment of the Light Camel regiment. The road led past an isolated rocky hill of curious formation, its upper *stratum* of sandstone resembling the foundations of a ruined castle. Its name is Jebel Zobrick-el-Kelb in Arabic, the polite equivalent adopted for which in English being 'Mountain of the Dog's Tongue.'

When we halted for breakfast at eleven o'clock, everyone seemed the worse for our disturbed night at El Howeiyat The spot being shadeless, the hot sun increased our misery. Then when the water ration was being served out it was discovered that our reserve supply had again been seriously decreased by the leakage of the iron tanks. This caused great anxiety, as the excessive heat and dry atmosphere combined had provoked such a thirst as the limited supply carried by the men in their water-bottles was insufficient to allay, and now their water-bottles could not be refilled.

In order to economise the store of the precious fluid laid in at the El Howeiyat wells, and especially on account of my horse, I had during this morning taken alternate sips from my water-bottle and from a bottle of pure lime-juice carried in one of the holsters of my saddle. I had also acted on experience gained under similar circumstances in the prairies west of the Missouri, keeping my mouth closed and resisting the temptation to drink in the earlier hours of the day. Still the thirst suffered was intolerable. Water *per se* never before seemed so valuable, and I began to feel a supreme contempt for those fussy people who make such an ado about the impurities of our London supply.

As the day wore on this water question became more and more serious. The Aden camel drivers were recklessly improvident of their water, and began buying it at the rate of a dollar (4s 2d.) for a bottle holding about a pint and a half. I had strong suspicions that some of our reserve water supply had thus been surreptitiously converted into coin, and felt quite certain that some of my own had also been thus disposed of by my Greek servant, for when we bivouacked at sunset my water-skins were so reduced in bulk as only to afford a gallon to my thirsty horse and another for him next morning, and even only then by limiting my own supply for supper and breakfast.

When I took the fellow to task about the mysterious decrease in the size of my water-skins, he tried to persuade me that like the iron tanks they had also leaked out part of their contents, and then with an air of offended dignity asked if I thought he would sell our water. This made me certain he had done so, and to resolve that in future when on the march I would look sharper after him.

The detachment of Egyptian soldiers sent with us as camel drivers also became demoralised over this water question, for they stole each other's and even their officers' supply. These men, if men they really can be called, wore white linen tunics with brass buttons, and over their red *fez* a white linen covering with a flap behind as a protection to their neck from the sun. In appearance they were thus military swells as compared with our fellows in their travel-stained suits of dingy grey. The contrast between them in other respects was most marked, for the latter bore the heat and thirst with true soldierly endurance, while the former pitifully succumbed to the trying circumstances of the hour. Gordon called the Egyptian soldiers 'hens,' and so they now appeared alongside of our fighting cocks.

While inspecting the straw hut stumbled upon by our scouts, Lieut. Stuart-Wortley, accompanied by one of our guides, rode on ahead for Jakdul with a despatch from Colonel Clarke to Colonel Boscawen, asking him to prepare a defensible post outside of the gorge, and also if possible to send some water to the convoy next day.

Sir Herbert Stewart had ordered Colonel Clarke to form a *zereba* for 1,000 men close to the caravan camel track near the gorge. In this despatch he asked Colonel Boscawen to choose the position and commence its construction, as he had only 100 men of the light camel regiment with him, and he knew they would be fully occupied on the afternoon of the 11th watering their camels, unloading and arranging the enormous number of boxes of stores and other supplies carried by the transport animals.

CHAPTER 13

The Crisis of the Expedition and How it Ended

Early next morning (January 11) we resumed our march, and halted at 10 a.m. for breakfast where the road from Abou-Halfa wells joined the caravan track. Finding my water supply so reduced by leakage or pilfering as to leave only a quart for my thirsty horse, I bade Colonel Clarke good morning and pushed on ahead of the convoy towards Jakdul. We had ridden about three miles when we fortunately met Captain Crabbe, of the Grenadier Guards, and Lieut. Stuart Wortley, with three camel-loads of water on their way to meet the convoy. Replenishing my water-bottle from this supply, I pushed on again, and soon met a Greek in the employ of Mr. Rees, the contractor, accompanied by a native on a camel with a large skin of water. A dollar secured the prize for my horse and camels. This brightened things up a bit, for, as the old adage goes, if a hungry man is an angry one, a thirsty man is a desponding one. It seemed now as if I could join more heartily than ever in some of the temperance songs in praise of water, the desert looked more cheerful, and Villiers's much-admired bluish-purple haze again decked the distant hills.

After riding seven or eight miles further on, our road diverged from the caravan track to the left, up to the Jakdul gorge. For some distance it led through a gravelly tract, pretty thickly covered with trees and scrub, and cut up by numerous narrow channels, through which in the rainy season torrents of water make their way down to the plains below. Then came a narrow pass opening into the gorge, at the opposite extremity of which were the celebrated wells. Until the road made by the Guards, by clearing it from the loose stones, was reached, the riding was very rough. Hence the Guards and Marines had cleared a broad pathway up to the wells, with side roads leading from this main thoroughfare to other parts of the amphitheatre. Locomotion was thus not only made less uncomfortable, but, what was of more importance, much less ruinous to shoe leather.

After this first sign of civilisation in this howling wilderness, the next met with was the Guards' mess, cosily arranged under a clump of verdant mimosas, and then, when riding past it, the hearty welcome by Colonel Sawle to luncheon.

Not liking the shadeless spot Captain Crabbe assigned to me for a bivouac, I removed to another near the wells and protected from the sun by a clump of mimosas. It subsequently turned out that what had thus been gained in shade was counterbalanced by the wind and dust to which the locality I had thus pitched upon was most uncomfortably exposed.

Shortly after my camels were unloaded, in came the Mounted Infantry from Stewart's column, which they had left at Abu-Halfa short of water. They rode up near where I had bivouacked, and soon Major —— rather peremptorily ordered me to pack up and move, for that the particular spot I then occupied had been assigned to them for officers' quarters. Tired as I was, I felt disinclined to comply with what appeared an unreasonable and unkind demand, for there was plenty of room for all. Besides, as a representative of the press, I felt annoyed at this cavalier treatment, and refused to move. After a parley, which, thanks to the kind courtesy of Captain Walsh and Major Phipps, soon assumed an amicable tone, I was left in quiet possession of my quarters.

I am pleased to say that not more than two or three other incidents of the same unpleasant nature befell me during the expedition. In each case I stood out for my rights and always came off victorious. These few collisions took place with officers of happily a very exceptional class so far as war correspondents were concerned.

The convoy I had left in the morning arrived later in the day at the *zereba* constructed on the caravan road abreast of the Jakdul gorge. Soon after it halted long strings of its eleven hundred camels came up to the wells to be watered. Poor brutes, their sore backs showed too painfully that they had had the worst of our weary march.

★★★★★★

Wells is a misnomer for the sources of water supply at Jakdul, for they are merely water-worn cavities in the rocks by whose precipitous sides they are in a measure shut in, and are supplied with water in the rainy season in sufficient quantity to secure a two years' supply for the ordinary demands made upon it.

There are three of these rock cisterns, one above another. The lowest is an irregular oval about a hundred feet long by sixty wide. Three quarters of its circumference is enclosed between perpendicular rocks. As it had been daily visited by a large number of animals, its water was hardly fit for any other use. Major Dorward, R.E., had constructed a long trough at right angles to it, into which its water was pumped. This, with the improvements he had made in the approach to its open side, very much facilitated the rapid watering of the camels, for it enabled fifty or sixty to drink at one time. The major calculated on January 13 that the lower pool contained a sufficient supply for twenty thousand camels, and, as subsequent results showed, his estimate was correct.

The next cistern, or pool, is about ten feet above that just described. It lies at the bottom of a channel two hundred feet long by forty feet wide, the rocky sides of which rise eighty feet precipitously from the surface of its water level. Its outlet to the lower pool is through a narrow passage about eight feet above the highest water level. The third pool is about five feet above the second, with which, in direction, it is at right angles, and is about eighty feet long by fifteen in breadth. A tortuous road, seventy feet long by three broad, leads down from it to the rocky brink of the second pool. Above these pools the gorge widens and bears the marks of the violent flow of water through it. It seemed like what had been recently the bed of a furious cataract, and such it certainly was during the seasons of the tropical rains which here prevail.

Major Dorward had constructed down below a number of tanks out of the lining of the biscuit boxes into which water from the upper pools was pumped for drinking and cooking purposes. But the supply thus obtained being inadequate, the men had to clamber up the rocks to the upper pools in order to replenish their water-skins and the iron tanks.

This climb up the steep sides of this rocky hill was almost as stiff a one as up the sides of the Great Pyramid, and over a surface almost as uneven. The water from the second pool had first to be drawn up by buckets from the depth below, and this made the process of watering the men a much slower and more laborious one than that of watering the camels.

It is impossible to decide absolutely whether or not any labour had been employed on these cavities. The probability is that they were formed by the action of water wearing out the softer portions of the rock in which they occur. Still the sides of the lower pool in several parts produce the impression of a human improvement on nature's work.

The sandstone rocks in which these cavities are formed have weathered a light brownish yellow, tinged here and there with dark reddish-brown, and when chipped present a curious appearance from the dark crimson-coloured veins by which they are marked.

On both sides of the minor gorge in which these pools are, there are several smaller ones leading down from the heights above, forming other channels. One of these bore the marks of the force of the torrent which periodically swept down through it. Its rock formation was very interesting, including a band of conglomerate composed of quartz and other pebbles bound together by a dark-coloured cement This conglomerate accounted in great part for the pebbles so thickly strewn on the desert plains over which I had ridden from Wady-Halfa up to Korti, and the black sand I had noticed along the shore of the river. Both were doubtless the result of the disintegration of this conglomerate. Subsequently I found fragments of the band at Tani, nine miles below Korti, and with it also fragments of the curiously veined sandstone rock of Jakdul.[1]

I must here bear testimony to the almost literal accuracy of the maps of the Bayuda desert compiled by the War Office Intelligence Department from various sources, but chiefly from Mr. Fowler's surveys of it for the proposed Sudan railway. The information contained in the letterpress descriptions on it was also remarkably correct. It was a most valuable guide to our force. And this illustrates the care with which such expeditions are sent out by our military authorities. It was not, for example, likely that Lord Wolseley would send General Stewart on a happy-go-lucky march to Jakdul, at any rate so far as the water supply was concerned. He had good reasons for supposing that it was

---

1. At the foot of Jebel Nasaib-el-Gereer, fifteen miles SSE. of Korti, I noticed a lilac-coloured sandstone thickly imbedded with pebbles, and between Ambukol and Tani the same formation crops out. At both these places there were also interesting tree petrifactions, some beautiful specimens of which I secured. At the latter place there was the greater part of the trunk of a tree—fifteen inches in diameter— of which, if transport facilities had been available, I should have liked to bring home a section. At Abu-Simbal, below Wady-Halfa, I also picked up a fragment of the lilac -coloured sandstone without pebbles— but I found another fragment with them, near Ambigol springs, fifty miles south of that place.

sufficient, his only anxiety being as to its condition when reached by our force of men and camels, for it was feared that the enemy might, in anticipation of our advance by the desert route, have polluted it

General Stewart's column arrived at El-Howeiyat a few hours after our convoy had left it As our convoy had drained the wells pretty dry, he was unable to obtain an adequate supply for his larger force, consequently he had to halt at the Abu-Halfa wells, half a day's march from Jakdul. The Mounted Infantry, however, had so economised their supply that they were able to continue their march, and reached the gorge, as already stated, shortly after I did.

This was quite in harmony with the remarkable efficiency of this corps all through this dash across the desert. It was ever to the front and ever ready for the duty assigned to it Its camels seemed always in better condition than those of any other corps. Whether standing in a *zereba* for hours together to be shot at, or facing the desert in a square as a mark for the invisible sharpshooter, or, as at Abu-Klea, shoulder to shoulder mowing down the Arabs when they charged, the fighting qualities displayed by our corps of Mounted Infantry cannot be too highly praised. It is hardly necessary to say that its discipline was admirable, and so also were its commissariat arrangements. In fact I never knew these brave fellows to be short of anything required for physical sustenance, nor was their mess larder even ever devoid of what were esteemed as luxuries under the circumstances of the expedition.

And as proof of this perfect regimental commissariat, while Stewart's column had to be halted short of its destination owing to want of water, this part of it was able to push on to Jakdul, actually bringing in with them a large unused supply of the precious fluid.

The acknowledged superior efficiency of the Mounted Infantry must be traced to the fact that it was composed of old soldiers commanded by picked officers, and who at all times and under all circumstances justified the wisdom of their selection. In fine, this corps had been formed on old and well-established military lines, and with an emphatic view to service in the field demanding such care in its formation.

The *zereba* constructed by General Stewart's orders on the caravan road, abreast of Jakdul, was commanded by rocky hills on every side. The two redoubts planned by Major Dorward, R.E., one to defend the entrance to the gorge and the other to protect the wells and the stores, were likewise overlooked by hills behind those on which they were built. Sir Evelyn Wood, when he went to Jakdul to aid in the withdrawal of the troops from El Gubat, improved these defences by the construction of other works, which, happily, were not put to the test, for, as will be remembered, the enemy did not advance after General Buller beyond Abu-Klea when withdrawing the troops from El Gubat.

When General Stewart reached this zere*b*a about midday on the 12th, leaving Colonel Stanley Clarke with his detachment of the Light Camel Regiment in defence of it, he marched his thirsty column at once into the gorge. The entry of this crowd of men, camels, and horses into the rocky amphitheatre presented a scene never before witnessed within its dreary and blackened walls. As each corps came up to the particular place already allotted to it, it wheeled into it with military precision. Halting in parallel lines to the main thoroughfare leading up from the opening to the wells, the men dismounted, and relieving their weary camels of their burdens led them in long lines to the lower pool to be watered.

The watering of so many animals was a difficult and tedious process, for only about sixty of the two thousand odd could find room to drink at a time, and this called into requisition all the patience and skill of the officers of the Guards and Marines and a large fatigue party working under their directions. The serious confusion which the crowding together of so many animals threatened was cleverly avoided by the officers as a jam often is on London Bridge by the skill of our Metropolitan Police. In fact, the military authorities seemed now to be acting out to perfection the part played by our 'bobbies' in dealing with a congestion of traffic, and continued this hard work long after sunset by the fitful light of lanterns.

The upper pools were immediately resorted to by fatigue parties for a supply of water for the men, and under the supervision of Major Carmichael, of the 5th Lancers, they were at it all night. Although, from the position of the second pool, as already described, obtaining a supply of water thence was a dangerous operation, particularly after dark, no accident happened to any one.

Early on the morning of the 13th I met the major clad in a scarlet tunic, when, with much indignation, he told me that he had caught two of the soldiers actually bathing in the third or uppermost pool. This was bad enough under the circumstances, but not so outrageous, after all, as the conduct of an officer who, during my return march to Korti, annexed an unwatched half camp kettle of water, which had been served out for cooking purposes, as just the thing for a 'tub.'

The 13th was a busy day. The men were engaged in filling water-skins and the iron tanks and in making other preparations for our march to Metammeh, and all this under a broiling-hot sun, for as not a breath of air found its way through the rocky amphitheatre it was like working in the stokehole of a steamer.

Under any circumstances Jakdul was not a desirable place for a residence; for while the heat was roasting during the day, at night the other extreme had to be endured, for then gusts of cold wind poured down into the gorge from all points of the compass. In fact, what with this heat by day and breezes by night, the melancholy barking of the jackals on the adjacent hills, when all had become still in the camp, its gloomy surroundings and the rocky debris strewn over its surface, and its scraggy, shadeless, thorny trees, it was of all places between Korti and Metammeh the most wretched and melancholy. The only redeeming point about this horrid hole was its abundant water supply; but even that was not so good as it looked or tasted to thirsty men. It would have afforded a London analyst a first-rate opportunity for a sensational report, for it was alive with *animalcula*.

As already mentioned, the water of the lower pool was only fit for animals when the wells were reached; but the upper ones later on showed unpleasant signs of 'wrigglers.' Whether from an incautious drink of the water of the lower pool on the day of my arrival or from drinking too freely of that from the upper ones, I cannot be sure, but on the 13th I felt very ill and feverish. Later in the afternoon I became anxious lest I should not be able to go on with Stewart's column next day, and therefore sent for Surgeon Allin, who prescribed the standard allopathic remedy in the form of a 'James's powder,' which I backed up with burnt brandy and a teaspoonful of the extract of Jamaica ginger, then lay down, piled on all my blankets, broke out into a profuse perspiration, fell into a sound sleep, and awoke at daylight all right again and ready for the march out.

Colonel Kitchener, who had accompanied General Stewart in his first march to Jakdul, had remained there when he returned to Korti. He had taken up his abode in a large cave in the side of the rocky hill which formed the south-western side of the gorge. It was quite open, and when lighted up after dark presented rather a singular appearance. Being for the moment the headquarters of the Intelligence Department, it became naturally to me a centre of considerable interest, and occasionally I dropped in to make inquiries. On the morning of the 13th the colonel told me that he could only confirm what we had already learned before leaving Korti—to the effect that the road was clear to Metammeh, but that this town was held by a force of two or three thousand of the enemy, with whom he expected we should have our first fight. This was all the information he had as yet been able to glean, but he hourly expected the return of some messengers he had sent out a few days previously.

When I returned to Korti in February I learned from an officer of the Intelligence Department there that on that very day (January 13) information had been received by Lord Wolseley that a large force had left Berber and Omdurman to oppose our march to the Nile, and that it was fully expected we should have to fight it before we reached Metammeh. 'But,' added my informant, 'anxious as we were, we had no means of informing you'!

The want of some means of rapid communication with his base thus added considerably to the risks of General Stewart's dash across the desert Field telegraphs and heliographs are now largely used in military operations involving considerably less danger than in so hazardous a march as his was, and it is difficult, therefore, to account for the omission now of some more rapid means of communication with Jakdul than by mounted messengers.

The continuation of the telegraph system to Korti from Dongola had been decided upon early in October, and provision made for it. Later on the contingency of a desert march on Metammeh must have impressed itself on our general, and especially after the receipt of Gordon's letter of November 4.

General Stewart, I know, did ask for a line of heliographs to follow his column, but for some reason or other he was refused, although all the materials for such a line were to my certain knowledge then in store at Korti. But no such provision had been made for a field telegraph because of the lack of transport upwards from Wady-Halfa. When Lord Wolseley bade us goodbye there after his hurried visit on November 17, General Webber, the chief of the military telegraph line, asked him for transport for telegraph stores, but was refused on the ground that 'men could do without information, but not without food.' The consequence was that the materials for a field telegraph which had been brought up the river to Wady-Halfa were left there.

Had they been sent on, El Howeiyat wells could have been connected with Korti in six days and Jakdul in twelve days, and only 130 transport camels would have been required for the work.

If General Stewart had anticipated having to fight a large rebel force before he could reach the Nile, he would have been in a better position to attack it than he was when unexpectedly obliged to do so. But a more unfortunate incident occurred when Jakdul was occupied on January 3, through the lack of rapid communication between its base and this desert column. Had such means of communication then existed, instead of halting there General Stewart would in all probability have pushed on to Metammeh, and for the following reason.

As already mentioned, he had private orders, if the supply of water at Jakdul was insufficient, to push on to the Nile. He had now ascertained beyond all doubt that there was no enemy between him and Metammeh. After examining the wells, he stood thoughtfully for some few minutes at the lower one, and then, shaking his head as he turned away, said, 'I cannot conscientiously report an insufficient supply of water here, and therefore I must return to Korti, although I fear that, before we are ready to move on to Metammeh, the road may be blocked.' It is a regrettable matter that General Stewart was not allowed such freedom of action as would have enabled him to take advantage then of the favourable circumstances of his position. Had there been means, however, of consulting Lord Wolseley, no one can doubt but that he would have ordered him to march on, and would have moved heaven and earth to despatch more troops across the desert to support such a movement, for, as he subsequently informed Lord Hartington:

'He was prepared at the time to incur great risk in order to extend immediate assistance to General Gordon, should his situation be found to be one requiring help without delay, and that, in pushing Stewart forward as he did, he went to the extreme limits of the risks to which a commander should expose his troops.'

If General Stewart had then taken the responsibility of marching on to Metammeh instead of returning to Korti, it is not difficult, therefore, to understand that the commander-in-chief would most heartily have approved the decision of his lieutenant, for whom he sincerely and deservedly cherished the greatest regard.

Had this responsibility been taken, it is certain that this desert column of the expedition could have reached the Nile without firing a shot.

General Stewart's double journey to Jakdul, however prudent it may be, looked at from a military point of view, may fairly be taken into account as the chief cause of failure in the attempt made to open communications with General Gordon. For reasons which will be given further on, it will be seen that despite this Gordon might have been reached before it was too late. The mistakes, however, which occurred to prevent this, and the loss of General Stewart at a critical moment, may be indirectly traceable to the incident to which I have referred. The expedition was so near a success that it may seem ungracious to some to call attention to anything which contributed to its failure. My narrative of it would, however, lack faithfulness if all allusion to such points were left out of it At the same time it must be borne in mind that the commander-in-chief of the expedition was placed in a most embarrassing position from the difficulties he encountered through the late date at which the expedition was authorised and for whatever mishaps occurred through this H.M. Government are primarily responsible.

CHAPTER 14

First Signs of the Enemy

Soon after the reveille sounded on the morning of January 14 the whole camp became alive in its final preparations for the march out at noon on Metammeh. The water-skins and tanks remaining unreplenished were filled and the last rations served out Soon after breakfast the transport camels were despatched to the *zereba* outside to be loaded with their burdens of commissariat stores and ammunition. Then, accompanied as usual by the dismal groanings and unearthly cries of the unwilling brutes, followed the saddling of the riding camels by the troops, and the mounting of the different corps and their marching to the appointed rendezvous in the valley outside of the gorge.

Just after sunrise Colonel Burnaby, who had come in the night before from Korti with a supplementary convoy, made his appearance at my quarters. He wore as usual his dark blue cavalry undress-cap. In appearance he reminded me always of the burly knights of the old days of romance and chivalry, and specially so this morning. After a hearty recognition he inquired where he could find one of my colleagues for whom he said he had been trying to procure a camel. This was the colleague who had come all the way from Dongola to Wady-Halfa in November last after a boat he had ordered up there from Alexandria to be used for the more rapid transport of news at the crisis of the expedition, and in navigating which up the cataracts he had lost his servant's life and was nearly drowned himself.

This craft had, however, for obvious reasons to be left in its native element at Korti, and now away out here at Jakdul he was trying to replace it by a ship of the desert. 'If you see him,' said the good-natured colonel, 'say that I cannot get him a camel, but I can supply him with a donkey!' The incident was characteristic of the man, which his sad fate a few days later indelibly impressed on my memory. Tired as he must have been after his four days' march through the desert, yet he had thus early come across the gorge, and by a cross cut too over its sharp stones, to do a kindness to a former fellow campaigner, for my colleague had been with him at El Teb and Tamai.

I reached the rendezvous in the valley about one o'clock, and had a weary waiting in the hot sun for an hour before the column was ready to move, detained as usual in getting the commissariat and transport into line.

And such a column was this one, for its elements were of the most heterogeneous character, in fact a regular hotchpotch of cavalry, foot, sailors, marines, and artillery, with the usual adjuncts of an army on the war path, of commissariat and field hospital corps &c. It may be said to have comprised representatives of nearly all the different corps of which the British army is composed.[1] Approximately it numbered 114 officers, 1,687 non-commissioned officers and men, and 343 native and Indian camel drivers and interpreters. For transport purposes we had 2,888 camels and 153 horses ridden by the 19th Hussars and including those belonging to the Staff.

Our actual fighting force, including the 58 sailors sent with us to work Gordon's steamer and 27 officers and men of the Royal Engineers, was 1581 officers and men. This comprised a detachment of 258 officers and men of the Royal Sussex Regiment under Major, now Lieut.-Colonel Sunderland.

Of the camels 1,565 were used for the transport of stores, ammunition, and hospital necessaries, and on some of the camels the detachment of the Sussex regiment rode, the animal carrying, besides its rider, a load of provisions and ammunition. The remainder of this pioneer regiment was left under the command of Colonel Vandeleur to garrison Jakdul.

Unfortunately there was only one driver to four camels, and the poor brutes had therefore to be tied head and tail together, that is the halter of one camel had to be tied to the tail of the one before it, and so on. Some few having lost their caudal appendages through this unnatural use of them, the halter was tied to the saddle instead. As these strings of camels came along, I remembered General Buller's repeated refusal at Wady-Halfa in November to send more drivers thence to

---

1. An intelligent commanding officer remarked to the author after the affair at Abu-Klea: 'Cavalry are out of place in a square, and moreover it is a mistake to try to have the whole British army represented in a small force. Taking a little of everything may be a capital way of making a salad dressing, but not an effective or safe fighting column.'

Dongola on the ground that 'the expedition would be over before they could reach their destination.' As results showed, this scarcity of drivers was a great mistake, and, as at Abu-Klea, nearly helped to secure a disaster.

A drove of horned cattle accompanied the column, sent with us by Mr. Rees the contractor at his own risk. Part of them were unfortunately lost at Abu-Klea, and the rest on the 19th in the battle near Metammeh.

Although, from its extraordinary composition, our column would have made a most unique march past the Queen, and afforded a spectacle such as had never before been witnessed by her Majesty's subjects, it had its heroic aspect, for this march out into the desert displayed under all its circumstances a courage and dash worthy of our best military traditions. Here was a handful of our soldiers sternly resolved, in the face of all the difficulties anticipated or unknown which might harass or endanger them, to carry out their orders and to save Gordon and release Khartoum. This was their object and hope, under the inspiration of which, as subsequent events showed, they did their duty as nobly as Nelson's sailors did at Trafalgar under that of his celebrated signal.

We had not gone far along the caravan road before recent horse tracks were noticed a short distance off it on the right This led to the impression that we were watched by the scouts of the enemy. Soon after this discovery, hearing the report of firing on our left, I rode to the front and found that it had only been caused by some of our ardent sportsmen trying to bag a few sand grouse for supper. One of them, I believe, had fired at a distant flock of gazelles.

The country which for several miles had been barren and desert became sparsely covered with *savas* grass and mimosa trees as we descended into one of the depressions covered by water during the rainy season. Shortly before sunset, 5 p.m., the column halted and bivouacked for the night, after having covered about eight or ten out of the fifty-two miles between Jakdul and the wells at Abu-Klea. Relying upon Colonel Kitchener's latest information, it was hoped when we marched today (14th) that this important position would be reached and occupied by us on the afternoon of the 16th. The recent horse tracks, however, made this now doubtful, and many of us went to sleep under the impression that on the morrow we might be delayed by an encounter with the enemy.

The reveille sounded at 4 a.m. on the 15th, and the column

marched at break of day. For some distance the ground was loose and sometimes sandy, but the going on the whole was not difficult. Right ahead of us was the Jebel-En-Nus, an isolated hill on the top of which a large stone was placed as a landmark.

In a previous chapter reference was made to the earlier experiences of our men with camels, and to the imposing appearance which a corps presented when mounted on them while on the march up the river. This morning (Jan. 15) our column was strikingly illustrative of this. The Guards and Heavy Camel Regiment were marching in open column of sections in front, with the buglers of the former slightly in advance blowing occasionally a warlike blast. On the left front face were the general's red flag and those of the several corps.

In order more fully to be impressed by the strange, unique scene of British troops mounted on camels and marching in such military order, I drew off a short distance to the right of the column. Its appearance was most imposing. The men seemed as if they had been accustomed all their lives to the steeds they now bestrode. The height of the camels, their red saddles, and stalwart riders clad in light grey, and wearing white sun helmets, produced an almost indescribably grand effect, not only from an artistic, but a patriotic point of view. Every face seemed to say, 'Here we are at length near the end of our toilsome work and ready for what remains of it.' Even the very camels seemed to enter into the spirit of the hour, for with their long necks gracefully curved out in front they moved steadily onwards with that swinging step which, to an onlooker at any rate, appears to be the very poetry of animal locomotion.

While thus engaged, a dog ran up along the right of the column, barking his 'Good morning.' This little fellow had been the pet companion of the grenadier section of the Guards all the way up from Assouan. He came thence to Wady-Halfa with a detachment of camels, and Sergeant Mortimer told me that he would trot ahead and, taking shelter from the hot sun under a projecting rock, wait until his friends came up to him, and then start off again to another shelter.

How he escaped in the fight at Abu-Klea is a wonder, for he was in the square with his regiment and in the thick of it. He was also in the square on January 19 at Metammeh, and amused himself during the fight by running after the bullets that struck the ground inside of it. The grenadiers took great care of their little pet, and during the march, when he happened to be thirsty or tired, some of them would give him a ride on their camels and a drink out of their water-bottles.

He was brought safely on the march back across the desert and to Wady-Halfa, where he was stolen from his friends. He resembled a colley dog in appearance, but was much smaller in size.

Then followed an incident which caused some amusement, changing the scene from the sublime to the ridiculous. While the column was thus grandly moving onwards, a man of the Coldstreams, having lost his camel, annexed as a substitute one of the drove of oxen. This new steed quietly submitted to the soldier's kit being tied on his back, but refused to carry him. In the struggle which ensued to secure a mount and to resist it, the Coldstream at last caught hold of the animal's tail in order to steady him, and in that fashion man and beast—the latter going full steam ahead—bolted through our stately ranks, amidst a burst of general merriment, in which even the general joined. Shortly after sunrise, the track led over a sandy belt cut up by watercourses, and very much broken by bunches of *savas* grass. This rough bit knocked the transport animals so much about that when the hard ground beyond was reached, the bugles of the rear guard called for the usual halt to repair damages.

Riding out to the advance scouts of the 19th Hussars, my attention was again specially attracted to the horse tracks noticed the day before, by their fresh appearance and increase. Dismounting to rest my horse when a halt took place, I examined them closely as well as the remains of fires near the track, and came to the conclusion that the scouts of the enemy had very recently been near us, and later on we saw some of his camel men. At sundown the column halted at the Jebel-es-Sergaim, or 'Mountain of the saddle,' and bivouacked for the night We were now within about twenty miles of the wells of Abu-Klea, having so far covered thirty-two miles in our march from Jakdul.

General Stewart was now quite convinced that we had been closely watched by the scouts of the enemy, and gave Colonel Barrow orders to push on ahead next morning (January 16) and reconnoitre the neighbourhood of the wells of Abu-Klea.

At 2 a.m. on the 16th, Colonel Barrow and his squadron therefore marched on ahead in its usual advance-guard formation— with scouts well out to the front and on its flanks; Major (now Colonel) French being in command of the more advanced troopers. About 9 a.m. the latter observed a small camel party of the enemy, two or three miles on his right front. Colonel Barrow coming up at the moment ordered Major French with a patrol of a few men to pursue them. In consequence of the undulating character of the ground the Arabs managed to get away out of sight from their pursuers. The chase after them had, however, taken the major and his men three or four miles in advance, and in fact right into the gorge or *wady* leading to the wells. Here were nine other men mounted on camels and small groups of others on foot, some armed with spears and others with rifles. What thus appeared to be a look-out outpost retired rapidly into the plain as Major French came in sight. Having now reached the foot of one of the hills overlooking the *wady* of Abu-Klea, he left the patrol with ten men and a corporal to support him in case of necessity and rode ahead to reconnoitre.

More footmen were now seen, and the major resolved, if possible, to capture one or two of them. He therefore with a corporal started in pursuit, and coming up with one of the men seized him, when small bodies of the enemy's horsemen were observed coming towards them followed by groups of footmen armed with spears and rifles. As their evident intention was to surround the major, he said to me, 'So we had to drop our prisoner and bolt.' The reconnaissance had, however, discovered the main position of the enemy. This prisoner was seized on the very spot where the square was charged next day by the Arabs.

Major French retired leisurely, halting occasionally further to observe the enemy. Colonel Barrow with the main body had now reached the entrance to the gorge, and, learning from Major French the state of things ahead, resolved at all hazards to hold the hills overlooking the *wady* leading to the wells. No sooner had he disposed his small force in order to secure this object than the position was attacked by the enemy's cavalry on both flanks. These attacks were repulsed, however, by the dismounted fire of the Hussars, who maintained their ground until the column came up.

There can be little doubt that Colonel Barrow by this prompt decision and the skilful disposition of his men had thus completely checkmated the enemy in his intention to occupy those hills, in order to check our advance.

The column marched at 5 a.m., three hours after Colonel Barrow. It was quite dark when we started, and soon it was discovered that part of the host had wandered away to the left, and we were obliged to halt until the mistake was rectified. Then came more halts and further delays. This was not very encouraging, and the imagination began to picture the nice scrape we should get into were the enemy to swoop down upon us in some of these moments of semi-disorganisation.

Before daybreak the road was most uncomfortably uneven and

strewn over with hillocks or bunches of *savas* grass. Matters, however, improved with the dawn, and soon we reached better ground in what appeared to be a vast plain. Just before sunrise and in the distance could be discovered the hills of Abu-Klea.

The region we had now entered bore the singular designation, according to our map, of Op-mit-Handel, whatever that signifies. After sunrise I rode out ahead of the column, and when it halted dismounted as usual to rest my horse, and again examined the horse-tracks. These had now visibly increased and led both ways, and some of them seemed very fresh.

Shortly after 11 o'clock the 'halt' was sounded, accompanied by 'rations' indicating breakfast Cameron and I alighted together, apart from our colleagues, and about fifty yards from the general's flag. Whether gloomy or tired I cannot say, but he seemed unusually reticent.

It was very hot, so after despatching a frugal breakfast I rigged a *tente d'abri* with my plaid and opened sun umbrella. It was a failure, however, for the gusts of wind upset it, making a siesta impossible.

Soon Cameron called out to me that Colonel Barrow had come in, and wouldn't I go over with him and hear the news? So off we went, and when we met General Stewart, he said to us:—'Well, gentlemen, the enemy is ahead of us! Barrow has exchanged shots with his outposts, and I am going to attack him at once.' The tone of quiet determination in which this was uttered is still fresh in my memory, as well as Sir Herbert's appearance. He had that carriage peculiar to cavalrymen when on foot which gives them an air, at any rate, of being bandy-legged. In his hand he carried a short stick with which he sketched in the sand for the direction of his *aides-de-camp* the formation in which he intended to advance, and they hurried off to carry out his orders.

My colleague and myself having despatched our men with the baggage to their designated place in the column, we mounted our horses and followed the General as he rode out to the front to reconnoitre.

The place where we had halted for breakfast was near the foot of the hills which separated us from the *wady* leading to the wells of Abu-Klea. The caravan road, after leading up between two of them, dipped into a small basin-shaped valley, and then rising between two higher hills gradually descended into the *wady*. The road thus formed a pass as it were, which, if Colonel Barrow had not taken prompt measures to prevent their doing so, might have been occupied by the enemy to block our further advance.

Chapter 15
Stewart's Decision and Sunset

The whole force was now dismounted, and the camels and transport animals with their loads of stores, ammunition, &c., were formed into a close column and placed under the protection of the Sussex regiment and the Naval Brigade. The fighting portion was formed into a line of columns at half distance, with the Guards' Camel Regiment on the right, the Heavy Camel Regiment in the centre with the guns, and the Mounted Infantry on the left.

So promptly had General Stewart's order been carried out that when Cameron and I had reached the basin-like valley referred to we found the troops already in battle array and the usual inspection of rifles being carried on by the officers and non-commissioned officers. The men seemed to enjoy this inspection, and some of them eased their exhilaration by using more breath than was necessary in order to clean the locks of their Martini-Henrys from dust. Had they been going to a singsong, instead of into a life-and death struggle with a savage foe, they could hardly have evinced more cheerfulness. The tired and weary travellers of our desert caravan had all at once been transformed into a band of stern warriors, ready and anxious for the fray.

Riding on a little further, a passing change came over the scene—and one verging on the ridiculous. A pair of donkeys came frisking over the hills on my left, one dragging his saddle after him by its girths, and both seeming stupidly unconscious of impending trouble. Soon their owners leisurely followed from the same direction, one a short Greek from Berber, clad in a flowing white cotton robe, which might be taken either for a shroud or a bed-gown, and the other his sable attendant from whom I had bought the skin of water beyond Jakdul. They seemed rather surprised when I told them the position of affairs, and at once hurried off in pursuit of their truant steeds.

When the crest overlooking the *wady* was reached, we caught sight of the general and his staff as they rode up one of the light-coloured gravel hills to the left of the road, and putting spurs to our horses reached its summit with them. Colonel Burnaby came riding up after us on a donkey, and leaning over to me said in an undertone:—

'M——, if any disaster happens to us, not one will ever see London again.'

'Why, Colonel,' I replied, 'you are the very last man here that I should suspect of dreaming of disaster. What do you mean?'

'Well,' said he, 'our chances of pulling through all right are twenty to one.'

'Say a hundred to one, and if I were a betting man I should take you up.' Perhaps he was chaffing me, or feeling my pulse, but I think not, for he looked troubled and excited.

The conversation dropped, as our attention was then called to a force of the enemy's horsemen riding in single line on the edge of the steep ridge which rose abruptly from the north side of the *wady*. Then a few flags were observed amongst the scrub some distance off in front.

Sweeping the ground with my glass to the right, I detected numbers of the enemy armed with rifles running rapidly down our right flank towards a conical hill. Owing to the undulation of the ground and the shallow depression they were following, sometimes they would disappear for a moment and then rise head first into sight again. It was evident to Cameron and myself that their object was to occupy this hill, and we therefore called General Stewart's attention to the movement. He, however, allowed them to do so, probably judging from its distance that they could not seriously injure us from it, and that from its isolation it would be hazardous to detach a force from the main body to occupy it.

It was difficult from this reconnoitring point to make out with certainty the exact position of the enemy, and as but three hours of daylight remained. General Stewart yielded to Colonel Burnaby's suggestion and decided not to attack until next day. The column was therefore halted in a low gravelly plateau, and the following measures taken for its defence. (See plan.)

One end of a long, oval-shaped hill 450 yards on our left was occupied by the Naval Brigade who held it during the night of the 16th. On the 17th both ends of the top of this hill were held by the Mounted Infantry.

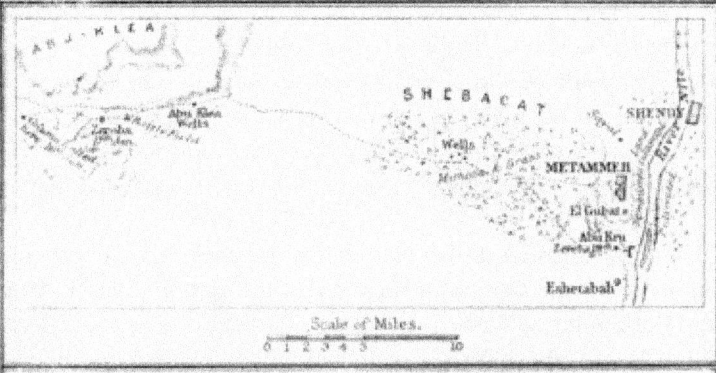

ZEREBA AT ABU-KLEA, Jan. 16th & 17th
From a sketch by Lieut. Lawson, R.E.

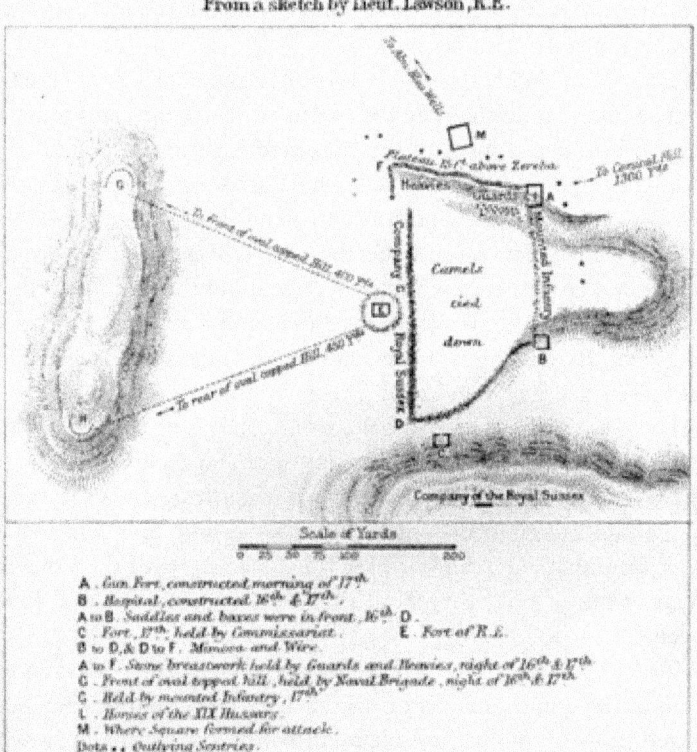

A . Gun Fort, constructed morning of 17th.
B . Hospital, constructed 16th & 17th.
A to B. Saddles and boxes were in front, 16th. D.
C . Fort, 17th, held by Commissariat.   E . Fort of R.E.
B to D, & D to F. Mimosa and Wire.
A to F. Stone breastwork, held by Guards and Heavies, night of 16th & 17th.
G . Front of oval topped hill, held by Naval Brigade, night of 16th & 17th.
G . Held by mounted Infantry, 17th.
I . Horses of the XIX Hussars.
M . Where Square formed for attack.
Dots .. Outlying Sentries.

A stone breastwork was rapidly thrown up in the fading daylight by the Guards Camel Regiment on the plateau in front of that on which the camels had been halted and tied down. It was about fifteen feet higher than the latter and divided from it by a narrow depression in which the horses of the Hussars were picketed.

A breastwork of camel saddles and boxes was also immediately constructed on the right face with wire entanglements in front The left face was defended only by a few straggling mimosa branches over which the engineers stretched a single wire to represent an entanglement.

The front breastwork was held by the Heavies, who lay two deep behind it with the Guards in their rear; the right left face by Company G of the Royal Sussex, with only one man to every four feet of ground allotted to the detachment Another company of this regiment occupied a hill in rear of the *zereba* during the night. The right front was defended by the Mounted Infantry. The three screw guns were placed at the right front corner.

During the night a hospital fort of boxes was constructed on ground a little higher than the *zereba* and in rear of the right front, and occupied by a detachment of the Mounted Infantry.

Early on the morning of the 17th a fort was constructed on the right front corner of the position with saddles and biscuit and 'bully' beef boxes, in which one of the three guns was placed in position. Another was constructed with boxes only, about the middle of the left front, nearly opposite to where my horse and camels were. This was held by the Royal Engineer detachment. A fourth fort was similarly constructed at the rear and held by the commissariat.

After General Stewart had halted the column he went out to the advance picket of the Hussars to reconnoitre, and on his return he told me that he had seen a long row of flags stretching across the caravan road, behind the right of which there was a large tent, and that the enemy were making a din with their *tom-toms*. When I then met him he had come to order the Naval Brigade to occupy the oval hill on our left.

Nor had the enemy been idle, for no sooner had they taken possession of the conical hill on our right than they could be seen busily engaged in fortifying its summit by throwing up a stone breastwork. Like a swarm of ants they ran rapidly up and down the hill collecting materials from its rocky sides for their fortification. It seemed strange as I watched them that they were allowed to continue their work without interference. Where, I mentally asked, are Captain Norton's screw guns? I was immediately answered by the report of one of them, and, to my relief, saw the shell which had been fired from it burst right amongst a swarm of the busy Arabs, and some weeks later I learned that it had killed and wounded twenty-seven of them. This was in the glow which followed sunset, but no more shells were fired, and until darkness hid the hill the Arabs could be seen going on with their fortifications.

Soon after sunset, they opened fire on us from it, and as the darkness deepened, the summit of the hill would have afforded an interesting study to an enthusiastic pyrotechnist, as it sparkled all over with jets of fire. Unfortunately for the poetry of the occasion, these jets were followed by the whistling of bullets overhead and accompanied by the beating of *tom-toms*.

The surface of the plateau, where the camels were tied down, was strewn over with loose angular stones, and therefore did not afford a very comfortable resting-place either for them or for tired travellers. Before I could find a comparatively easy place for my hip-joints and shoulders, I had to shift my position several times, and remove not a few stones from beneath them. The particular spot I had stumbled upon was, however, well protected from the fire of the enemy by three large camels lying tied down between me and the conical hill. Its sanitary condition was not, however, all that could have been desired, for the camels around me reeked of the carbolic oil with which their sore backs had been treated, combined with the sickly odour of over-perspiration. There also seemed to be a prevailing epidemic of flatulency amongst them. Happily, when the poor tired brutes had become fairly settled down on their uncomfortable beds, they ceased their usual harsh gurgling groans.

After a while, fatigue got the better of these surrounding discomforts, and I dozed off, but was soon roused by a disturbance in my rear. Looking round I discovered that one of the camels, which was suffering from mange, had risen. One of his forelegs still remained tied up, and the poor brute was trying to scratch himself with one of his hind feet, while maintaining his perpendicular on the other two. Twice I got up and tied him down. The second time a bullet whizzed uncomfortably past us both. Generally, however, they flew so very high that their cutting through the air sounded like the humming of bees, or the singing of a cloud of gigantic mosquitoes, bent on a foraging expedition. Sometimes this music had a wailing tone about it, just as if these leaden messengers of death had hearts and mourned over the errand on which cruel men had despatched them. Taking into account the rapid and continuous firing of the enemy up till midnight, when it slackened and almost ceased, and the fact that but two or three of our men were hit and about as many camels, it would appear, as has been alleged, that it takes half a ton weight of bullets to kill a single man in battle.

As the mangy camel did not again rise to disturb the neighbourhood, I dozed off once more, but was soon suddenly roused by the startling cry, 'Stand to your arms!' Somebody had given a false alarm, for shortly all became quiet save a restless colleague who was wandering about in the dark, trying to persuade some one to lend him a rifle on the plea that we should all lend a hand to defend our lives!

This alarm occurred about nine o'clock, judging by the stars, for, as lights were forbidden, watches were unavailable. Shortly after midnight there was another false alarm.

Both these alarms were caused by the outlying sentries of the Heavies on the left front running in. Each time they did so the sentries of the Royal Sussex, touching them on the left front corner, naturally withdrew with them. At the time of the second alarm Colonel Burnaby happened to turn up at this corner of the *zereba*, and asked a Sussex sentry why he had left his post The man replied that he and the others had done so because the sentries of the Heavies had run in. 'Never mind those fellows,' said Burnaby; 'there is no danger. Stick to your post, my man!'

After the second alarm, the fire of the enemy had almost entirely ceased, leaving us some hopes of a quiet nap. In this, however, we were disappointed, for occasionally they would fire three or four shots apparently in response to the groaning of some disturbed or uneasy camels. One surgeon also drew their fire by an incautious exposure of his lantern while attending to a wounded man. The enemy was evidently on the alert, and their quietness at length produced the suspicion of intended mischief.

About 2 a.m. the conical hill presented a strangely wild sight. Several fires were lighted simultaneously near its top, round which could be discerned groups of the enemy, engaged in a war dance to the rub-a-dub-dub of their *tom-toms*. Sleep was impossible under the circumstances, and so we waited anxiously for daylight, making the most of our hard beds.

At daybreak many of the enemy, emboldened by our inaction, came running down the hill, and crept up towards the *zereba*, while their less courageous companions began blazing away at us from behind their stone breastwork. The fire now became so hot that skirmishers from the Guards and Mounted Infantry were sent out to keep it down.

Soon after sunrise the bullets came thicker than ever from the hill, and from the edge of the shallow depression running parallel with our right front. Amongst the hits was Colonel Burnaby's horse. He was complimented after he obtained an early remount, but gloomily responded, 'I am not in luck today.'

The enemy now appeared to concentrate their fire on the right front—taking in flank the shallow ravine in which the horses of the 19th Hussars were picketed. Many of these were soon disabled, and some of them killed.

Noticing the general's red flag in motion near the gun-fort, I made towards it, but had no sooner reached this ravine than a man of the Mounted Infantry just before me was hit by a bullet in the left breast, which came out at his back and whizzed past me. The poor fellow turning round exclaimed, 'I am badly hit, sir,' and fell into my arms. As I laid him gently down I noticed that the hole made in his grey tunic by the bullet had a scarlet and a black ring round it. A file of the bearer company soon came along with a stretcher and carried him off to the hospital. I then heard several voices calling out to me to get under cover, 'or sure as anything you'll get hit!' These friendly warnings were almost immediately emphasised by the whiz of a bullet past my head. This decided the matter, and hoping the squall of lead would soon blow over I sought cover.

Noticing Cameron making his way up to the hospital fort, I followed him thither in order to discuss the situation. We saw that a square was being formed for the purpose of attacking the enemy, and I asked if he intended going out with it. 'No,' he replied, sternly, 'I do not think it is the right thing to do. It will be a mob of camels, sailors, cavalry, and artillery, all mixed up together.' So we quietly arranged that one should go out with Colonel Barrow and his squadron, and that the other should remain in the *zereba*, for, said he, 'we are going to have a hot time of it here when the square goes out, for those fellows on this hill and those horsemen on our left mean mischief.'

During our conference more wounded men were brought in, and amongst them Major Dickson, who had been sent with us to accompany Sir C. Wilson to Khartoum. He had been hit below the knee, but the bullet had fortunately missed both bone and arteries. One of the surgeons told me that human skill would be puzzled to take a bullet through a man's leg in so harmless a direction as this one had gone. Then Major Sunderland's groom was carried in, hit by a bullet which had passed through both his thighs. The surgeons could do nothing for him, as arteries had been cut in both, and in agony the poor fellow bled to death. Shortly before this groom was hit, a bullet passed through the nostrils of his master's horse. When any of the wounded died, a blanket was placed over the stretcher on which they lay, and before I left the hospital fort there were seven poor fellows thus covered up.

Leaving the hospital in order to look after my men and camels, several bullets struck the gravel slope down which I was walking. One came very nearly securing for me the notoriety of being returned amongst the wounded, for it drove a pebble against the calf of my left leg, but not with force sufficient to leave even a mark on the leather of my top boot.

I found my Greek fellow quite cool and happy, and my camels and horse untouched. In fact this part of the *zereba*, which was nearly abreast of the engineers' fort, seemed well out of range, for no casualties had occurred there to either men or animals.

Cameron now seemed anxious to go out with the Hussars, and I therefore consented to remain in the *zereba* and watch events. After saddling my horse and dividing my remaining water with him, I returned to the hospital fort, as its comparatively elevated position afforded a good view of everything going on.

Just as I entered, young Lieutenant Lyall, R.A., was brought in unconscious, having been wounded by a bullet passing through one of his lungs. Then Major Gough was brought in stunned by a bullet, which, after passing through his *pugaree* and helmet, had not sufficient impetus left to break the skin.

About this time a body of the enemy's horse were noticed moving in the direction of our right flank, but were soon sent to the rightabout by two or three of Captain Norton's skilfully fired shells. If all our artillery officers are as efficient as those with our half-battery of screw guns were, we have good reason to be as proud of that arm of the service in the present as we have been in the past.

The hospital was now quite full of wounded officers and men, and some fourteen who had died in it were lying in a row outside. It did appear high time for something to be done in order to check the harassing fire of the enemy. Up till nine o'clock, and for two long hours, we had been a target for his sharpshooters, who having fairly got our range were now making good practice. It was, therefore, a relief to learn that General Stewart had given up hope of the enemy pushing home, and was going to march out at once to attack them, and had given orders for the formation of a square for the purpose. And this was how the square was formed.

Front face,—Right: Two companies Guards Camel Regiment (Grenadiers and Coldstreams). Left: Two companies Mounted Infantry.

Right face.—From front to rear. Two companies Guards Camel Regiment, Scots Guards, and Royal Marines, detachment of Royal Sussex Regiment (128 rank and file).

Left face,—Right: Two companies Mounted Infantry. Left: 5th Company of Heavy Camel Regiment (5th and 16th Lancers).

Rear face,—Four companies of Heavy Camel Regiment as follows, from left to right faces: fourth company, Scots Greys and Royals; third company, 5th and 4th Dragoons; second company, Bays, Royal Horse Guards; first company, 2nd and 1st Life Guards.

The half-battery of screw guns were placed in the middle of the front face; and the Gardner, with the detachment of the Naval Brigade, in the centre of the rear face.

When the square began to move, it was found necessary to strengthen the left face, for, as will be seen, it was a whole company weaker than either of the other three. In order to effect this, the Greys of the fourth company Heavy Camel Regiment were moved from the rear face into it

The centre of the square was so seriously crowded by the 120 camels carrying spare ammunition, and those of the bearer company, that more than one officer assured me that it was almost impossible for any one at the front to be usefully cognisant of what was taking place in the rear. Sir Charles Wilson, in a note to his observations on the accident to the square, with his usual candour, says, 'I was in the front part of the square, and could not see what occurred behind the camels.'

If rightly informed, I believe that General Stewart, in order to obviate this serious difficulty, sent Colonel Burnaby to the rear to report to him, but without any executive authority. To both Cameron and myself the square appeared too unwieldy a formation to meet and repel successfully the attack of a daring and active enemy, such as he supposed that in our front to be from his experience at El-Teb and Tamanieh. As already stated, we therefore decided not to go out with it

CHAPTER 16

Dangerous Position of the Naval Brigade

The defence of the *zereba* was entrusted to Major Gem of the Royal Sussex, with a mixed force of two hundred officers and men, composed of detachments from his own regiment and from the Mounted Infantry, and a few men from other regiments.

A part of the Mounted Infantry were sent to occupy the small stone-work on the top of the oval-shaped hill on our left (see plan), and Lieutenant Kane, with forty-seven men of the Sussex Regiment, held the small defensive work on the right front corner of the *zereba*. The engineers and the commissariat were left in charge of their respective forts, and a few of the Mounted Infantry garrisoned that of the hospital.

The enemy's horsemen, foiled in their attempt earlier in the day to work round our right flank, began about 8.30 a.m. to threaten our left. General Stewart then ordered Colonel Barrow and the Hussars to move out in that direction, with general instructions to aid the square when it advanced, to use dismounted fire, but by no means to charge the enemy.

The Hussars left the *zereba* about 9 a.m., and as they advanced diagonally from our left their progress was watched with much interest. They soon reached the slopes of the round gravel hills below the ridge which formed the sky-line in that direction, and along which the line of the enemy's horsemen could be seen slowly advancing to meet them. They halted as the Hussars approached them, and soon after a part of them took ground to their right, and disappeared beyond the ridge.

About 10 o'clock, or an hour after the Hussars had moved out, the square advanced to fight our way to the wells. Up till then I had had my misgivings as to the prospects, but these were soon dispelled by the appearance which the square itself now presented. How grandly imposing was that mass of armed men! At first sight it suggested a moving fortress, but with walls of such material as to bid defiance to the assaults of any ordinary foe. Then, under the ocular deception produced by the prevailing mirage, it was lifted above the ground and seemed to float away from us, now firing a gun from one side and then from the other, when an enthusiastic fancy converted it into a line-of-battle ship sailing into action.

Many of the enemy's sharpshooters followed the square along the ridges on the right of the line of its advance, and from 400 to 800 yards distant from it. Taking advantage of every rock and tree, they kept up a hot and telling fire on it from their safe commanding positions. Others of them, moving along the same flank, availed themselves of the inequalities of the ground and of the cover afforded by the sparsely scattered shrubs and grass. On the left flank the Arab sharpshooters had plenty of cover among the tall grass in that direction, and also kept up a hot fire.

Skirmishers had therefore to be sent out from the front, rear, and flanks to check this galling fire. Sometimes, however, it became so hot from all directions that the square itself had to be halted in order to reply to it by Martini and screw-gun fire. This had the desired effect, and on one of these occasions, after several shells had been fired in the direction of the enemy's right, strings of Arabs could be seen running rapidly to the rear. Another shell fired to the right burst over a squadron of the enemy's horse which I had been anxiously watching, for they were then moving past our square under cover of a swell in the ground, evidently bent on paying a visit to the *zereba*. This shell, however, threw them into confusion, when they retired out of sight Others of Captain Norton's shells seem to have done some execution at the point marked K on the plan, for forty-eight dead were found lying there after the battle.

Whatever has been said and written about the bad shooting of our soldiers was not applicable to the skirmishers sent out on this occasion, if only half the incidents told me of their firing can be depended upon.

Many of the single men of the enemy's sharpshooters were, I was told, killed at ranges from 600 to 800 yards. In another instance, when twelve of the Arab spearmen were making a rush at ten men of the

Sussex, under command of Colour-Sergeant Kelly, they were met by two volleys at 400 yards—seven of them falling at the first and three at the second, when the other two bolted.

Captain Campbell's company of Mounted Infantry—all picked shots—did excellent service on the left flank, for as the square advanced it almost silenced the fire of the enemy's sharpshooters. Looking down at the motionless line of flags which marked the position of the enemy. Captain Campbell and some others imagined that the Arabs had bolted, leaving their colours behind them as a blind. An officer with the captain who had been at El Teb and Tamanieh knew all about it, for he positively declared that there was no enemy there, and that the flags only indicated a native burial-ground.

These illusions were however soon dispelled, for when the Captain and his skirmishers came within 200 yards of what had thus appeared to them to be a deserted camp, suddenly a large mass of Arabs in battle array came up from it To General Stewart this was no surprise, for he recognised in it the result of the masterly flank movement he was then making (see plan) on the position of the Arabs.[1] In fact, he had completely outgeneralled the Dervish commanders. The latter had declined attacking him in the *zereba*, in order to do so in some position of their own choosing as he was advancing to the wells. They had also evidently calculated upon his following the caravan road from the *zereba*, for they had constructed (see plan) stone loopholes along the dry watercourse which runs abreast of the road and at a distance from it of only 150 yards. As this watercourse was thickly fringed with tall grass and scrub, it afforded a capital ambuscade for a large force. On its north side the caravan road was dangerously commanded by high and broken ground. Here then was the trap into which it was designed to lead General Stewart, but which was so skilfully avoided by the line of advance followed by the square.

The ground over which General Stewart was advancing now became very uneven and covered with loose stones. This not only made it difficult for the heavy-laden camels to keep their places within the square, but also seriously impeded the work of the Naval Brigade in getting their Gardner gun along. Consequently the former began to

---

1. Referring to this period in the advance of the square in his despatch about the engagement, General Stewart says: 'The enemy's main position was soon apparent, and by passing that position clear of its left flank, it was manifest that he must attack or be enfiladed. As the square was nearly abreast of the position, the enemy delivered his attack in the shape of a singularly well organised charge.'

lag behind, and when the square was moved obliquely to the right, as shown in the plan, they pressed so heavily against its rear left corner as to force it open, when many of them drifted outside the formation through the gap they had thus made in it. The native drivers, as usual being non-combatants, preferred the rear of the square to its front, and this in no small measure contributed to what we have described as now taking place.

In order to meet the impending attack of the Arabs the square was now halted on the face of a hill sloping towards the position of the enemy, and a hurried attempt was made to close up its rear to the front. An incident then occurred which largely contributed under the following circumstances to the only serious disaster of the day. When the order to close up was given, the Naval Brigade had begun to move the Gardner gun from its position in middle of the rear face and put it into action outside of the left rear corner of the square. In order to do this it had to be taken through the camels that were now crowded together between these positions, and in this confusion when the rear closed up the gun and its sailors round it were left outside of the formation.

The enemy were now close at hand, and Colonel Burnaby, perceiving the dangerously exposed position of the Naval Brigade, ordered the company of the 4th and 5th Dragoons to wheel out from the rear face in order to cover them. Before this movement was accomplished, the Gardner gun had been drawn back into the square, taken through the left face between the Greys and Lancers, and put into action a few paces in front of it.

No sooner was Colonel Burnaby assured of the safety of the gun than he ordered the men he had wheeled out from the rear front for its protection to fall back into their places. From all accounts he seems to have had some difficulty in getting them to accomplish this backward movement, and while thus engaged the enemy came up and he was unhorsed, and as he lay on the ground was killed by a spear-thrust, which severed his jugular vein.[2]

The Arabs advanced to the attack in compact, oblong columns of spearmen, each having a wedge-shaped front or head. The form of these fronts or heads suggests that of the Greek *ἔμβολον*, which had three sides representing the letter Δ, and probably like it was designed to pierce and forcibly enter an enemy's formation.

---

2. When Colonel Burnaby ordered the 4th and 5th Dragoon Guards to wheel up and protect the Naval Brigade, it caused great confusion, as the latter got mixed up with the former.

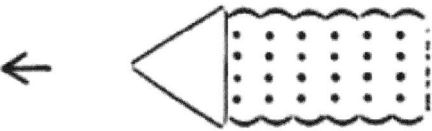

The oblong form of the columns which closely followed these wedged-shaped heads, made them less vulnerable to fire as they advanced, but when they charged they did so in a broad front, bringing up their right shoulders. Each column was led by either an Emir or Sheik on horseback carrying a flag, and accompanied by mounted attendants.

There were five of these columns, three of which had evidently been formed up under cover of the steep bank shown in the accompanying plan of the engagement. These advanced to the attack along the dotted lines 1, 2, and 3. The columns which moved along lines 4 and 5 had probably been concealed in the dry watercourse behind this bank, and which, curving round the right of the position in which the enemy waited for our attack, protected it in that direction.

The enemy came on very rapidly, in fact at a quick run, and in such regular order as to excite general admiration. Their masses or columns charging along lines 1, 2, and 3 were at once met by the Guards and Mounted Infantry with an independent fire, which at first does not appear to have been effective, for it did not check their progress. On still came these compact masses of spearmen with a low, murmuring cry like the sound of many waters. They are now within a hundred yards diagonally of the left front corner. The masses, charging along lines 1, 2, 3 had been exposed all the time to the full fire of the Guards and Mounted Infantry on the front face, while line 2 was also exposed to the Mounted Infantry companies in the left face.

The effect of this sharp fire was soon seen in the gaps made in the ranks of these brave Arabs. The masses moving along the lines 1 and 2 were so checked by this fire that they did not press home their charges. That moving along line 3 swerved under it to the right, and although taken in flank at the positions indicated between the sectional (red) lines B and D, still continued its advance, reaching the left face of the square, according to Captain Verner's lines on the plan, at or near the company of the Lancers. Information from other sources, however, leads me to the conclusion that its actual point of first contact with

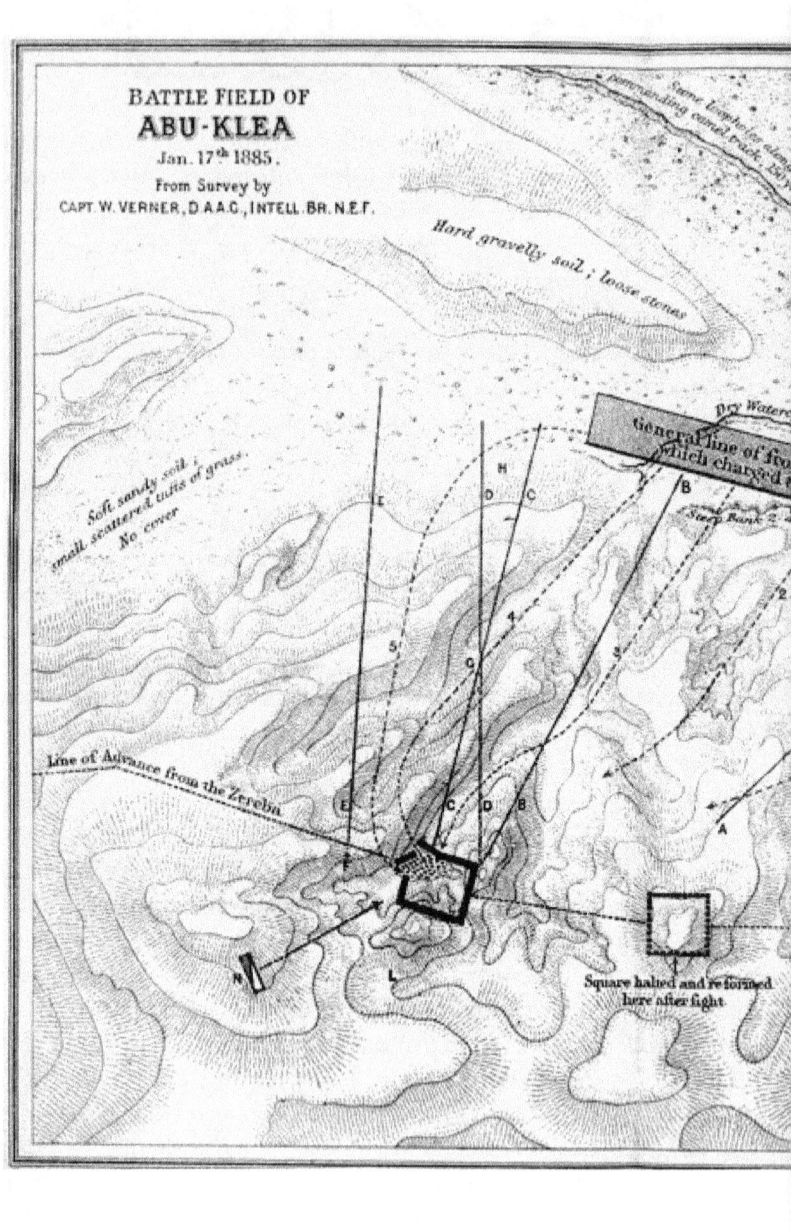

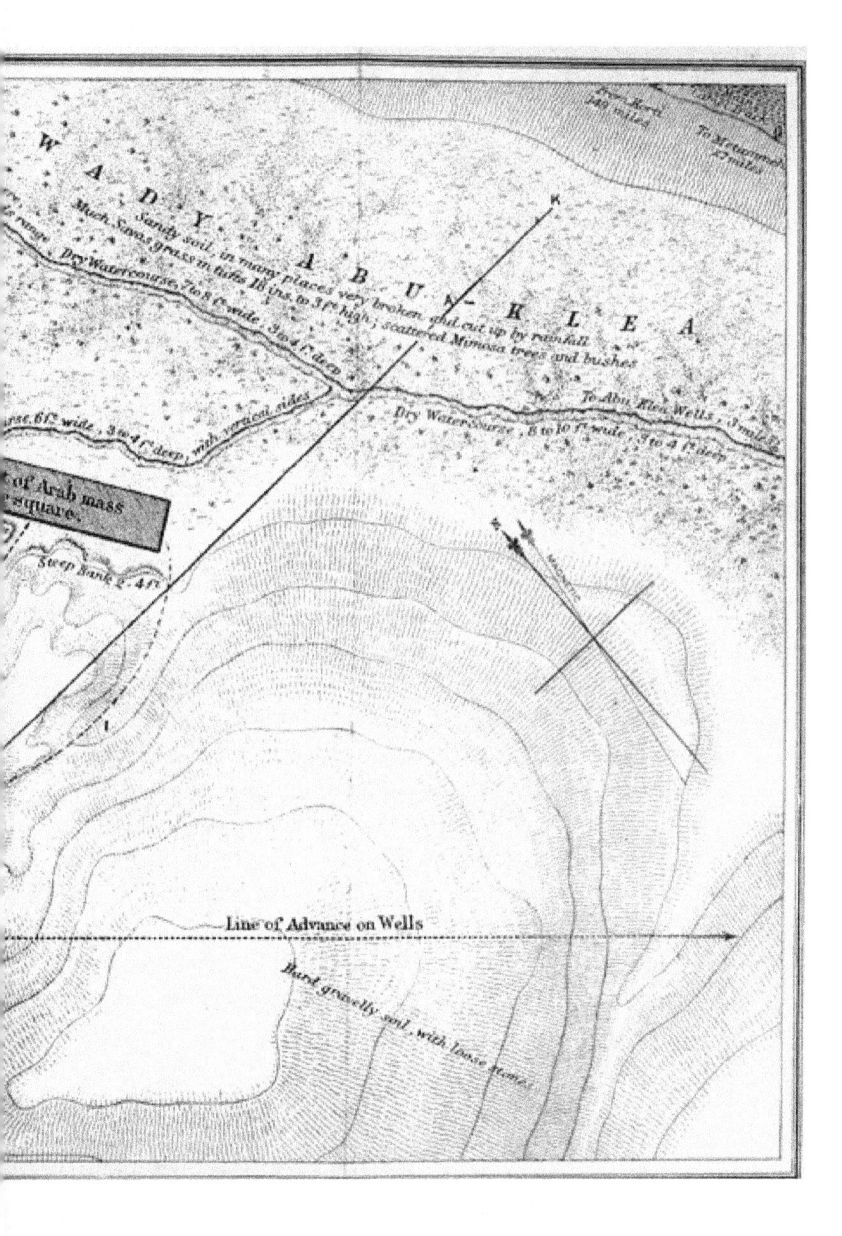

the square must have been nearly in rear of the Gardner gun. The masses charging along lines 4 and 5 were also taken in flank by the fire of the Mounted Infantry, as the sectional (red) line D D on the plan shows, and at the point G when it inflicted heavy losses on the mass moving along line 4.

This flank fire must not only have seriously checked the Arab masses advancing by their lines to support those which had already reached the square, but also from its demoralising effect must have largely contributed to the final early repulse of the enemy and their sudden retreat.

The Dervish commanders showed their usual military skill on this occasion by their quick perception of the vulnerable points of the square, for when checked in its advance towards the left front corner of the formation the mass charging along line 3 swerved to the right, and made for the weakest place in the left face, namely, that in rear of the Gardner gun. The weakening of that portion of the line, by its deflection forward through the pressure of the camels against its rear, must also have attracted their attention. The Arab mass charging along line 4 penetated the square through the opening made in its left rear comer by the drifting of the camels, and the mass charging along line 5 took advantage of the opening made in the formation by Colonel Burnaby as already described. No other parts of the square were assailed by the enemy, for their lines remained unbroken, and from their sharp fire discouraged any attempt of the enemy to penetrate them. Even when the Arab mass surged up against the left face and drove in the Lancers, Royals, and Greys, although it overlapped the Mounted Infantry companies on their right, it made no other impression on that portion of the face than to force it back a couple of paces, but when bayonet crossed spear these companies stood their ground like a wall of rock.

It must, however, be pointed out that the charges of the Arabs along the dotted lines 4 and 5 were from the very first but little exposed to the fire of the Lancers, Royals, and Greys, and especially at the points G and H, for, as shown by the contours on the plan, they were part of the time under cover of two intervening swells in the ground. These companies were therefore not in so good a position to meet promptly these charges by Martini fire as the companies of the Mounted Infantry on their right had been with respect to the charges along lines 1, 2, and 3.

That the fire of these companies as well as that of the whole force was weakened by the jamming of the cheaply made regulation cartridges with which they were supplied, and also by some imperfection in the cartridge extractors of their rifles, has been abundantly proved. But that these defects contributed, to the extent which has been alleged, to the giving way of a portion of the square, cannot be fairly maintained in view of the facts of the case we have already given. It must not be overlooked that the right half of the rear face, which was formed by cavalry on foot, repelled by their sharp fire a large body of the horsemen of the enemy (see plan); not a single Arab penetrated through their line, which, unlike that of their less fortunate comrades on the other half of the face, had not been disturbed by either camels or sailors.

It is also evident that a fatal mistake was made in not recalling earlier the skirmishers who were out on the left front, for it not only resulted in some of them being killed by the advancing enemy, but also masked the fire of that face of the square. The skirmishers also unfortunately did not promptly obey the order of the recall when it was given, for many of them when retiring halted to fire, and when they realised what was taking place and began to retire rapidly they were met and confused by contradictory calls to run this way and that way, or to lie down so as to give a chance to fire over them.

When the enemy entered the square by the gap in its left rear corner, the Lancers, Royals, and Greys were placed in a most critical position. Hampered and pressed by the camels, they had now not only to repel an attack in front, but also to meet another from the rear. In fact, they were surrounded. The company composed of the 4th and 5th Dragoons, which Colonel Burnaby was moving back into the rear face then in the position indicated on the diagram, was similarly surrounded by those of the enemy who had penetrated the square round their left. A hand-to-hand fight then ensued between these companies and the Arab spearmen, which during the ten minutes it lasted was a soldiers' battle—in fact, an Inkermann on a small scale. British pluck and strength now as then, and as it had often done before under similar circumstances, gained the day, and soon every Arab who had penetrated the square was bayoneted or shot, including the *emir* who gallantly led the charge along line 3, and who coolly rode into the square reading a book of prayers.

There was unfortunately at this moment some irregular firing into the square from the rear face which it is feared killed and wounded some of our officers and men and several of the Aden camel-drivers.

General Stewart had also a narrow escape. His orderly was killed at his side, and when rising from his horse which had been shot from under him, three Arabs were noticed rapidly making for him. One of them was shot by Sir Charles Wilson with his revolver, and the two others were despatched by some of the Mounted Infantry.

What has thus far been described appears to have occurred when the wedge-shaped fronts of the enemy's columns charging along lines 3, 4, and 5, reached and penetrated the square.³ The compact body of spearmen led by their ἔμβολον heads now came on, and rapidly bringing up their right shoulders in the most orderly fashion hurled their masses against the left face. The first to feel the effects of this charge were the Naval Brigade, who had, as already stated, put their Gardner gun into action outside of the square.

After firing eight rounds at the advancing enemy, Lord Charles Beresford noticed that its elevation was too great. This was immediately rectified, but after six rounds (that is, six turns of its lever) the gun jammed and became useless.

While Lord Charles was attempting to clear it with the assistance of his chief boatswain's mate, the enemy came on them, spearing the latter and in their crush knocking him down behind the gun, and eventually driving him against the front of the square, when he fortunately escaped further danger. His two officers, Lieutenants Pigott and De Lisle, were speared while heroically defending their gun from capture. An officer of the —— thus summed up to me this incident:

'The Naval Brigade were driven back and had to leave their gun; however, we all made a rush and got it back.'

Under the sharp fire of the Mounted Infantry this surging mass of Arabs turned to the right, and by sheer weight of numbers forced back the companies of the Heavies forming the rear left corner of the square, until they were brought up by the crowd of camels in their rear. Although the latter had prepared the way for what had now happened by weakening this corner of the formation, they thus op-

---

3. The confusion which prevailed in that part of the square which felt the full force of the attack of the enemy has made it most difficult to obtain a perfectly satisfactory or clearly consecutive account of what then took place. Both the officers and men who were in the thick of the fight, as well as those of my colleagues who were in the square, differ in their statements about the leading incidents in this crisis of the engagement. The author, therefore, has been obliged carefully to compare and weigh all the information he received after the battle with that he has obtained since, in order to give his readers as accurate a description of the engagement as is possible under the circumstances.

portunely prevented it from ending in a disaster to the whole square, for like a wall they resisted its further penetration by the Arabs. As the square had been halted on sloping ground, the right face from its elevation was enabled to turn round and fire over the left at the advancing Arabs. It now concentrated that fire at point-blank range upon the mass of baffled Arabs, and with such effect that they immediately broke and withdrew. This decided the fate of the day, for suddenly the enemy on all sides began to slowly retreat; and their pace, as they thus sullenly withdrew, was quickened by Martini and artillery fire.

As may easily be imagined, this final hand-to-hand struggle with the enemy threw the square into considerable disorder, during which, however, the men did not forget to cheer heartily at their victory. Its centre was filled with killed and wounded men, and hampered by dead camels. Before the square could therefore be reformed, it was moved to the point indicated on the plan.

The wounded now naturally claimed the first attention, for the poor fellows were found to be in a sorry plight, as many of the camels on which they were placed in *cacolets* had been speared by the Arabs who penetrated the square. Others of them had also been very much knocked about in the crush and confusion which then ensued, during which Lord St. Vincent had a narrow escape. The camel carrying the *cacolet* in which he had been placed after being wounded was shot and fell over him, thus saving him from being speared. The wounded soldier in the *cacolet* on the other side of the animal had had a very rough time of it. He had been wounded after the square had begun to advance, and soon after he had been placed in the *cacolet* he was shot again in the wrist, and now, poor fellow, he was speared

Those of the wounded who were on the camels which drifted out of the square just before the Arabs charged, were also speared, and when the bearer company were going over the field after our wounded, many of the enemy who lay simulating death rose up and attacked them. A few of the older wounded Arabs, when approached by our fellows with a view to their assistance also showed fight. One whose leg was hanging to his body by a shred of flesh, when our men came near him, struggled to secure his spear. Another fired his rifle at two of the bearer company, happily missing them, but knocking the roller off one of the short fore legs of the stretcher they were carrying.

The mass of our dead were buried in a long trench, at the point L on the plan. The bodies of Major Gough of the Royals and Lieutenant Wolfe of the Greys were interred separately at the point F, and as their surviving and sorrowing brother-officers stood round their open grave. Major Byng read the Burial Service over them.

The hospital record of the casualties in the square were as follows: killed, officers 9, and non-commissioned officers and men 56; wounded, officers 5, and non-commissioned officers and men 56. The latter do not include the slightly wounded, but only cases which required hospital attention.

The Heavy Camel Regiment, which had borne the brunt of the fray, lost in killed 6 officers and 46 non-commissioned officers and men. The Mounted Infantry had only 4 men killed, the Guards and Marines together but five. The Sussex Regiment got off with the loss of only 2 men.

Nearly all the camels in the square had been either shot or speared by the Arabs, and a number of boxes of ammunition, for which there was no transport, had to be burned; most of the rifles of the killed and wounded were collected and broken. The burning cartridges set fire to some of the pack-saddles of the dead and wounded camels, thus adding to the horrors of the battlefield.

The number of the enemy killed in the action was estimated by General Stewart at 800, but one of the officers who went carefully over the field stated that at least 1,150 of them had fallen. The prisoners told us that their wounded were exceptionally large. The total force which we had fought was estimated at from twelve to fourteen thousand, of whom 3,000 operated on our right flank and 3,000 at least in the main attack. Further on reference will be made to the composition of this large force, which was thus defeated by one not much stronger than a battalion of British troops on a war footing, a mere handful of cavalry, and a half-battery of seven-pounders.

The square arrived at the wells at 5 p.m., or about half an hour before sunset. After what the men had gone through during the day this march of about two miles was very trying, for owing to the loss of the camels the wounded had to be carried by hand, as well as a number of heavy boxes of spare ammunition. There was plenty of water to be had, but no other food save the biscuits carried by the men in their pockets. Tired and hungry, they lay down in a square formed around the wounded. What with the groans of the latter and the bitter cold from which they had no protection, the poor fellows, officers and men alike, spent a wretchedly uncomfortable night.

And here I feel constrained to record my protest against the unwarranted charge made against this force by Mr. Bright in a recent speech at a meeting of Quakers. His authority for making this charge he then stated was that of an officer who had been with the force this night at the wells. His story was that, hearing shouts and noises, he was told upon enquiry that they proceeded from the English soldiers who had gone out to the battlefield to shoot or bayonet their helpless wounded Arab foes.

In the first place, this story carries with it its own contradiction, for how could noises and shouts be heard from a battlefield which was over two miles distant from the wells?

Then, the only part of the force which left the bivouac at the wells that night was a detachment of volunteers sent by General Stewart about 8 p.m. to bring in the stores, &c., left at the *zereba*. Their orders were to take a circuitous route in order to avoid the battle-field, and to march in a column of companies, so that if attacked they could at once form square, for, as one of the officers who went with it told me, it was not thought unlikely 'that the enemy might have another go at us.' Writing to me recently with reference to Mr. Bright's statement, this officer said:

> The only English soldiers on the battlefield that evening (January 17) were those poor fellows who are there now!'

And further, I must say that so serious an incident as that related by this anonymous officer could hardly have taken place unknown to either my colleagues or myself, and certainly a sense of duty would have led us to make it known. On the contrary, all of us who have witnessed the conduct of our officers and soldiers in the field can bear testimony to a self-restraint, often exercised under the most aggravating circumstances, unsurpassed, if even equalled, by that of the troops of any other nation. On this occasion, instead of shooting and bayoneting the wounded Arabs, as alleged by Mr. Bright, they picked up many of them found lying helpless in the grass, and carried them to our field hospitals at Abu-Klea and El Gubat to be cared for.

We must now recall our readers to the *zereba*, where, from the time the square moved out from us, we had a hot time of it until 2 p.m., owing to the continued attacks of the enemy, specially on our right. Squads and groups came over the slight rise in the ground in that direction, and attempted to rush us, but they were promptly met by the sharp fire of the detachment of the Sussex under Lieutenant Kane, and so promptly and successfully repulsed that none of them ever got nearer the *zereba* than 600 or 800 yards.

Early in the day the enemy also attempted to get round our left flank, but were quickly repulsed by volleys from the detachment of Mounted Infantry who occupied the position on the oval-shaped hill. The Arabs on one of these occasions came stealthily along in considerable force, but were unexpectedly saluted with a shower of lead, when those of them who could do so bolted.

About 2 p.m., when the firing from the conical hill had almost ceased, four of the enemy came in from that direction and gave themselves up. One of them was an ethnological curiosity. He was black as ebony, short of stature, and clad in the *Mahdi*'s uniform, which consisted of a white cotton robe trimmed with black round its skirts and elsewhere. He spoke Italian with all the volubility of a darkey, and told us that he had been in Hicks's army and had joined the *Mahdi* in order to save his life, and with the hope of being able eventually to get back to Egypt. He had not only lived in Cairo, but had visited Europe and been employed in some hotel at Naples. During the night he had been on the conical hill, and in reply to my enquiries about the bad practice they had made, he tried to persuade me that, in firing at us, he and the other soldiers with him from Hicks's army had not taken aim but fired in the air, illustrating his assertions by rapid gestures.

We had, he continued, killed two hundred of them by skirmishers we had sent out early in the morning, and by the volleys from our right. With respect to the strength of the force by which we had been attacked, he stated that it numbered from ten to twelve thousand men. From him and our other prisoners we learned that this force was made up of 2,000 Ababdeh, Bisharin, and other Arabs from Berber and 60 Egyptian soldiers belonging to its garrison before the place had fallen into the hands of the rebels. These men arrived at Abu-Klea on the 12th of January, and were joined there on the 14th by 2,000 Arabs and others from Metammeh. From 5,000 to 6,000 Arabs of different tribes, with 1,000 riflemen from the army of the *Mahdi*, had arrived on the morning of the engagement.

The prisoners also asserted that the *Mahdi* intended to offer a stubborn resistance to the British advance on Khartoum, and that having now taken Omdurman he was able to detach a large body of troops to oppose us. From the severe defeat we had inflicted on the force we had met, the prisoners did not think that any of them would be inclined to fight us again. They also told us that the horse tracks we had noticed were those of their scouts, who had watched our advance from Jakdul.

We also elicited from the prisoners that Gordon's steamers were at Shabluka and visited Metammeh occasionally.

The leading spokesman, however, talked so glibly about some things of which he could not possibly have a personal knowledge from his position on the conical hill, that a great deal of what he said had to be taken at a discount. Still we were now assured that the enemy had been sharply defeated by the square, and that our way was now open to the wells of Abu-Klea, and probably also to the Nile beyond them. This was fully confirmed about 5 p.m. by a heliograph from General Stewart to Major Gem, stating that he had occupied the former.

All that we knew previously about the square is soon told. It had marched out at 10 a.m. For some time it moved steadily, but slowly, forward; now it appeared to halt, then it moved on again, but to the right with more cannon firing, when suddenly it disappeared from our view behind an intervening swell. The moments of uncertainty which then followed were soon relieved by the appearance of a column of smoke rising up from among the trees and scrub on our left front. It was blue smoke, and therefore not from gunpowder but from burning wood, and for this reason we concluded that the camp of the enemy had been captured and destroyed and that our way had been opened to the wells.

This was soon made more certain by the cessation of the firing from the conical hill and by the sudden disappearance of the enemy all around the *zereba*. Nor did we lose sight of the Hussars, for as they approached the horsemen of the enemy the latter suddenly moved off over the ridge on our left and soon disappeared. Before the column of smoke was seen a part of them then dismounted and began firing at the sharpshooters of the enemy. They then continued to advance, and soon also moved out of sight During the day it had been hot, sultry, and hazy; but in the afternoon, soon after the firing of the enemy had ceased, a change of wind made it cooler. The sun now shone brighter, and everyone seemed in buoyant spirits. Nature began to crave a supply of food, and soon camp kettles were called into requisition, and full justice done again to biscuits, bully-beef, and tea.

Major Dorward kindly offered me quarters for the night in the Engineers' fort on a pile of large sacks filled with flour; so, spreading my portable cork mattress over them, I laid me down to sleep, thankful for the mercies graciously vouchsafed to us during the past twenty-four hours and trustful for the coming events of the morrow.

My slumbers were, however, soon disturbed by talking and movements outside of the fort, and I soon learned that General Stewart had sent a force to remove us, bag and baggage, to the wells.

It was now ten o'clock and pitch dark, yet all the boxes of stores built up in the walls of our three forts, &c., had to be collected and loaded up on the camels, and their saddles brought in from the breastworks for which they had been used.

The camp which had become so still was soon now all alive, and fires were lighted here and there. One of them near my quarters was soon surrounded by groups of Aden boys in a shivering condition, for it was bitterly cold.

When roused and while half asleep I jumped to the conclusion that we were at once to vacate our present premises, and, in order not to be left behind, directed my man to load up. This impulsive hastiness cost me another wretchedly uncomfortable night, for when my camels were ready and my horse saddled I learned that our 'baggage master,' Lord Dundonald, who had come with the force from the wells, had lain down for a 'nap,' and that several hours would elapse before we could remove. So wrapt up in my plaid, and with the cushion of the riding-saddle of one of my camels for a pillow, I lay down for the second night on the hard rough gravel of the *wady* of Abu-Klea for a rest. Continuous sleep or even a decent doze was out of the question, for when I fell off into one I was roused either by the groan of some camel near me, or the chattering of the Aden camel-drivers, or the shouting or squabbling of the men fumbling about in the dark after saddles or something else, interlarded with expressions unpleasant to 'ears polite.'

The eastern sky was well aglow with the rosy dawn before we were ready to move to the wells. Riding ahead of the convoy in order to view the battlefield of yesterday, I soon reached the place where the square had repulsed the charge of the enemy. Their dead lay in heaps, and in all imaginable forms of contortion. A few, however, had died without a struggle, for they lay on their gravel death-bed as if they had been laid out by loving hands. Others, who had crept away from where they had received their mortal wounds, were seen kneeling in the Mohammedan attitude of prayer.

Some were aged men, but the majority of the slain were in the prime of life. One of the former, who lay dead near the watercourse where so many of the Arabs had lain in ambush, had a wooden leg of the rudest description.

Amongst the slain were also many mere lads, armed only with the short curved stick commonly carried by the natives. One of these poor fellows, lying with his arms outstretched, still grasped his little stick in his right hand. His face was turned towards me as I rode past, and his unclosed eyes seemed to look up piteously at me.

Near the body of this lad was that of a man in the *Mahdi*'s uniform, lying in a reclining position against a bush. He presented a terrible sight, for some one had driven a native battle-axe into his skull between his eyes, and left it there with the handle sticking out from his face! Who killed him? From the weapon used for the purpose, certainly none of our soldiers.

Shortly after passing over the battlefield, hearing rapid firing in the rear, I rode back to the convoy to ascertain what had occasioned it. My first impression was that we were in for another brush with the enemy, but it only proceeded from the shooting of a number of exhausted and severely wounded camels. These poor brutes had been only allowed eight pounds of *dhura* each on the march from Korti to Jakdul, and but few of them had tasted food for three days, and this was the fourth since they had been watered.

Riding on again ahead of the convoy, we came to one of the gravel pits which comprise the wells of Abu-Klea, and which are similar to those already described at El Howeiyat This one had a good supply of water, and it was only four feet deep. Somebody had left a calabash in it, which came in handy for a hearty drink from its cool though turbid water. My horse, who stood on the edge of the pit watching me as I filled it for him, kept me busy for some minutes, for he was very thirsty. My camels and man then coming up, we gave them a drink all round.

The *wady* had now opened out into a plain sparsely dotted over with scrub and clumps of trees, and bounded to the left by a low ridge of rocky hills. Whether owing to excessive fatigue or to the depressing effects of the terrible sights I had just witnessed on the battle-field I cannot say, but the landscape seemed to lack the wild beauty of other similar plains over which we had already ridden in this desert

Riding on we soon reached the bivouac at the wells, and halted near a couple of low mimosa trees, and after unloading the camels my man set to work to prepare for breakfast—the first regular meal we had had for forty-eight hours. Twenty yards off was a deep well, and near it a long rope; so, borrowing a tin pail, I busied myself in the meantime in replenishing our water-skins.

The morning was very hot, and the scanty foliage of the mimosa, under which my portable table had been set up, afforded but little shade from the hot sun. The comfort of breakfasting under a tree was therefore purely imaginary. When I returned to the well to continue my watering operations, I found it had been taken possession of by some thirsty soldiers, who soon emptied it of its precious contents.

CHAPTER 17

The Nile at Last

The first person I met when riding into the bivouac at the Wells on the morning of January 18 was Sir Herbert Stewart. He was alone, and although looking very tired he accosted me in his usual cheerful manner. After exchanging congratulations over the results of the engagement of the previous day, I asked him if he intended sending a messenger at once to Korti with the news of our victory. 'No,' he replied; 'my orders are to take Metammeh and secure a position on the Nile, and when that is done it will be time enough to communicate with Lord Wolseley.' Later in the day he said to one of his *aides-de-camp*, 'Tomorrow I intend taking Metammeh, and if Gordon's steamers are there I will the day after send them up to Khartoum with Wilson!' And no one can doubt, who knew his quiet determination, that if he had not been severely wounded at a critical moment, next day he would have kept his word.

About 11 a.m. I received a message from him, stating that he had now decided to send a messenger back to Korti, and would be pleased to forward with his despatch anything I had to send, but it must be ready by 2 p.m.

Sitting beneath my shadeless tree in the glare of a January midday tropical sun, and worn out by two sleepless nights and two days' intense excitement, I was more fit for a nap than for writing a graphic description of our fight and victory of yesterday. But do it I must, and as well as I could under the circumstances. It was by no means a satisfactory performance when completed, but revision was impossible, time was up, and go it must just as it was, or not at all.

Shortly after my despatch was handed in at headquarters, several of my colleagues informed me that they proposed to return at once to Jakdul, and asked me if I would accompany them. Three of them had the unpleasant reminiscences of El Teb and Tamanieh revived by what had happened the day before, and had been further perturbed by a report that the enemy we had fought then was but the advance guard of a much larger force on its march from Omdurman, and that we should have to fight it before we reached the Nile. Nor were they alone in their gloomy conclusions, for when Sir Herbert Stewart held an informal council of war with his commanding officers, one of them on the ground of this rumour advised him to fall back on Jakdul and wait for reinforcements. The only notice of this suggestion taken by our lion-hearted General was a contemptuous stare at the man who had ventured to make it.

I did not credit this report, and had a feeling akin to contempt for the enemy which our small force had so easily defeated yesterday. Nevertheless, owing to the manner in which the square had been handled then, and the serious catastrophe which might have followed, the situation was anything but assuring. It appeared, however, safer to go on with the column, on the principle that 'the coach never breaks down two days running,' than, by leaving it, to run the risk of encountering bands of the enemy, which we had reason to believe were hovering on our flanks and rear.

From a brotherly feeling, however, towards my colleagues, and after a few moments' anxious thought, I agreed to go back to Jakdul with them if all went. Cameron, to my surprise, was not amongst those who had made this proposition, because I knew he felt more keenly than any of us our critical and dangerous position. To his credit be it recorded that when approached on the subject he refused to return. His keen sense of duty made it a matter of honour with him to go on and face all the dangers that he feared still threatened us. And so this proposition to return broke down, and we all went on together.

Although active preparations were carried on throughout the morning for our march to Metammeh at 2 p.m., the column was not ready to move until 3.30 p.m. This vexatious delay was chiefly due to the insufficiency of the water supply. The wells, which were not very full at first, were soon emptied, and then as at El Howeiyat the men had to wait until they refilled by percolation. Then a fort had to be constructed in order to provide for the defence of the position and for the protection of the wounded we were obliged to leave behind here.

Several of the commanding officers had strongly advised General Stewart to postpone marching until early next morning, in order that the men might have a rest after their two sleepless nights and the excitement of the battle on the previous day. He resolved, however, to push on in order not to give the enemy time to recover from the effects of their recent defeat. His intention was to keep the Metammeh road as far as the Shebecat Wells (see Map), and thence to make for a point on the Nile three miles above that town, and after breakfasting to attack it. So out we marched at half-past three o'clock, with the Guards and Mounted Infantry in front, and the Heavies and Sussex Regiment bringing up the rear of the column, and the Hussars as usual out scouting in front and on our flanks.

We marched in open column with the artillery, baggage, commissariat supplies, and the bearer company and medical stores in the centre, in the same formation. The total number of camels was, roughly speaking, 2,500, of which 1,350 were ridden by the fighting part of the force, and 210 used in the transport of *cacolets*, or litters for carrying the wounded and medical stores and a number of these ominous-looking 'stretchers.'

The position assigned for the baggage of the correspondents was with that of the brigade, although personally we were at liberty to ride anywhere in the column, and usually did so independently of each other; on this occasion we kept together. Even poor Cameron, whose last march this was to be, rode more with us than was his usual habit.

An hour after leaving the wells we reached the summit of a gentle rise, beyond which lay a wide plain descending southwards, the horizon of which in that direction was formed by the purple-coloured mountains beyond the Nile. Right and left, at a distance of two or three miles, were ranges of low hills along which the Hussars were scouting. Later on they could be seen on the sky line on our left in groups of two or four or nine. Tiny-looking figures they appeared in the distance; but assuring us that no enemy could approach either flank without our being duly warned.

Sunset came, and still we marched on. This was disappointing; for although it was understood we were to make a night march of it, it was generally supposed we should now halt for refreshments, for we had had only one meal during the day. Still on we went, hoping for a halt, but in the meanwhile taking stock of the supply of biscuits carried in our pockets, in case of being disappointed. At last the 'halt' was sounded, and word was passed down the column, from the front, that there were to be no more bugle calls that night, and forbidding all lights and loud talking. So farewell to supper, to sleep, and even to the solace of a pipe, and on we marched continuously for some time, and over a capital road.

Shortly after darkness had set in, the light of a small fire suddenly appeared about half a mile off to the right and as suddenly disappeared. Soon after another similar fire was seen away off ahead on the right front. These were no doubt beacon fires announcing to the enemy, at Metammeh, our march out from the wells. Shortly afterwards an Arab was picked up said by some to be badly wounded, and who had got thus far in his struggle to reach the Nile; and he was ordered by the general to be placed on one of the *cacolets*. Soon after another order came from the front that he should be tied down on it lest he should escape. But, if suspected, the fellow ought to have been gagged, for no sooner was he tied down than he began to cry out loud enough to be heard half a mile off.

On and on through the bright starlight[1] we marched for two hours, the silence only now and then being broken by a groaning camel or the demand passed from mouth to mouth from the rear asking the front to halt. Faintly at first it came up the column: 'Tell the front to halt,' then louder and louder until it reached us when we passed it on ahead, and the column halted. Whenever the front halted, all in its rear did so without the necessity of being thus signalled. About eleven o'clock, judging by the altitude of the planet Jupiter, which rose shortly after sunset, the road became much broken owing to the tracks leading over soft ground covered with tall grass. The halts now became very frequent and apparently urgent, for if the front did not promptly respond to the request from the rear it was quickly repeated.

These halts were chiefly caused by the exhausted condition of the camels. For five days they had been without water, and almost without any other food excepting an occasional bite of the long grass through which the column was passing at the time, or when it halted for the night.

It is not therefore to be wondered at that during this night's march one-tenth of their number gave out and had to be left behind. I have already described the manner in which they were tied together head and tail. Often as I rode along the column by daylight I saw the poor tired brutes towed along thus, with their necks drawn out forward

---

1. The starlight was very brilliant on account of the large number of stars visible of the second, third, and fourth magnitudes, and on account of several bright nebulae, of which the great one in the constellation of Charles's Oak was the most remarkable. The planet Jupiter also shone in the clear atmosphere like a miniature sun.

and at such a tension as to suggest that soon their heads might part company with them, or that the tail to which the halter of the lagging brute had been tied would give way. By-and-by some exhausted camel, though apparently willing enough to go forward, could not With his fore legs he appears to be treading the air as if marking time. At last his utmost limit of endurance is reached, and down he goes gracefully enough, for he sinks kneeling as is his wont.

The column is then asked to halt until his load and saddle are hastily removed, often from a bruised and bleeding back. Sometimes a Martini bullet put an end to the pain and suffering of the discarded camel, but as firing was not allowed tonight they were left behind uncared for in the desert, to live or to die. Relieved from this used-up means of transport, the word was passed up to the front: 'The rear is ready,' and on we marched again until some other camel had to be similarly abandoned.

Some of our halts were, however, caused by the straggling of the column, through the exhausted condition of many of the camels; others by some of them drifting from their places in front to the rear, through the sleepiness of the native drivers. This gave the rear guard plenty of work, and we had often to halt until the column had recovered its normal compactness.

What was now happening to delay our progress confirms the observation made in a previous chapter on the camel-transport question. Almost the last words of General Stewart to one of the commanding officers with us in this column were, 'You see, if this expedition fails it will be owing to the government's parsimony in buying camels!'

So far as could now be judged by the stars, our course for some time had been about south-west by south; and some of the uninitiated supposed that General Stewart was making for Khartoum direct.

As the native guides who had brought us from Korti to Jakdul were unacquainted with this part of the desert. General Stewart took with him Ali-Loda, the desert robber he had captured during his first march to the latter place, as it was ascertained he knew the road so well to Metammeh that he could take us to the river clear of that town. His doubts about our being able in the darkness to pass through a thick band of trees which he stated would be met when the Shebecat Wells were reached, were silenced by the promise of a good reward if he took us safely through to the Nile. Measures, however, were taken against his playing false with us, and he was not only guarded, but Captain Verner was instructed to use his compass frequently during the march.

On still we went, but now over ground covered with tall *savas* in bunches or on hillocks, between which, on account of the sandy soil, the camel-tracks ran like gutters. This so tumbled the camels about as to make the halts more frequent Our progress now became very slow; for we were only able to creep along at the rate of about a mile an hour. And so we went on until the small hours of the morning of the 19th (Jan.), when the column all at once became sadly confused by the transport camels crowding out of their places and streaming up both flanks to the front My colleagues and myself, who were then riding together on the left flank, attempted to drive back those which came up that side; but our efforts, I need hardly say, were useless, excepting when we came across a sleeping Aden driver and woke him up. The officers of the Mounted Infantry now became very anxious; for in the case of attack their movements would have been hampered by the crowding round them of this mass of camels.

The confusion increased when we reached a place more thickly covered than ever with tall *savas* grass, for now the starving camels broke away in every direction to browse upon it An active enemy, though even in small force, could then have easily taken advantage of our condition and brought the expedition to an end. As we were then nearing Shebecat Wells, it was also thought possible that some of the enemy might be prowling among them. In view of the danger General Stewart deemed it prudent to dismount the Guards.

We now struck the band of trees about which we had been warned by Ali-Loda, when the road became so contracted that we could only advance in half sections. This change of formation from our broad front threw the column into greater disorder than ever, and many of the heavily laden camels became entangled in this bush, through their leading-halters fouling with the trees, and often so jammed together that we had to leave many of them behind, some said a hundred at least. The halts now became almost incessant until we reached open ground. Here we made a long halt, of which I availed myself to get 'forty winks' on the hard gravel, with part of my plaid for a pillow.

It was then calculated by Captain Verner, our topographical authority in the expedition, that we had come fifteen miles, leaving but ten more between us and the Nile. This was the point at which General Stewart had decided to turn off the Metammeh road as already stated. Lord Wolseley had suggested to him in his instructions to *zereba* his stores here and then march on. Had the water supply been more abundant at Abu-Klea, I have reasons to believe he would have left the greater part of them there; and his resolution, not to halt now may have arisen from his anxiety to get to the water as speedily as possible.

All hopes, however, of being able to reach the Nile before daybreak had now to be abandoned, and our robber guide was told to take us to it well clear of Metammeh. After leaving the caravan road our route led over a trackless region. As it was thickly covered with trees, the column soon became more confused than ever, and the halts more frequent and longer than ever. When the mass was supposed to have come to a standstill, strings of loaded, driverless camels kept on coming up to the front, adding to the embarrassments of the moment. The prohibition against loud talking was now virtually repealed, for the groaning of the camels and the shouting of the drivers made a noise loud enough to be heard a mile off.

Everybody seemed so thoroughly done up that when we halted many lay down on the ground for a nap. Several times I caught myself dozing off while riding. How my little horse stood the fatigue of this night's march so well as he did has been a marvel to me ever since. Once while I was lying on the ground and holding his bridle he roused me just in time to move on with the column, by rubbing his nose against my pocket, asking in his fashion for his accustomed mouthful of biscuit. Two men were lost during these halts. It was supposed they had dismounted and fallen asleep, and, not awaking when the column moved on, were left behind. One, a Guardsman, found his way back to the wells at Abu-Klea; but the other poor fellow, a lance-corporal of the lancers, was supposed to have ridden into Metammeh and to have been killed by the enemy.

It was now half an hour before daylight, and General Stewart ordered a halt to allow the rear to close up and to enable him to ascertain whereabouts we then were. Ali-Loda the guide, on being questioned, said that we were still some distance from the river, in fact, further from it than had been calculated by Captain Verner. Finally General Stewart ordered him to take the column by the shortest cut he could to the Nile, hoping to get there without being observed by the enemy. We were then, as was supposed, about six miles from the river, and evidently near some habitations, for the well-worn tracks on the hard gravel became very numerous and seemed to converge to some adjacent centre. After advancing two miles further the column halted, and Captain Verner was sent out with some of the hussars to reconnoitre. It was now quite daylight, and we saw several flocks of goats, one of which was 'annexed' by the Hussars. Then, through the barking of a dog, we discovered a goatherd's hut in a clump of trees with several well-filled water-skins lying in a shed outside of it, which I need hardly say were quickly emptied by us. A detachment of the hussars now put in an appearance with a young man dressed in the *Mahdi*'s uniform, who was most profuse in his compliments to the English, but soon afterwards disappeared. Then we stumbled over a slave boy, who followed us for some time.

As the column began moving on again. Captain Verner returned and reported that he had seen Metammeh, and that troops in regular formation were moving out from it, and that the *tom-tom*s were going. He had also observed horsemen moving in our direction along the ridge on our left. The head of the column had. now reached a shallow depression, having between it and the river a slight rise in the ground forming the continuation in our direction of the ridge referred to, which effectually screened it from observation. We were now halted again, and General Stewart ordered Colonel Barrow to move out to our left and threaten Metammeh in order to mask our advance in a more direct line to the river. Cameron and I then rode on ahead together.

This was our last and never-to-be-forgotten interview. He seemed unusually anxious and depressed, and said to me: 'Well, I would give a five-pound note if our backs were to the Nile; wouldn't you?' When the crest of the ridge up which we were then riding was reached, we caught a first glimpse of what we supposed to be Metammeh on our left and some smaller place beyond it which was taken for Shendy. Cameron now brightened up a little, and General Stewart coming up with his staff to where we had halted, we all rode forward to an isolated high knoll in order to obtain a more unobstructed view of the country before us.

On our left was unmistakably Metammeh, looming against the pale yellow light of morning like a gigantic fortress. Some three or four miles in front and on our right glistened the waters of the Nile, Casting wistful looks in the latter direction, the question was anxiously asked,

'Which is the nearest point of the river to us' and then, 'How long should we be in reaching it?' Having with my glass distinctly recognised the upper end of the island marked on the map opposite to Eshetabah, I pointed in that direction and ventured the opinion that we could reach the river in an hour and a half Sir Charles Wilson seemed to doubt this by asking me if I really thought we could reach the Nile in so short a time. Feeling that an important crisis had arisen requiring decisive action, I reaffirmed my opinion with all the vehemence allowable to one in my position. General Stewart then questioned the slave boy through his interpreter about the roads leading hence to the river, and even went so far as to ask him if he could take us to it, for no beaten road was visible from where we were, as the tract between us and the Nile was covered by trees, scrub, and, so far as could be seen, by a thick undergrowth of tall *savas* grass. Beyond this and between it and the river we could see the bare gravel ridge on which Metammeh and the villages of El-Gubat, Abu-Kru, and Eshetabah were built, and looking to the left in the direction of the former town there were but few trees near us, and further on they almost entirely disappeared. The ground gradually rose from the river to the ridge we had just crossed, which,, as will be noticed on the accompanying plan, not very far from where we had halted, rose to a height which commanded Metammeh. Had we come out there instead of where we now were, how different might have been the results of this day's fight!

Before any satisfaction could be obtained from the slave boy about the best road to the Nile from where we were, our attention was suddenly arrested by the renewed beating of the *tom-toms* at Metammeh and by the numbers of the enemy which were now streaming out from the town and running rapidly along the gravel ridge to the cover on our right. General Stewart then quietly remarked: 'After all, we shall have to fight our way to the Nile. We ought to have been here two hours ago, and should have been but for these unfortunate camels.' As our night march had failed, it appeared important that some effort should at once be made to reach the river, for the enemy were evidently now preparing to oppose us, A bold advance if promptly made was the safest and surest way out of the difficulties which evidently threatened to block our further progress. Lord Airlie and some other young officers, who had in the meanwhile been reconnoitring the enemy through their 'binoculars,' had, however, come to a less hopeful conclusion as to our situation, and expressed themselves accordingly.

After a few moments' apparent indecision. General Stewart ordered the column to halt, and, pointing to a patch of bare gravel near us surrounded by tall *savas* grass, said: 'I will occupy that position!' Turning to me he remarked, 'I intend attacking the enemy as soon as

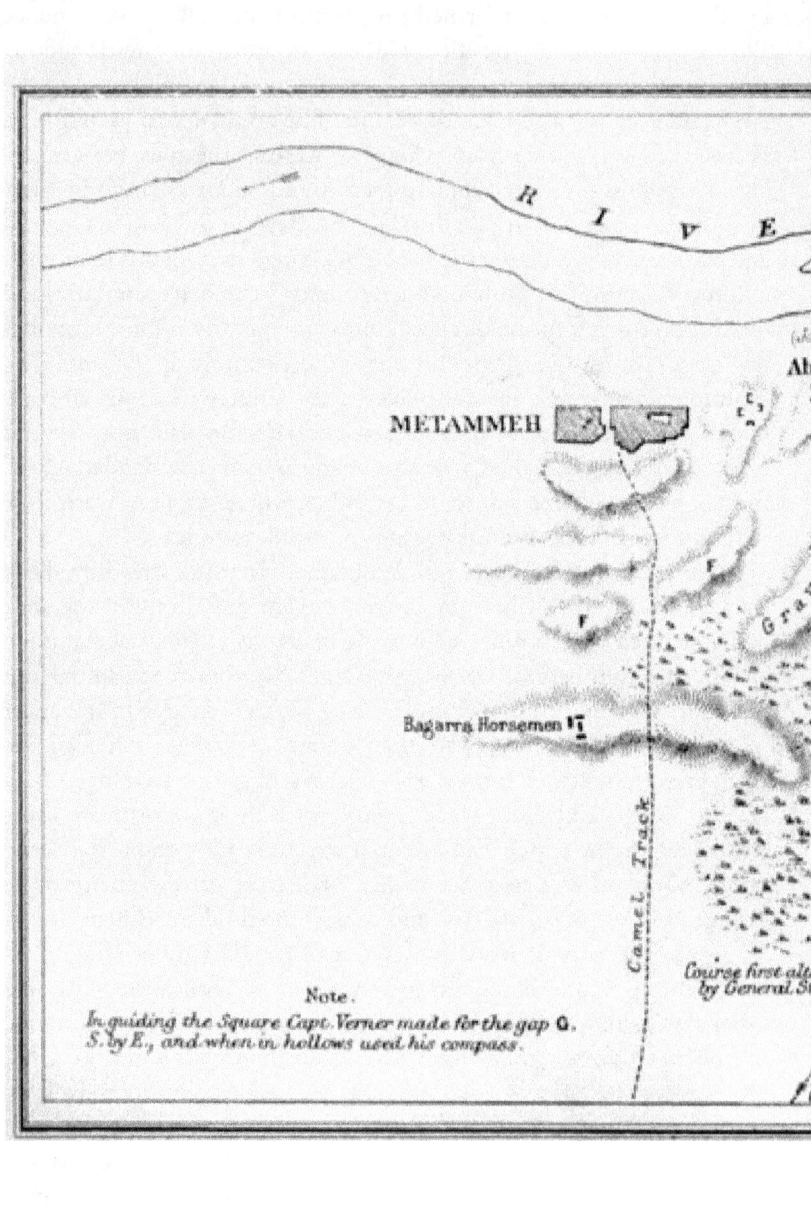

NIGHT MARCH TO METAMMEH
Jan. 18th-19th
after daylight 19th
from original sketch by
CAPT. W. VERNER, D.A.A.G., INTELL. BR., N.E.F.

English Miles
0   1   2   3

the men get something to eat!'

'For any sake,' I ventured to reply, 'do not halt the column here, but defend your left flank and boldly advance.' I received no answer to my impulsive appeal, excepting an anxious look.

As the enemy's sharpshooters could be seen making their way rapidly to the cover on our right, it appeared to me that the position he had thus hurriedly selected for a *zereba* would soon be very much exposed to their fire. It was also dangerously commanded from the rising ground in its rear, and the gravel spot itself was not even level but convex. Altogether it looked an uncanny and dangerous place to halt in under the circumstances, as it eventually proved to be. All that can be said in defence of its selection is that it was only intended to be temporarily occupied—that is, until the men could get something to eat before attacking the enemy.

When the column came up, the transport and riding camels were at once crowded together on the bare gravel spot which had been selected for the *zereba*, and the Guards, Heavies, and Sussex immediately formed a cordon round them. The Hussars then came in, and, having picketed their horses, formed up in line before them. After a short hunt in the crowd I found my man with only two camels, the third having died during the night. The only place I could squeeze into with them and my horse was on the very crest of the gravel mound; when the camels were tied down they would be comparatively safe, but my poor horse standing up above them would, I was afraid, afford a capital mark for the enemy's sharpshooters.

My Greek fellow took matters very coolly, and soon managed somehow or other in the prevailing confusion to make a canteenful of tea. It was now about eight o'clock, and before I had finished my hasty meal, bullets from the cover on our right began to whistle over us. Anxious to ascertain what was taking place outside the crowd of camels by which I was hemmed in, I made my way through them and came out where the lancers had halted. The prospects of any breakfast for the men seemed now hopeless, for many of them were being wounded and a few killed. A man of the 16th Lancers was killed near me as I passed, under rather painful circumstances even in a battlefield. He had asked a comrade of the 5th Lancers to give him some of the tea he was preparing. While the latter was trying to plug up the hole which one bullet had made in the kettle in which he was boiling the water for it, another struck the former on the head and killed him instantly.

A few men of the Heavies had been sent out to the high knoll from which we had reconnoitred before halting, in order to prevent the enemy occupying it. This was all that had been done as yet, so far as I could ascertain. Our halt seemed to have emboldened the enemy, who were evidently actively massing round us, for their bullets now came from several directions.

I had not gone very far before I heard the sad news that our general had been wounded under the following circumstances. He had sent his *aide-decamp*, Major Rhodes, in one direction, while he went in another, to tell the men that only half an hour would be allowed them for breakfast. He had hardly, however, gone a dozen yards on this errand before he was wounded. This occurred, as I am assured, between 8.30 a.m. and 9 a.m. The seriousness of his wound was soon apparent in the physical and mental prostration by which it was quickly followed, and which utterly incapacitated him from taking any further part in the direction of affairs. As he told Sir C. Wilson at the time, he felt his soldiering days were now over.[2]

The loss of our general at such a crisis was a serious matter; for although next to him I had full confidence in the judgment of Sir Charles Wilson, who as senior officer had succeeded him, it was to be feared that the change of commanders might dangerously delay our advance. Under the circumstances I therefore resolved to seek cover until arrangements were completed for an offensive movement, and returned at once to where my horse and camels were. Lying down under the load of one of the latter, which I propped up with a stick, I instructed my man to look out for any movement of troops, and to waken me if I fell asleep. Well, I did fall asleep, and slept for over an hour before he came near me. He was then very excited, showing me his wooden water-bottle, which had been perforated by a bullet, and telling me that my horse had been hit thrice, and that the other side of the camel behind which I was lying had been grazed by a bullet which had afterwards wounded an Aden boy. The bullets, he said, were now flying about in all directions, and I soon found he had not exaggerated the state of affairs, for a few minutes after he left me, the box under which I was lying was hit twice.

This was a hint to move, and after changing my position several times with as many narrow escapes I caught sight of a breastwork

---

2. In confirmation of this it may be mentioned that a post-mortem examination revealed that the wound General Stewart had received was much more serious than the surgeons had at first supposed it to be. See A. M. D. Report for 1884, p. 291.

and made a dash for it. It was the hospital redoubt, which had been constructed under the heavy fire while I had been asleep. It was full of wounded men lying on 'stretchers,' some of them in great agony. General Stewart was amongst them, and, although not suffering much pain, was very weak and apparently much depressed.

Outside of the hospital redoubt there was another breastwork, where two of the screw guns were then in position, and where the Gardner was placed later on. Looking in the direction of Metammeh, two large masses of the enemy with flags could be seen on the gravel ridge, one in the rear of the other. Another mass, nearer to us, could be seen to the right of what appeared to be the direct road. All were in the regular wedge-shaped formation we had noticed at Abu-Klea.

The breastwork on the knoll some fifty yards off, where the men of the Heavies were, was now a fort of biscuit-boxes, which, I learned, had been constructed under a heavy fire by the 2nd Life Guards and the Greys.

Glancing at the ridge on our left rear, I noticed that it was now occupied by a squadron of Baggara horsemen, probably that which Captain Verner had reported to General Stewart as advancing along earlier in the day. The enemy's sharpshooters on our right and front were keeping up a hot fire, but it was seldom any of them could be seen. Our only guide in replying to it was the puffs of smoke from their rifles, and volley after volley was fired from the redoubt, and from the fort in the knoll, at all such indications of their whereabouts.

These views of the situation were by no means reassuring, for it was now nearly 2 p.m., and we had halted shortly before 8 a.m. After our night's march, undertaken to prevent the enemy from recovering from the defeat we had inflicted on them at Abu-Klea, here they were again in strong force, and evidently resolved to dispute our further advance to the Nile.

The general impression seems to have been that the Arabs had received large reinforcements from the south, and that we had the prospect before us of another hard fight. How far this impression and the hot fire under which we had been for several hours contributed to delay our advance it may be difficult to say. Both combined, however, had no doubt something to do with the extensive preparations for the defence of the *zereba* which it was thought necessary to make before marching out to fight our way to the Nile. It took some time, for example, to construct the hospital redoubt, as the camels were so crowded together as to make it slow work collecting their saddles.

This was also done under a heavy fire, as well as the construction of the fort on the knoll in front of the *zereba*. The enemy had evidently no intention to attack us where we were, but were formed up nearly two miles off waiting for us. The wiser and safer course would have been to march out and fight them, and not to remain cooped up where we were as a mark for their sharpshooters. Even if the square had moved out at noon, we could have saved one day in our march to join hands with Gordon.

A square, however, was now being formed for attack, and the defence of the *zereba* was entrusted to Colonel Barrow under Lord Charles Beresford as senior officer in rank, with a force of about 300 rank and file made up as follows: Royal Artillery and three guns under Captain Norton; half the R.E. under Major Dorward; the Naval Brigade under Lord Charles, and half of the Heavy Camel Regiment under Major Davison of the 16th Lancers.

The square when formed comprised the Guards, Mounted Infantry, half the Heavies and the Sussex Regiment, who occupied the same positions in it as they did in the square at Abu-Klea. Only camels for carrying *cacolets* and reserve ammunition were taken with it, and no guns. In order to avert a similar catastrophe to that which occurred at Abu-Klea a reserve force of Engineers and dismounted Hussars was placed at its angles. As will thus be seen, in its organisation it contrasts most favourably with the latter. It was in fact a square of British infantry only, and as such proved its efficiency. When the square was ready to move, Sir Charles Wilson gave Colonel Boscawen its executive command, and entrusted Captain Verner with its direction, so far as the topography of its line of advance was concerned.

At the time of its formation the fire of the enemy had become very heavy—so sharp indeed that as the various corps came up to take up their position it lay down until all was ready for the advance.

Lieutenant Crutchley, of the Scots Guards, was unfortunately wounded during this preparatory state of affairs, while giving a receipt to Lieutenant Lawson for some entrenching tools; Mr. St. Leger Herbert (correspondent of the *Morning Post*) on General Stewart's staff, who had left him to go out with the square, was struck by a bullet in the head and instantly killed while beckoning to his servant to bring him his horse.

Shortly after General Stewart was wounded, Cameron was killed by a bullet which struck him in the back and passed through his heart, while in the act of taking a box of sardines from his servant From the time his camel had been tied down until then he had lain alongside of it armed with a rifle. Although my camels were only a dozen feet from him, I knew nothing of his death until I saw his body with St Leger Herbert's and those of two officers lying together outside of the hospital fort. But more of them anon.

The square had been formed on the edge of the *zereba*, nearly in rear of the hospital redoubt. When it was moving round, it attracted a sharp fire from the enemy, and we noticed that as it advanced it left several men in the ground behind it wounded who were quickly picked up and brought in by some of the Heavies in the redoubt on the knoll under the command of Lord Dundonald. Having rounded this point it made for the gravel ridge as already described, on which two of the masses of the enemy were formed up to receive it. Between us and this ridge there were a number of bare gravel patches connected with one another, and the square had to move in a zigzag fashion to keep on them and out of the thick *savas* grass. On the right of its line of advance there were other gravel patches enclosed by the grass, along which we could see groups of the enemy moving in parallel lines with it. They no doubt had calculated that our advance must lead through some of these enclosed spots.

The fire from the cover on the right seemed to follow the square, and occasionally to become so hot that it halted and lay down to reply to it Then it moved on again as before.

In the meantime we were not idle in the redoubt, for Captain Norton made splendid practice, and pitched shell after shell right amongst the masses of the enemy, both on the ridge and below it, in the cover on the right; we followed the explosion of these shells with hearty cheers. On one occasion one of them burst right amongst the mass referred to when we supposed it was about to attack the square in flank, and drove it towards the gravel ridge.

Lord Charles was in his element, and, if I remember rightly, also in his shirtsleeves, and one of the Naval Brigade went about cracking jokes. Colonel Barrow would occasionally have the 'attention' sounded, and mounting a biscuit-box or water-tank harangue the men on the progress of the square, always winding up with the caution, 'Now, men! No single firing! Give them volleys!' And volleys the sharpshooters all round us got with such a will as not only sensibly to check their fire, but with such a deterring effect as to keep them at long range from us. In fact, they never came within 800 yards of the *zereba*.

The crisis of the engagement occurred about 4 p.m., when the enemy charged the square. We saw the large mass coming over the crest of the ridge, with their banners fluttering. Almost at the same moment a shell fired from one of our guns laid by Lieut. Du Boulay burst amongst the mass in rear of it and threw it into disorder. Then followed several rapid volleys from the square, when the charging Arab mass broke up and disappeared beyond the gravel ridge. The square then moved steadily onwards, and after we had lost sight of it we heard two more volleys and all was quiet in that direction.

Next day we learned that when the square got within 600 yards of the gravel ridge, the fire of the enemy from the cover became so very hot that seven men were killed in a few minutes, and the *cacolets* and stretchers were all filled up with the wounded. Several officers who were with him in the square told Sir Charles Wilson afterwards that things then began to look so ugly that they thought he would certainly have to turn back to the *zereba*.

'That, however,' he characteristically writes, 'we never should have done, as failure meant annihilation!'[3] The men had such a set determined look about their faces, that he further says, 'I knew they could be trusted.' No officer ever commanded a finer body of men than were the officers and soldiers in that square. Nor was ever a square better handled, and from my intercourse with both officers and men I gathered that the confidence thus expressed by their commander was heartily reciprocated.

Before the enemy charged the firing of the Arab sharpshooters ceased. The spearmen of the enemy then came rapidly down the ridge towards the square, led by men on horseback with flags as in the charge at Abu-Klea. The square was at once halted. As an officer of the Guards told me:

> Suddenly, we began to see men's heads as the Arabs crested the ridge, and I cannot describe the feeling of relief that we all experienced as we knew the game of the enemy was up. The men burst into a cheer which we immediately silenced, as we were afraid the enemy would then turn back without coming on. On this occasion the firing was excellent, but then the enemy were charging down a nice slope, while at Abu-Klea they were charging uphill.

Sir Charles tells us that after the men had 'given vent to their feelings in a wild spontaneous cheer,' they set to work firing as they would

---
3. *From Korti to Khartoum*, 2nd ed.

have done at an Aldershot field-day. As the firing at first appeared to have little effect, the bugle sounded 'Cease firing,' which steadied them; and they then opened fire at 300 yards with such deadly effect that all the leaders with their waving banners went down at once, and in a few minutes the whole of the front ranks of the Arabs were swept away.

My informant who was in the front rank also said to me: 'What struck me most was that during our firing there seemed a particular zone beyond which no one could pass, viz., from about one to two hundred yards; and of all the men that entered that zone I don't think more than half a dozen got away.'

The enemy left behind them 300 dead, but carried off the field all but a few of their wounded. The body of spearmen who charged the square was estimated at from 800 to 1,000 men. The masses of the enemy assembled on the adjacent hills were, however, as numerous as those which met us at Abu-Klea. They had then evidently had enough of it; for on this occasion they allowed the new comers to try their hand at fighting a British square, while they stood looking on. That the bursting of our shells amongst the masses of the enemy as the square advanced prevented a greater number of their spearmen charging it is also very probable.

Not a single man of ours was lost in this last charge of the Arabs nor a single man wounded by a spear throughout the fight. No wonder, then, when it was over, that our fellows gave a hearty cheer; and that both Sir Charles Wilson and Colonel Boscawen were complimented on the successful issue of the gallant fight they had so ably conducted.

When the gravel ridge was reached by the square the sun was setting, and much disappointment was felt at not seeing the Nile—which, it was supposed, was just behind it. The tired men, after a short but weary march, struck the river, and succeeded in the dark in finding a safe and comfortable camping ground on its bank. They were so exhausted that after coming up from their drink many of them 'fell down like logs and were with difficulty got into their places for the night'

We were in very much the same way, almost in a worse condition, in the *zereba*, for we had no refreshing Nile water to drink; that was a luxury yet to be enjoyed. However, we made the best we could of our position after the enemy's fire ceased from all directions about 4.30 p.m. My man could nowhere be found; and the reason, I am afraid, was that he was engaged with a number of other men, both civil and military, in plundering. General Stewart's private stores were stolen, as well as a quantity of brandy of the Medical Department, and lots of other things. It seemed for a time as if all military discipline was at an end. My stores had, with my camel saddles, been requisitioned for the breastworks of the hospital redoubt, and in this way fortunately escaped pilfering; but as I could not then get at them I had to depend on the charity of friends around me for a meal. I am chiefly indebted to Major Rainsford, of the Commissariat, for the loan of his tin of preserved beef and a handful of biscuits; and with my back to the breastwork next the hospital, I actually fell asleep with them, one in each hand.

We had a hard bed of it in the redoubt that night, and were pretty closely packed together. First, on the right, lay Colonel Barrow, then Major Dorward, myself, and then Rainsford. After we had lain down a colleague came along and begged for a share of our bed, and squeezed in between me and the latter. Major R. said during the night, while my colleague was snoring, 'I wouldn't mind a bit if the fellow would only keep his legs still.'

Twice during the night we were called to stand to our arms—but they were false alarms. Then the groaning of the wounded behind us was most painful. One poor fellow who had been hit in the abdomen had become delirious. Late in the evening I noticed him getting up on his knees and heard him raving—talking of friends at home, as I gathered from what he said; and then in his agony he would lie down again and moan. The first time we were roused I heard him still. The second time not hearing him, I learned upon enquiry that he was dead. I could not help thinking then, as I have often done under similar circumstances, that a night alongside of a field hospital after a battle would do much to moderate the tone of those who clamour for military expeditions in defence of national interests or for the maintenance of British prestige.

We had no chaplain with us, although there were two of them at Korti. The reason of this was. that the chief of the Staff refused permission for either of them to accompany the Desert Column. The Royal Irish, when they marched from Korti to Metammeh, took their good Father Brindle with them; and the Gordon Highlanders who formed part of the Nile Column had their Presbyterian chaplain, Mr. McTaggart, with them. But no Anglican chaplains were, as stated, allowed to leave headquarters. Surely more consideration ought to have been shown to the spiritual wants of our troops, when exposed to wounds and death, than was manifested on this occasion. Our chaplains are appointed and paid by the British public for certain religious purposes; and where could their services be more useful or appreciated than in a field hospital after a battle? Our wounded men were nevertheless allowed on this occasion to suffer or die without the consolations of religion so far as chaplains were concerned. Many of them, I was glad to see however, had their Bibles with them; and some of the officers as well as others did all they could to make up for this mistake of those in authority—to call it by its softest name.

CHAPTER 18

Junction with Gordon's Troops

At daybreak on the 20th, all eyes were anxiously directed towards the gravel ridge beyond which our square had disappeared on the previous day, after its gallant fight. That it had reached its destination we felt assured, but it was still uncertain whether the defeat it had inflicted on the enemy was so complete as to open our way to the Nile without further fighting.

At first the indications were not very reassuring, for groups of the enemy could be seen moving about the battlefield. Then columns of blue smoke began to rise beyond the gravel ridge, followed by a light cloud of white smoke in the same direction, and then, much to our relief, we saw the square coming towards us over the crest of the ridge. Every glass was now put into requisition, and soon the word passed round 'They are marching in open column!' This settled the question of the success of Sir Charles Wilson's fight of yesterday. No foe could now be seen from the *zereba* in any direction, and it was evident that no foe existed in a condition to interfere with his march back for our relief.

At last the column came within hearing, when we gave expression to our feelings of admiration and thankfulness in lusty cheers, and when it came up in hearty personal congratulations to Sir Charles Wilson and the officers and men he had so gallantly and successfully led. They also were pleased to find us in safety, for although, in looking back with their glasses, they supposed we were all right, the crowds of the enemy hanging round us made them anxious. Our congratulations and joy were therefore mutual, or, as Sir Charles expressed it:

'The garrison received us with hearty cheers which I think were more grateful to us than any after-rewards will be. We felt that under the trying circumstances we had done our duty like men, and that the lusty cheers were the spontaneous vote of thanks of our comrades for having pulled them and us out of an awkward position.'[1]

We then ascertained that the square, after a cold and hungry night's bivouac on the bank of the river, had occupied the deserted village of Abu Kru (see plan), built on a gravel ridge and about three-quarters of a mile from the Nile, and that measures had at once been taken to put its houses in a state of defence. Leaving the wounded there, with the Heavies and Sussex Regiment under Lord Arthur Somerset for their protection. Sir Charles Wilson then marched for the *zereba* with the Guards and Mounted Infantry. As large numbers of the enemy were seen on the gravel ridge and about the battlefield, he moved the column so as to threaten Metammeh. This had the designed effect, for the Arabs rapidly withdrew in that direction, followed by several volleys at long range. The column then marched on without seeing any more of the enemy, and reached us as already described.

As soon as the force had breakfasted, preparations were immediately commenced for removal to our new position on the Nile. And then we began to realise what we had suffered through our unfortunate halt for breakfast in an exposed position on the previous day. The hospital was filled with wounded men, and outside of its breastworks lay eighteen dead bodies. A number of our camels had been killed and a large number wounded, and what were left of them were in a wretched condition, for they had now been six days without water, and during that period almost entirely without food. In fact, so done up were the poor brutes that they could just stagger along when loaded up.

The horses of the Hussars were also completely done up, for with the exception of a drink at Abu-Klea, they had had scarcely enough water to wash their mouths since we had left Jakdul. The manner in which Colonel Barrow managed to get them along so far and so well as he did, excited the admiration of every one. After reaching the Nile, they were, however, so done up as to be only available for scouting at short distances from the camp.

The escape of my own horse from the enemy's sharpshooters was marvellous. Although he had stood on the very crest of the hill during the engagement, and above the tied-down camels, they only managed to graze both of his fore legs, and to put a bullet in the flap of his saddle, which happily, however, went no further than the girth beneath it.

---

1. *From Korti to Khartoum*, 2nd ed.

It took some time to get the living camels out from amongst the dead, and to disentangle the saddles and stores and other things from the confused mass into which they had been piled up in the breastworks round the hospital and gun redoubts. My portable table and chair could not be found in the confusion thus caused, and consequently we parted company, much to my subsequent discomfort.

Owing to our heavy loss of camels, and the wretched condition of those which remained, Sir Charles Wilson was compelled to leave a great part of the stores in the *zereba* under the protection of a small force commanded by Major Davison of the 16th Lancers.

Before marching our dead were buried in two pits, one of which was filled by fourteen bodies, laid side by side, and another in line with it by those of Quartermaster Lima of the 19th Hussars, Conductor Jewell of the Commissariat, St. Leger Herbert (correspondent of the *Morning Post*), and Cameron of the *Standard*. I followed the body of the latter alone from the hospital to within a few yards of the pit, where it was met by my colleagues. Melton Prior, Pearse, Villiers, and Burleigh, when we joined in carrying it to its last resting-place. Sir Charles Wilson, Colonel Barrow, and several officers then gathered round the open graves of our dead, and stood uncovered while Lord Charles Beresford in feeling tones read the Burial Service over them. Stern as had been

those warriors in the hour of battle yesterday, they now mourned as British soldiers always mourn over comrades whose lives have been part of the price paid for the victory they have achieved.

Two out of our little band of eight had fallen. One who had been esteemed by all who knew him personally had now been cut down by a Sudanese bullet on the threshold of what it was hoped would be a brilliant career. The other had been our companion and friend, and we could not, therefore, take our last look at his stem but honest face without feelings of sorrow and of sympathy with his widowed mother in her irreparable loss. I could not help then recalling the Duke of Somerset's sarcastic remark about war correspondents, when he called them 'a noble army of martyrs.' The joke he thus intended to make at their expense was after all no joke, for here was one of them at any rate who, without the hopes of military honours or decorations from the hands of his Sovereign, had risked his life on more than one occasion, and who had now lost it in the public interest.

The latest incidents in his distinguished and eventful career were connected with the recent military operations in the Sudan. When

Baker Pasha's force was crushed by the Arabs, he very narrowly escaped losing his life, and he subsequently accompanied the British expeditionary force in its advance from Suakim upon Tokar, and was also present at the battles of El Teb and Tamanieh.

In a private letter from Suakim at the period of these events, and from a very high source, he was thus characterised:

> Of the correspondents, Cameron is first favourite. Everybody likes him, and his work is honest and sincere. Some of the men think nothing of romancing, but Cameron tells the true story, and makes it much more interesting than the fiction of others.

No commendation can be higher than this, and all who knew Cameron will acknowledge it was deserved. The *Standard* newspaper recognised the value of his services by settling a handsome annuity for life upon his widowed mother. Writing to me on March 16, 1886, she bears this testimony to him:

> My son was born this day thirty-five years ago. He had from his earliest boyhood a love for the army, which was strengthened by his passion for music, as military bands had always a great attraction for him. In disposition he was most amiable and sympathetic, and he was the most tender and devoted son that ever a mother mourned for.

Our Column began its march for the Nile at 2.30 p.m., with a square of the Guards and Mounted Infantry on its left front, and another square at the rear composed of the balance of our force and the Artillery and Gardner gun. General Stewart and Mr. Crutchley were carried on stretchers in the former, the other wounded in a similar manner in the latter; and so shorthanded were we, that the servants of my colleagues and my own had to bear a hand in their transport. We marched very slowly and with frequent halts, and when passing the battle-field. Major Poe was sent by Sir Charles Wilson to bury the dead. They were found stripped of their clothing, and three of them much cut about with spears and swords. As all of them bore bullet-wounds, death must have been instantaneous. It was a relief also to find that none of their bodies had been mutilated by our barbarous foes. Although during the night the Arabs had buried many of their dead, over two hundred of them were still lying on the ground. We picked up three of their wounded, and, burdened as we were, carried them along with us to be cared for with our own poor fellows.

We reached Abu Kru about sunset, hungry, thirsty, and thoroughly worn out by our four days' hard work and want of proper sleep. Leaving the column when it reached the village, I was met and taken kindly possession of by some men of the Heavies which had been left to hold the position. They appeared to regard me as if I were on my last legs, for with a kindness never to be forgotten, after seating me with my back against the wall of the house, they brought me a bowl of hot mutton broth made from a looted sheep.

Although this village bore the name of Abu Kru, it was subsequently designated El Gubat lest, as I was officially informed, our position there should be confounded with that at Abu-Klea. It comprised six or eight houses, with walls of Nile mud as hard as concrete, and with heavily thatched roofs. As the one assigned to the 'Press' contained but one very small room, we bivouacked in the open air round it. All of us were very much knocked up by the fatigue we had undergone, and therefore hailed with satisfaction the prospect of an undisturbed night's rest

The Guards lay down under arms in front of the village, in which the Sussex were quartered with the wounded. The Heavies occupied a similar position on its left, and the Mounted Infantry on its right. The Hussars bivouacked in its rear.

The result of yesterday's fight had such an inspiring influence that we all supposed no great difficulty would be encountered in the proposed attack on Metammeh. We therefore hoped for better quarters next night within its walls. No sooner had we settled down for the night than we were roused by a fire which had broken out in the thatched roof of one of the adjacent houses. Major Poe with his men, however, soon got it under, and then all became quiet again.

At the very dawn of day on the 21st, I was awakened from a sound sleep by the tramping past me of some of the soldiers marching from their bivouac to the point 4 on the plan, where the column was about to be formed up for the attack on Metammeh. I was just in time to see Colonel Barrow and the Hussars move out to reconnoitre the town. Their horses were evidently all the better for their drink of Nile water, but still unfit for cavalry work such as that now required of them. In fact they could not do it effectively, for instead of riding round Metammeh, as under ordinary circumstances they would have done, they rode up together to the high ground to the north of the town and waited there for the attacking force. This comprised the Guards, part of the Heavies, the Mounted Infantry, the Naval Brigade

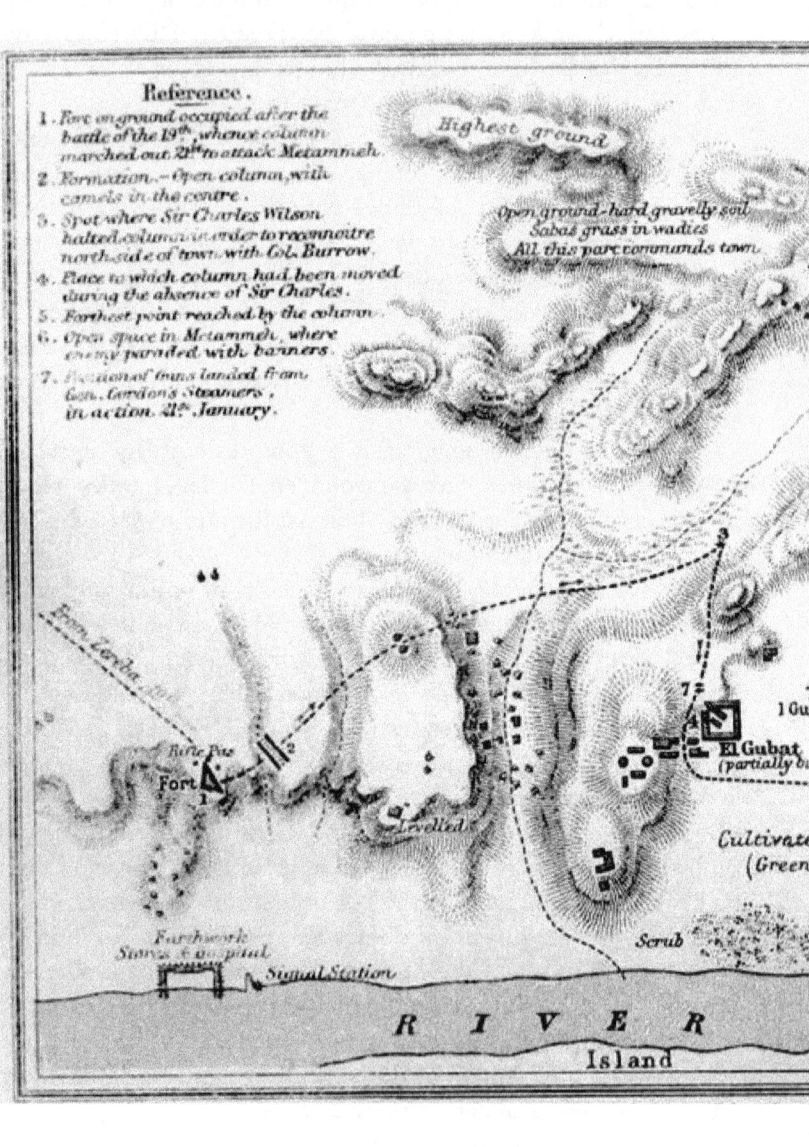

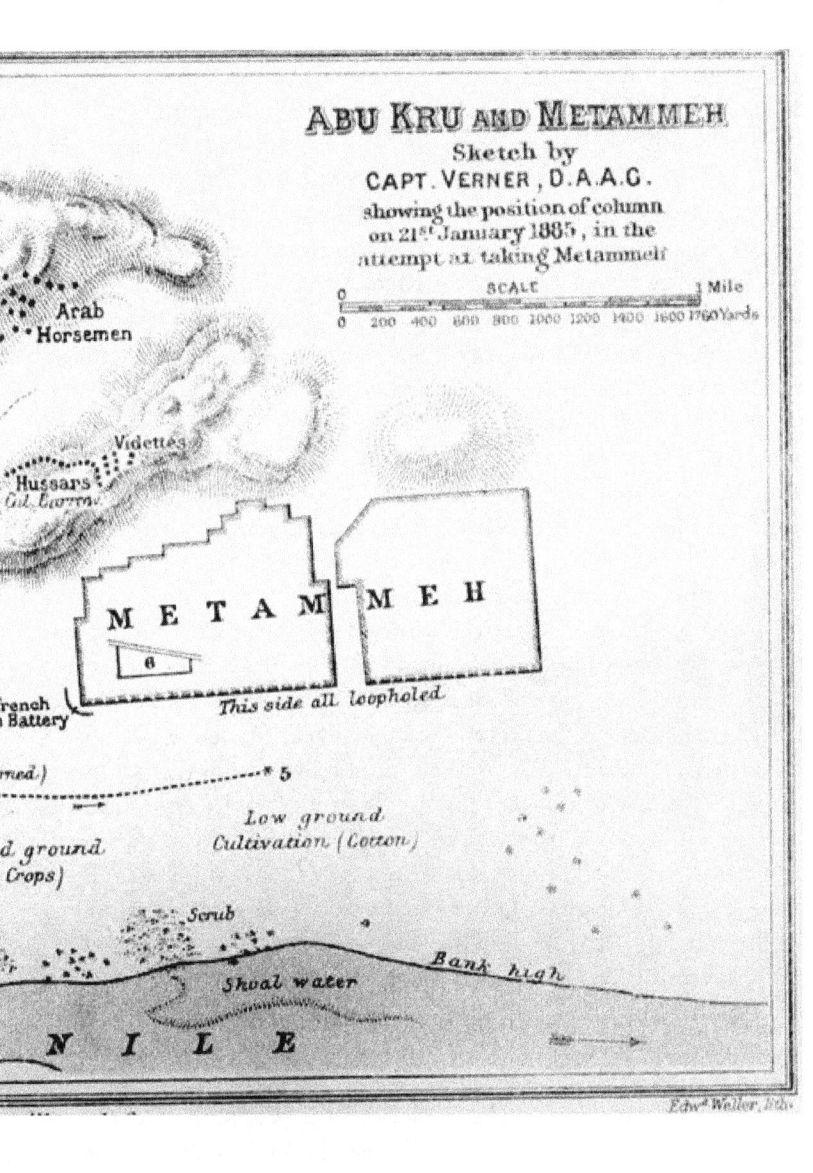

with its Gardner, and the Royal Artillery with the three screw guns, and a detachment of Engineers. In order to ensure a rapid advance it was formed in a double column, with the guns and camels, carrying ammunition, water, and *cacolets*, between them.

Not anticipating any serious resistance on the part of the enemy and still feeling very fatigued, I remained behind. The roof of the house used as a heliographic station afforded me, however, a capital place for observation, for it commanded the whole position.

The Sussex Regiment with the Royals, 4th and 5th Dragoons, were left to protect the wounded, and soon after daylight they set to work to fortify the place and loopholed a number of the houses.

Sir Charles had ascertained on the previous day that there was a large Government building in Metammeh which could be easily reached from the desert side of the town, that there were some defences on its river side against the steamers, but that the place was not held by the enemy in any great force.

He, therefore, moved the column in the direction marked on the plan, and halted it at the point 1 in order to communicate with Colonel Barrow. Being the only mounted officer, he rode out alone to him and found the Hussars dismounted and watching a body of Arab horsemen who were in close proximity to them, but whose further advance they had discouraged by their fire.

Having ascertained that the position occupied by Colonel Barrow commanded Metammeh, and that the gun battery at its S.W, corner could thence be taken in reverse by artillery fire, he returned at once to order up the column for the attack. His horse was now so thoroughly done up that he had to dismount and lead it. After having gone a short distance in this fashion, he noticed to his great surprise that the column had been changed into a square and was moving off towards the river and firing. An officer then met him with a message from Colonel Boscawen, to the effect that having seen a body of dervishes moving between the force and the river towards the camp he had moved the column in that direction in order to intercept them. Sir Charles, delayed by his worn-out steed, did not catch up the square until it had reached the point 2 on the plan, where it had been halted behind the houses of the village.

From this position, which overlooked the ground between it and the river, no dervishes could now be seen by Sir Charles or anybody else. Their present invisibility was, however, sought to be accounted for by their probable concealment amongst the thick growth of *dhura* and cotton bushes which covered the cultivated ground in that direction. Our readers will, no doubt, be surprised to learn the slight grounds upon which Colonel Boscawen was urged to move the square as already described. As given to me by one of the most trustworthy officers in it, and in his own words, they were as follows:—

> As we were advancing we saw some flags below one of the villages near the river, and the column was diverted in that direction so as not to leave the camp open to attack. As we advanced we found only a few of the enemy, the flags we had seen being stuck over the graves of some of the chiefs who had fallen on the 19th.

This strange error of judgment at a critical moment can only be accounted for on two grounds. Both officers and men had not then recovered from the extreme fatigue of their four previous days' hard work. Men under such circumstances become unduly nervous and excitable. Nor was the Camel Corps, from its organisation, the kind of force to be employed in an attack on a town. Sir Charles Wilson has been criticised for having planned an attack from the desert side of Metammeh because the camp, it was said, would thus be exposed to an attack of Arabs passing between these attacking columns and the river. How far such views may have prevailed in the square when it was moved by Colonel Boscawen from where it had been halted by Sir Charles I am not in a position to say. Subsequent events showed their fallacy if they were entertained.

There were also good reasons at the time for concluding that the Arabs would not attempt such a movement as these critics have suggested. In the first place, the enemy were too much demoralised by two consecutive defeats to attempt anything of the kind. For example, had they not rapidly retired from before our square without firing a shot when it was returning to the *zereba* on the previous morning? Then we had no reason for believing that the enemy would act otherwise on the 21st than they had done on the 17th and 19th, for on both these occasions they had confined their main attention to our attacking force, and never attempted any real counter-attack on our two *zerebas*.

Influenced by the positive assurances as to the appearance of the enemy between the square and the river, and by the possibility of their moving on the camp through the thick growth in that direction, Sir Charles deemed it prudent to move the force southwards instead of carrying out his original plan of attack. Soon after it reached the point 5 on our plan, the enemy opened a hot fire upon it from behind loopholed walls. So brisk was the fire, that the men were ordered to lie down while skirmishers went out to check it. Our guns also opened fire, but without effect, as their shot passed through the mud walls without injuring them.

While all this was going on at the front, we were startled in the camp by report of cannon from the opposite direction. Our alarm was further increased by the falling back of the Hussars, who had been scouting along the left bank of the river under the impression that they were about to be attacked. A few minutes later we caught sight of Gordon's four steamers flying the Egyptian flag. It is difficult to describe the joyous excitement which then spread through the camp. When the news of their arrival reached our wounded general, he said: 'Thank God I have done my duty!'

As the steamers passed abreast of the camp they were welcomed by hearty cheers, and all who could get away marched down to the river to greet them. No sooner were they moored to the shore below the signal station than Khasm-el-Mus, the *melik*, or king of the Shagiyehs, landed with a detachment of black troops and one of artillery, with two small handy brass guns throwing a 9-lb. shell. The blacks were armed with Remingtons, and for the most part with swords. Having loaded their ammunition on camels brought down from the camp by Lieutenant Burn-Murdoch, off marched our welcome auxiliaries to the front to take part in the attack.

Sir Charles, having failed to make any impression on the town from the south side, decided after effecting a junction with Gordon's troops, of whose arrival he had been made aware, to attempt it from the west. He therefore withdrew from the position marked 5 on the plan, and reoccupied the village of Gubat after uniting below it with the force under Khasm-el-Mus. The latter were then sent to a position above the village, and immediately opened a hot rifle and artillery fire on the town; but their *canons rayés* had no better effect on its concrete walls than had our own guns.

While we were watching this cannonade from the heliographic station, a messenger came in from Sir Charles, with orders to hurry on the defences of the camp, as a large force of the enemy was marching upon us from the direction of Khartoum. Orders were also given to send out for Major Davison and the stores we had left with him at the *zereba* on the previous day. We were also informed that this force of the enemy, when seen by Khasm-el-Mus from the steamers in the morning, was only twelve miles from the camp, and its arrival might therefore be looked for in the evening or early next day.

The cannonade and rifle fire, however, still continued at the front, and apparently with some effect, for numbers of the enemy could be seen streaming out from the north side of Metammeh. Some were women, but a large number of these fugitives were men. To our surprise and disappointment there came the heliographic signal, 'Force withdrawing.' Soon after columns of black smoke rose from the village between us and the town, for it had been fired by our troops as they withdrew, in order to prevent its occupation by the enemy.

It was not until after Sir C. Wilson was informed of the approach of these fresh troops of the enemy that he abandoned the attack on Metammeh and ordered our force back to the camp. There can be no doubt that this order was given with great regret, for no one knew better than he did that the political effect of not taking the place would be bad. He had therefore resolved to make the attempt, and hoped to capture it before the enemy received reinforcements. He failed to do so, as has been described, and now had to direct his attention to making preparations to ward off the new danger with which we were threatened.

Colonel Boscawen, who had distinguished himself by the masterly manner in which he had handled the square on the 19th, now so conducted the withdrawal of the force as to prevent the enemy from imagining that we had failed in our object in attacking them. He retired slowly, as if inviting them to come out from behind their loopholed walls and fight him in the open, but they declined the challenge, and made no attempt to annoy the square in its march back to the camp.

When Sir Charles came in he gave orders for the removal of the greater part of the force and of the wounded down to the Nile, leaving, however, the Guards and Marines with the Artillery to hold Gubat, as we must henceforth call our position on the Nile.

The place where this new camp was pitched was by no means either safe or comfortable, for it lay on ground sloping rapidly down to the river from the edge of the cultivated plain between it and the gravel ridge on which the village stood. While thus concealed from the land side, it was exposed to an enemy occupying the island opposite to it, from which it was only 400 yards distant. Although we slept the first night under the protection of one of Gordon's steamers and twenty-five men of the Mounted Infantry under the command of

Lieutenant Maxwell, many of us expected to be shot at from that direction before morning. Part of the ground we occupied was covered at high Nile, and was consequently damp; and when the wind blew from the land side we were smothered with dust from the cultivated soil above us.

As the few tents put up for the wounded did not afford accommodation for the whole of them, a number had to be protected from the sun by blankets hung over them. Some idea may be formed of their suffering through this exposure from the fact that the temperature at noon was 91° Fahrenheit in the shade. Under these circumstances it would certainly have been much better to have left them at Gubat, where there were houses enough to shelter them, and where on the hard gravel terrace they would have been comparatively free from dust. Surgeon Ferguson, however, did what he could to remedy these discomforts by the construction of straw huts, the material for which was plentiful in the luxuriant growth of *dhura* which covered the island.

In the hurry and confusion of removal to our new camping ground we were left by the military authorities each one to shift for himself. Several of my colleagues took up their quarters at its upper end, while Melton Prior, Burleigh, and I settled down below it near the signal station. The former, guided by his artistic instincts, selected a commanding site for his residence on the high bank of the river, but Burleigh followed my example and sought shelter from the north wind and protection from stray bullets beneath the bank below the cultivated ground. Four stakes, picked up somewhere by my man, driven into the ground and covered on three sides and overhead with a spare blanket; two empty canvas sacks, and my cork mattress with its waterproof flaps, provided a house long enough to hold my portable bed and broad enough to leave room to get in and out of it.

After our fortnight's wandering and stirring adventures in the desert it was a comfort to find oneself even thus housed, and to feel that although Metammeh had not been seized and occupied as Lord Wolseley had intended should be done, we had at any rate secured a position on the Nile which would enable us to carry out successfully the ultimate objects of the expedition. As some misconception has prevailed with regard to the nature and scope of these objects, it is desirable to recall them here by a concise reference to the orders given to General Stewart and to Sir C. Wilson by Lord Wolseley, as well as to his statements in his despatches to H.M. Government

General Stewart's orders were to seize and occupy Metammeh and then to return to Jakdul with the Heavy Camel Regiment only, and from there to continue to forward convoys of stores back to it. Lord Wolseley expected it would be in his possession on January 16, for he did not anticipate any serious resistance at the place itself. It would also appear from the tone of the despatch in which he expresses this hope, that he further anticipated Stewart's second march would be as great a surprise as had been his previous one when he seized Jakdul.[2]

In the same despatch he told Lord Hartington that his future line of action would depend very much upon the information he hoped shortly to obtain from General Gordon, adding that, as Khartoum was then sealed to native messengers by the troops and spies of the *Mahdi*, he had sent Sir C Wilson with Stewart's column 'with orders to proceed to that place as soon as possible for the purpose of conferring with General Gordon.' We learn from a later despatch to Lord Hartington that his chief object in occupying Metammeh was 'to be prepared to march at once, even at considerable hazard, to the assistance of Gordon, should it be found that he required immediate assistance.'[3] From a calculation made by the chief of his staff it appears Lord Wolseley did not expect that General Earle's Nile column would reach Shendy before March 5, nor that his own force, which was to cross the desert, would be concentrated at Metammeh before March 2.

From Sir C. Wilson's instructions we learn that Lord Charles Beresford was sent in command of a small party of seamen with Stewart's column to Metammeh, 'where if there are any steamers' he was to take possession of one or two of them; and that when he reports to Sir C. Wilson that he was ready to proceed to Khartoum the latter was to go with him to that place.

Sir Charles's mission was to deliver an open letter to General Gordon, from which Lord Wolseley tells him he would learn the object of his mission. He was, however, only to remain long enough in Khartoum to confer with General Gordon on the political and military-situations. He might, if he liked, march through it the small detachment of infantry General Stewart was ordered to send with him, but they were not to sleep in the place, and he was peremptorily ordered to bring them back with him to Metammeh. He was, however, to leave three officers with General Gordon to assist him until Lord Wolseley informs us he was able to relieve him. So ill-informed was he at the time when these instructions were given of his endangered position,

---
2. Parliamentary Paper, Egypt, No. 2, 1885, pp. 3, 4.
3. *Ibid.*, p. 5.

that he even expresses the opinion to Sir Charles that 'it is always possible that when Mahomed Achmet realises that an English army is approaching Khartoum, he will retreat and relieve the siege.'[4]

Our readers will learn from the foregoing references that General Stewart's column was not primarily sent for the relief of Khartoum, and that, so far as Lord Wolseley's plans were concerned, on the date of its despatch to Metammeh neither he nor the chief of his staff appeared to recognise any immediate or pressing need of an armed intervention for that purpose.[5]

If any further proof of this state of feeling at headquarters be necessary, reference may be made to Lord Wolseley's despatch to Lord Hartington of Jan. 29, enclosing Sir C. Wilson's despatch of the 22nd describing the operations of our column subsequent to the 18th.

'The result of these successfully executed operations has been to place us in possession of the desert route from this place (Korti) to the Nile, in the vicinity of Metammeh, near which place we are now fairly established, cutting off in a great measure the enemy's forces north of Shendy from those besieging Khartoum, thus rendering still more difficult than before the feeding of the *Mahdi*'s army, already short of provisions.'

He also congratulates himself on being thus able to capture Berber, as Gordon's steamers, manned by the Naval Brigade, will assist him in that operation. So far, however, as Gordon himself is concerned, these steamers will enable him to communicate direct with him and ascertain the real condition of Khartoum.

If such was the feeling at headquarters up till January 12, it certainly is excusable that it should have prevailed at Gubat on January 21, as I am quite certain it did amongst our officers—Lord Charles Beresford and Major Wardrop included.

On the 22nd, however, our hopes were somewhat damped by Abd-ul-Hamid, the commandant of the armed steamer *Bordein*, who reported that when he left Khartoum on December 14 Gordon had told him that unless he returned in ten days with British troops it would be too late. It also became known that a letter had been received from Gordon for Colonel Watson of the same date, stating that a catastrophe in the town was not thought improbable within ten days. As a set-off to this discouraging news we knew from our prisoners at Abu-Klea on the 18th that, although Omdurman had fallen,

---

4. Parliamentary Paper, Egypt, No. 9, pp. 11, 12.
5. See end pages chapter 1.

Khartoum still held out We therefore hoped that though:

Late, late, so late! but we can enter still;

. . . . for after the two crushing defeats we had inflicted on the troops he had sent to oppose us it seemed probable that the *Mahdi* would now hesitate to attack Gordon in his stronghold.

Prudence, however, suggested that we should at once communicate with him at the earliest possible moment, and no one felt more anxious in this respect than did Sir C. Wilson himself. In his despatch to Lord Wolseley of January 22 he said, referring to Colonel Watson's letter from Gordon:

> The important news received from Khartoum rendering it in my opinion imperative that I should carry out my original mission and proceed at once to that place, I handed over the military command to Lieut.-.Col. the Hon. E. E. T. Boscawen.[6]

This was in accordance with the original programme of the expedition, but there are other parts of it which either had not or could not now be so effectively carried out as Lord Wolseley had anticipated. He had, for instance, relied upon Lord Charles Beresford and his seamen to facilitate Sir C. Wilson's mission to Khartoum. The condition, however, in which this division of the so-called Naval Brigade reached Metammeh on January 21, was most deplorable. Lord Charles Beresford was so ill that he could not stand without support Not only were two of his officers killed and the third severely wounded, but he had lost all his petty officers and a number of his men. For the moment our sailor corps was thus in a virtual state of collapse, and Sir C Wilson had to do the best he could to get to Khartoum without its assistance.

General Stewart's wound incapacitated him for any further control of affairs; Colonel Burnaby, to whom Sir C. Wilson was to have handed over the command at Gubat when he left there for Khartoum, was dead. Sir C. Wilson was thus placed at a critical moment in a position involving serious responsibility, not merely on account of his seniority of rank, but also in consequence of the important duties which had been assigned to him in connection with the expedition itself.

The difficulties which now confronted Sir C. Wilson may be thus further summarised. Instead of an unopposed march to the Nile from Jakdul as Lord Wolseley had anticipated, we had had to fight our way

---

6. Parliamentary Paper, Egypt, No. 9, 1885, pp. 12, 13.

to it, and as the result our fighting force had been reduced by losses in killed and wounded in the engagements of the 17th and 19th to 1,322 rank and file.[7]

Our commissariat supplies were so short as to necessitate their replenishment by the despatch at the earliest possible moment of a convoy to Jakdul. At least 400 men would be required for this service, and after their departure we should be left with only 54 officers and 868 non-commissioned officers and men to hold our dearly bought position until they returned or we were reinforced from Korti. This was the serious position of affairs at Gubat on January 22. Urgent as was the need for Sir C. Wilson's departure for Khartoum, it would manifestly have been a reckless act on his part to have left our decimated and virtually disorganised force without reasonably assuring himself of its safety. His attention was therefore directed to the immediate dangers to which it was exposed from attack by the force from Khartoum under Feki Mustafa and by another which was coming up from Berber, and which it was reported was now concentrating at Sayal just below Metammeh.

The Hussar scouts having sent in word on the morning of the 22nd that nothing could be seen of Feki Mustafa's force, Sir Charles went down the river in the *Talahawiyeh,* accompanied by Lord Charles Beresford and two companies of the Mounted Infantry under the command of Major Phipps. Captain Verner followed in the *Bordein* with a detachment of Sudanese. The captain of the *Es Sofia,* without orders, got up steam and also went down the river after them.

Nothing could be seen from the steamers of the enemy at Sayal, and Sir Charles ascertained from two men of the Khasm-el-Mus tribe that when the fugitives from Abu-Klea met the force from Berber it had halted.

Having noticed the force under the Emir-Wad-Hamza, which had followed Gordon's steamers along the right bank when they were coming to meet us, riding into Shendy, Sir Charles hauled out into midstream and shelled the place.

When near the lower end of the island opposite the camp, men were noticed crossing to it from the right bank, and a party of Suda-

---

7. Our losses in these engagements were, according to Surgeon Ferguson's statement at the time: 101 rank and file killed, 167 wounded, or a total of 268 out of a force, including native drivers, of 2,144 rank and file. On the 19th our wounded numbered 10 officers and 94 non-commissioned officers and men, or a total in hospital at Gubat, on January 22, of 104.

nese were landed who drove them back and took possession of their boats. As it was now about sunset, the flotilla returned and reached its moorings shortly after dark.

Sir C. Wilson tells us that on their way back from Shendy Lord Charles asked him to appoint young Ingram, who represented some small paper, to the Naval Brigade, as he had no officers and could not go about himself. He also informs us that, before starting on this reconnaissance, and in consequence of what Gordon had said unfavourably about Nashi Pasha, the commandant of the *Talahawiyeh*, he had replaced him by Khasm-el-Mus. These facts, together with what we have already stated about the Naval Brigade, show that Lord Charles Beresford unaccountably exaggerates the part he played in the proceedings of this day in his report to the Admiralty.[8] He was also inaccurate in stating at the same time that he had on the 22nd reported the steamers ready for Khartoum, for to my personal knowledge the naval artificers did not touch them until the following day, and Lord Charles, when I called his attention to the matter, frankly acknowledged his error in date, and said that I was correct in my statement.

Early on the 22nd Major Dorward and Lieutenant Lawson, with their sappers, began the construction of defensive works at the village, and at our camp on the river. At the former place several houses were blown down with gun-cotton, and the triangular fort marked on the plan was constructed with their debris. The position was well chosen, for it was sixty feet higher than the surrounding plateau, which it thus effectually commanded. It was also surrounded by rifle-pits. Two of our screw guns were placed on it, for which, unfortunately, we had then only 83 rounds out of the 300 we brought from Jakdul. The Guards and Marines held this fort, and from the comfortable quarters they made for themselves in one of the houses which had been left standing it came to be called the 'Guards' Club.'

Before these works were commenced at the village, General Stew-

---

8. Under January 22 he says:—'After some repairs to the engines reported the steamers ready to proceed to Khartoum at 3 p.m. Took command of Gordon's steamers. Proceeded to Shendy, distance seven miles, in *Bordein* and *Tull-Howeiya*, taking *bashi-bazouks* and the crews I found in the vessels. Fired a few shells into Shendy and cleared a small earthwork. Received no opposition.'—*London Gazette*, April 28, 1885, page 1915.

(N.B.—There were ten shells fired into Shendy from each of the six guns on the steamers, and the earthwork Lord Charles here refers to was a battery constructed in a *sakeeyeh* pit, from which upon examination it was found the gun had been removed.)

art was taken on board the little steamer *Tewfikieh*, where he was tenderly nursed by Major Rhodes.

The construction of entrenchments on the river (see plan) was also commenced, and vigorously prosecuted during the day by a succession of fatigue parties. By evening that portion of them parallel with the river and on a level with the cultivated ground was completed, and surrounded outside by what are termed wire entanglements. These, as their designation suggests, are simply wires stretched over the surface of the ground from pegs driven into it. Their object was to trip up the enemy, and they were, to judge by my own experience on one unguarded occasion, most effective for the purpose.

Just after sunset Burleigh, Melton Prior, and I were ordered to pull down our houses and move inside the new entrenchments. This was decidedly uncomfortable, for we had in the hurry to put up with a bed on the hard gravel in the open. The whole force lay down that night under arms, but were not disturbed by the enemy.

Chapter 19

All Lost

In accordance with Sir C. Wilson's orders on the previous evening, work was commenced at daylight on the 23rd, to prepare the *Talahawiyeh* and *Bordein* to take him to Khartoum that day. These steamers had been selected because they were the largest and best protected of the four. They were bullet-proof except at ranges under 150 yards, but were not shot- nor shell-proof. There was a turret at the bow constructed of rough planks of wood fastened together with iron pins in which there was one gun, but the porthole of the turret only allowed it to be fired right ahead. Amidships there was another turret similarly constructed, the floor of which was just high enough to allow the gun in it to be fired over the paddle-boxes on either side through its two portholes. A sort of iron bucket was slung from the foremast for a look-out man. On the top of the saloon or deckhouse a place had been prepared for infantry, by a bulwark formed of boiler-plates round it The helmsman was similarly protected. The sides of the ship, the bulwarks and saloon, or deckhouse, were also protected by boiler-plates fixed to wooden stanchions.

A wooden beam was placed above these plates sufficiently raised to leave a long loophole to fire through. The caboose was at the foot of the bow turret, where all day long slave-women were busily engaged baking *dhura* cakes for the soldiers and sailors. The ammunition, provisions, with a quantity of loot, were all stowed away down in the fore and midships holds. The engines were old and worn, but appeared to be in fairly good order, and during the day the naval artificers remedied some trifling defects which were found in overhauling them. A great deal depended on the machinery of these half-armed 'penny boats,' as Gordon called them, for they would have to run the gauntlet of several of the enemy's batteries while steaming up against the current of the river.

The last and most formidable of these batteries, as the captain of the *Bordein* told me, was just above the cataracts; but beyond it only rifle fire would have to be encountered until Hal-fi-yeh was reached. The steamers, in passing from the White Nile into the Blue, would, however, have to run the gauntlet of the fort at Omdurman, now known to be in the hands of the enemy. As, however, their smoke could be seen fifteen or twenty miles from Khartoum, the captain was certain that on their approach Gordon would make such a diversion as would render a safe landing possible at Tuti Island, by which the town could be reached by Sir Charles. When Abd-ul-Hamid Bey referred to Gordon seeing the smoke of the steamers afar off, I was reminded by the date of the following notice, hung up in the *Talahawiyeh*, of the length of time he had evidently waited and watched, but all in vain, for some such sign of our coming to his relief:[1]

> N.B.—These men do not understand English, consequently I hope any of my countrymen who come on board will be considerate to them, as they have done good service.
>
> C. E. Gordon.
>
> September 30, 1884

Gordon reckoned each of these steamers equal to 2,000 men, and his letters and journals show how valuable they had been to him on many occasions, and yet, in order to facilitate the movements of our expedition, he had sent four of them to meet us. Colonel Kitchener tells us, in his official report on the fall of Khartoum, that Gordon had so weakened himself by sending them away that he found it impossible to check the Arabs on the White Nile, and therefore to keep open communication with the fort of Omdurman, and hence its falling into the hands of the enemy was owing to our delay.

In his letter to the commander of H.M. troops, sent down with the steamers. General Gordon laid great stress upon the removal from them of the Egyptian officers and soldiers, these 'hens' or heroes of Tel-el-Kebir, as he contemptuously called them. The first thing then, in preparing the *Bordein* and *Talahawiyeh* for their risky trip to Khartoum, was to get these men routed out from amongst the crews. It took some time, and a large amount of talking through interpreters, before this could be accomplished, so mixed up were they amongst the Sudanese.

---

1. See chapter 9

The fuel question was also a serious one, for wood was scarce, and the old-fashioned engine boilers of the steamers consumed a large quantity of it Our only sources of supply were the beams of the houses blown down by the Engineers at Abu-Kru on the previous day, and the wooden remains of two adjacent *Sakeeyehs*. Then, after the wood was carried down to the steamers, it had to be sawn or chopped into handy lengths for stoking.

Although every possible effort was made to get the steamers off by midday on the 23rd, it was found impossible to do so, and Sir Charles had therefore most reluctantly to postpone his departure until next day, when he hoped to start at daylight The twenty men of the Royal Sussex under Captain Trafford, who were to accompany him, lay down on the shore alongside of the steamers, ready to go on board in the morning. These men, in accordance with Lord Wolseley's orders, were to be clothed in scarlet to show the garrison at Khartoum that they were really British soldiers, and in order to produce a deterrent effect upon the *Mahdi*. Unfortunately the red coats, sent up with us for the purpose, had either been lost in our night march from Abu-Klea or looted in the *zereba* during the night of the 19th-20th. Anyhow, as they could not now be found, others had to be obtained from the Guards and Heavies. This foraging for red coats with which to frighten the foe, and to prove our force was a British one, excited some merriment in the camp, for had we not already proved our nationality to the consternation of the Arabs, though clad in grey in our recent fights with them?

In the evening a convoy with an escort, under the command of Colonel Talbot, started for Jakdul for provisions, and Mr. Pigott of the Mounted Infantry, with despatches for Lord Wolseley, accompanied it The latter was under orders to proceed to Korti the day before, but could not get away, as neither horses nor camels were in a condition to travel fast, and our guides were afraid to go with him. His orders now were to go on with the convoy as far as Abu-Klea, and then push on ahead of it alone. Unluckily, he lost his way after leaving it, and did not reach Jakdul until after it had arrived there. His subsequent progress was very rapid, for my despatch, which he took with him, giving an account of the battle of the 19th, was telegraphed to London from Korti at 2.30 p.m. on the 28th. During the day we were, as a precautionary measure, put on half-rations, and, in view of the low state of our commissariat, it was somewhat of a relief to be depleted of one third of our force by the departure of this convoy.

Although Sir Charles had given orders for steam to be got up at daylight on the 24th, he did not get away until 8 a.m. Critical as we now knew Gordon's position to be, we yet watched with hopeful hearts this little flotilla as it steamed away from us up the river, bound for Khartoum, and when it passed out of sight round the green point above the camp, many began to calculate the date of its probable return. Nobody then anticipated that any ill would befall it, and no one high or low, including my colleagues—for in their telegrams and letters sent from Gubat to Korti on the 23rd the suggestion was never made— then hinted that its departure had been unduly or unnecessarily delayed.

The opinions which have been since expressed to the contrary are, therefore, merely after-thoughts, or *ex post facto* reasonings. Even if General Stewart could have captured Metammeh on the 19th, he could not have sent Sir Charles off to Khartoum next day as he purposed, for Gordon's steamers did not put in an appearance until 10 a.m. on the 21st. It is very doubtful whether they could have been despatched that day; but if this had been accomplished they could only have then reached Halfiyeh on the evening of the 25th, too far from Khartoum to have prevented the catastrophe which occurred at 3.30 a.m. next day. If, however, Sir Charles had started on the 22nd or early on the 23rd, the results would to all intents and purposes have been the same as they unfortunately were when he left us on the 24th.

After we had seen Sir Charles safely off to Khartoum, our defensive works were pushed on rapidly. The ditch comprising the earthwork upon the land side, which was twelve feet wide by eight feet deep, was soon completed on the east and west sides. The Hussars were formed below the river-bank to the east of this fort, and for their protection an old *Sakeeyeh* mound was made into a small redoubt, and connected with the main work by a *zereba*-fence along the top of the bank. This redoubt came to be known as the ' signal station ' (see plan), as it commanded the best view of Metammeh from our camp and was occupied during the day by look-out men, and held at night by a strong detachment with outlying sentries.

On the 23rd, Sir Charles Wilson sent Captain Verner over to the island opposite to the camp with a force of Egyptian troops to hold it, in place of the Mounted Infantry which had been doing duty there since the night of the 21st. The former soon completed a strong breastwork—and cleared all the crops from around it—so as to prevent the enemy obtaining a footing there. The distance to the camp from the right bank across the island was 1,300 yards. It was thus of vast importance to us for tactical purposes, for above it the Nile was only 800 yards wide, and the country on the right bank was not only well wooded but also very populous. This would have made a post on the left bank above the island very dangerous, for it would have been within easy rifle range from the other side of the river. We could not, therefore, have stumbled upon a better defensible position than that we now occupied.

Fortunately, also, the island was covered with rich crops of dhura and barley, and also a few beans, which afforded an abundant supply of food for our camels and horses. Fatigue parties were, therefore, immediately set to work to cut down these crops and bring them over by a number of *nuggars* we had captured. When these were filled, the *Tewfikieh* towed them across. This made things pretty lively, and gave the river-side of the camp quite a harvest-home appearance.

Surgeon Ferguson and his staff, aided by fatigue parties, constructed a number of huts with the green *dhura* stalks on the top of the bank inside of the earthworks, in order to secure better and cooler accommodation for our wounded and sick. No terms of commendation can be too strong when referring to the kindness, care, and skill shown throughout this desert march by the medical staff attached to our column. Surgeon Briggs specially deserves honourable mention; for while he would not hesitate to give pain by cutting off a damaged limb if necessary, he was exceptionally gentle and kind, and especially so for an army doctor. General Stewart, I knew, appreciated his skill, as we all did, for the attention he paid to him.

In two other cases Surgeon Briggs also distinguished himself. One was that of Major Poe of the Marines, whose scarlet tunic, instead of cowing the Arabs at Metammeh, had drawn upon him a volley from them, resulting in a wound which necessitated the amputation of one of his legs, and for some days after the operation we feared he would not recover. The other case was that of one of the most popular officers of the force, Lieut. Crutchley of the Scots Guards, who had to undergo a similar amputation. Both these officers were, however, safely brought down to Korti and thence taken to England. I saw the latter soon after he was wounded on the 19th, when he told me with a sigh that he felt that his soldiering days were now over. During our march down to the Nile he was so weak as to be almost unable to speak.

When I saw him in the hospital at Korti upon his return from Gubat, he had resumed his accustomed cheerfulness, and when asked why they had not sent him down the river with the other convalescent wounded replied, 'I suppose I am kept here as a specimen of their skill!' And so in fact he was, for to get two such cases as were his and Major Poe's so successfully across the Bayuda desert, and subsequently to London, was an achievement quite in keeping with the other wonders of our wonderful expedition.

Before leaving Korti it was officially intimated that no correspondent would be allowed to go to Khartoum with Sir C. Wilson, because H.M. Government were unwilling that either the purport of the letter they were sending Gordon by him, or the reception which it was thought probable the latter would give to it, should be made public. The contents of that letter have been most scrupulously kept secret until this day, and perhaps it is well for the credit of all concerned. It is, however, mentioned here in order to account for none of us going to Khartoum with Sir C. Wilson. We had to submit to the inevitable under silent protest, and, while patiently waiting for the next event, to make ourselves as comfortable as possible under existing circumstances.

Melton Prior, Burleigh, and I settled down together again near the riverside, between the doctors' quarters and the hospital dispensary. Our huts this time were built with a view to a more lengthened sojourn at Gubat than our previous houses had been near the signal station. Prior and I stuck to the original pole plan of building, but Burleigh at first went in for a genuine native mud hut, but after getting his walls up a foot or so went back to our style. Coming into possession of a piece of looted native matting about 12 x 6 feet, I was able to build on such a scale as would enable me to set up a table or something equivalent to it. This I managed with two empty wooden boxes borrowed from the Commissariat and lent with great reluctance and only on the promise that they would be returned when wanted—that was for firewood. My camel riding saddle with its cushion made a comfortable substitute for my lost chair.

Burleigh managed to secure an '*angareeb*' or native bedstead. This article of Sudanese furniture was very simple in its construction, consisting only of four roughly made posts 30 inches in height, with head, foot, and side pieces let into them about two feet from the ground. The network of native grass rope supplied the place of a mattress. I always found them comfortable when long enough for a man to stretch himself upon, but this one of Burleigh's misfitted him by nearly a foot and was therefore to that extent uncomfortable.

Every morning, at sunrise, a strong detachment of our Hussars went out on picket duty. They scouted all round the camp, but their attention was specially directed to Metammeh. The enemy there seemed to have a wholesome respect for them, for, as a rule, their outlying pickets, some of whom could be seen in the early dawn on the top of a gravel-swell off the west side of the town, would immediately disappear when they caught sight of them. Sometimes, however, they waited to exchange shots with our scouts, but always with the same result.

Even the fierce *Baggara* horsemen appeared unwilling to cross swords with our Hussars, and contented themselves with observing them from a distance. This was fortunate, for although the horses had somewhat recovered from their fatigue, they were still unfit for a conflict with the enemy's cavalry, and our men would, if attacked, have been obliged to use dismounted fire. This was not the fault of Colonel Barrow or his officers, but the consequence of not employing men on dromedaries for scouting during our desert march. Our Hussars would then have travelled with the column along the caravan-track, where the going for horses was comparatively easy. Instead, however, of thus husbanding their strength, they were kept continually out on our flanks, riding over rough and broken ground. No horses could do such work without having their efficiency for more important services seriously impaired.

Not having immediate use for my own horse, I was glad to place him at the disposal of Lieutenant Young, of the Hussars. He was in better condition than any of their own horses, and through his steadiness under fire and other warlike qualities he secured for himself all the care the troopers could give him, and for his master the relief of providing for his wants.

The cruising of the *Es Safia* up and down the river helped to keep the enemy quiet, for they knew that she was now manned by us. Lord Charles Beresford took up his quarters on board of her on the 23rd, too ill, however, for service; and Captain Verner, who accompanied him, was for the time the fighting captain of our one 'ironclad,' aided by Mr. Webber, the 'boatswain.' On the 24th, the steamer started on a reconnoitring expedition down to Shendy, where they found the enemy in force behind a breastwork between the town and the river. A few turns of the lever of the Gardner gun, however, put an end to their rifle-firing and caused them to bolt

On the 26th the *Es Safia* paid another visit to the place, and when passing Metammeh was fired at, and replied by sending a few shells into the town. Later in the day, the steamer went five miles up the river beyond the camp, and had a skirmish with some of the enemy's sharpshooters. On the 27th she went down to Metammeh, and fired into the place her last twenty detonating shells, leaving for future requirements only those fitted with time-fuses, cut for 2,500 yards. On the river-bank below the town we could at certain hours of the day see the glistening of the bright rifle-barrels of the enemy. When abreast of this point they made it hot for her until a shower of lead from the Gardner gun was turned on them, when they quickly retired.

Jack was now himself again, and in these expeditions, being afloat, did excellent service in supplementing the fire of the Gardner. This recovery from the depressed condition into which what was left of the Naval Brigade was thrown by the loss of all their officers, is largely due to the presence amongst them of Captain Verner, and it is a strange omission on the part of Lord Charles Beresford that no mention is made in his published report to the Admiralty of the aid thus rendered him by that able and gallant officer. But such seems to be the custom in both naval and military circles, and as it has been from days of yore. Nelson, suffering from similar injustice done him, expressed the hope that one day he would have a gazette of his own. There were no war correspondents then sent abroad to do justice to our soldiers when in the field, as is the case nowadays, and so far as my colleagues—with one regrettable exception—and myself were concerned, no part of our duty affords us more gratification than supplying omissions of the kind just mentioned, which we believe may have been in this instance due to an oversight on the part of Lord Charles.

The enemy at Metammeh showed no inclination after our armed reconnaissance of it on the 21st to take the offensive, nor did they attempt to cut our line of communication. In fact, they seemed paralysed by the rough handling we had given them, and were also evidently demoralised by the number of wounded in the town. Some of its people who made their way into our lines said they would be glad to make friends with us, but were prevented by the dervishes. They also stated that the Arab force in Metammeh numbered between two and three thousand, of which 250 were horsemen and about 500 riflemen, and that they had three or four cannons, but were short of gun ammunition.

The only signs the enemy gave us of their existence was an ostentatious display of their force every afternoon, either outside of the town near its S.W. corner, or within it on the open space indicated in the plan. They also kept up an incessant beating of their *tom-toms* at night— beginning about eight p.m. or shortly after our 'last post' had been sounded. The rapidly repeated *rub-a-dub-dub* of this warlike music, softened by the two miles of distance between the camp and Metammeh, often reminded me of the wailing sounds of an Æolian harp; now louder, and then fainter, according to the force and direction of the wind. We always welcomed the commencement of this nocturnal concert, for it gave some assurance that the enemy would not molest us during the night

On the afternoon of the 28th our complacence was somewhat rudely disturbed by prolonged cannon and rifle firing in Metammeh. Ignorant that the enemy had heard of the fall of Khartoum, we connected these rejoicings with the arrival of the reinforcements which we knew the enemy expected from Berber, and from their liberal use of powder on the occasion we also inferred that they had received a supply of gun ammunition and an addition to their artillery. Anticipating therefore that the *dervishes* might now at any moment attack us, extra precautions were taken to prevent a surprise during the night. This was all we feared, for we felt confident of being able successfully to defend our strong positions as long as our food and ammunition lasted. We had a good supply of the latter, but our small pile of commissariat stores was daily growing most alarmingly smaller. Not only had we been put upon half-rations, but everything was being served out according to the regulation scale with scrupulous exactness.

Major Rainsford, the officer in charge of this important department, did what he could to eke out our limited supply of food. For example, he converted large quantities of the ripe *dhura* from the island, native fashion, into meal. This was mixed with flour and baked into bread. Captain Verner was able to purchase a few cattle and sheep from friendly natives six miles up the river, and this not only supplied us with fresh meat but helped to economise our preserved beef. Still the prospect was not reassuring, and we watched anxiously for the return of the convoy from Jakdul, sending up signal rockets at intervals in the evening, lest arriving near us after dark it might miss our position.

When our column left Korti on January 8, it was generally supposed that Lord Wolseley would follow it in a few days. This impression now deepened into a confident expectation of his arrival any day. If he still lingered in his sylvan abode on the Nile, we all felt absolutely certain that when he heard of our fight at Abu-Klea, and of the increased danger in which Gordon had been placed by the fall of Omdurman, he would at once push across the desert with reinforcements for his relief. As nearly a week had elapsed since he must, according to our calculations, have received this information, we concluded that he would put in an appearance at Gubat on the 30th or 31st. But, as our readers are aware, he never left Korti; and hereby hangs a tale.

The impression that Lord Wolseley would follow our column as stated was not without foundation, for on December 29 he actually telegraphed to Lord Hartington that he hoped to be able to start with all the Camel Regiments for Khartoum *via* Jakdul and Shendy on January 7.[2] As no reply to this telegram had been published, as was the case with regard to his similar proposal of February 11,[3] we may presume that H.M. Government disapproved of his intention to march on Khartoum.

This view is sustained by their instructions to him, in which Lord Wolseley was given to understand that they relied upon him not to advance further southwards than was absolutely necessary to attain the primary object of the expedition, namely, to bring away General Gordon and Colonel Stewart from Khartoum. In order to keep him as it were strictly within the lines thus laid down for his guidance in these instructions, he was directed to endeavour to place himself in communication with these beleaguered officers. Hence Sir C. Wilson's mission to Gordon, and the restraint put upon Lord Wolseley's movements until it was carried out

An injustice would be done to Lord Wolseley if we supposed that, with Gordon's letter of November 4 before him, and its confirmation by the intelligence he had received through his messenger on December 30, he did not on the latter date fully realise the critical condition of things at Khartoum. How otherwise can we reconcile his pressing anxiety about his friend 'Charley Gordon' in April and July with his inactivity at Korti at such a crisis, without supposing that he was officially prevented from hastening to his relief? No doubt Lord Wolseley would under these circumstances argue the case with the government

And there are reasons for supposing that he did do so, for during the first week in January (1885) several despatches were received from him, of so important and private a nature, that Lord Hartington deci-

---

2. Egypt, No. I (1885), p. 131.
3. Egypt, No. 9 (1885), p. 1.

phered them himself in order to prevent even the high officials at the War Office becoming acquainted with their purport.

Our expedition, therefore, as may be inferred from what has just been stated, was not—as we who accompanied it, and the British public, supposed at the time—sent across the desert for the immediate relief of Khartoum, but chiefly in order to ascertain if General Gordon's position was then so critical as to require an armed intervention for his rescue. In fact, this whole procedure was but the continuation of the efforts made in May, and subsequently, by H.M. Government to convey to Gordon the purport of their message of April 23 (see Introductory). Until his reply was received, Lord Wolseley's hands were thus virtually officially tied.

The wish for Lord Wolseley's arrival was also to a large extent father to the thought, for we were not only weak in numbers and limited in the matter of supplies, but were without a general. Colonel Boscawen, who had borne himself so bravely, was so ill with fever that he was obliged to hand over the command to Colonel Mildmay Willson, in whose soldierly qualities we had the fullest confidence; Colonel Barrow and his Hussars were fully occupied; and Lord Charles Beresford also, if he had been well, could not as a sailor be relied upon when infantry operations were required. Our staff officers were, without exception, cavalry men, and though gallant and zealous, were young and inexperienced in practical warfare.

Gordon's journal had been brought down by the *Bordein*, and two entries in it of December 13 and 14 when they became known had added to our anxiety. In his entry on the former date he told us that:

'If some effort is not made before ten days' time, the town will fall. It is inexplicable this delay. If the expeditionary forces have reached the river, and met my steamers, one hundred men are all that we require just to show themselves.'

It was now January 29, or over six weeks since these words had been written. Omdurman had fallen, the *Mahdi* had sent a large force to oppose us, and how could we now expect the twenty soldiers Sir Charles had taken with him, though dressed in red coats, to frighten him, and thus raise the siege of Khartoum? The terrible suspense and anxiety of this week at Gubat to which we have thus referred will not be forgotten by those who went through it Still, no man's heart failed him, for we knew, so far as we ourselves were concerned, we could hold our own, but if help and Wolseley did not soon come, what might not happen to beleaguered Gordon?

Early on the morning of the 21st, signs of unusual activity were noticed in Metammeh. About 10 a.m. a large force of the enemy formed up outside of the place, and we concluded that at last they were about to attack our camp. An hour later we were startled by the report of a gun, and hastened up to the signal station to ascertain what had happened. Watching a group of the enemy's horsemen on a height to the west of the town, I saw a shell burst among them, when they scattered with four of their saddles empty. The mass of the enemy formed up outside of the town, then disappeared in patches, and soon Colonel Talbot's convoy from Jakdul, accompanied by Major Hunter, with the other half of the battery of screw guns, and the second division of the Naval Brigade, under the command of Lieutenant Van Koughnet, much to our relief, came in; but no Lord Wolseley. We were now, however, in a better position to stand a siege if the enemy cut our communications.

Some anxiety was caused by a rapid fall of the Nile after the steamers had left us for Khartoum. In four days a pump, which had been originally placed upon its edge, was left a dozen yards inland by the receding water. By actual measurement on the 31st, we ascertained that the river had, within the period mentioned, fallen three feet. The *reis* of the *Es Safia* and her captain told us that while they feared Sir Charles' flotilla would, from their draught of water, have great difficulty in reaching Khartoum, they now felt they would run a greater risk in returning.

We have thus placed before our readers the condition of things at El Gubat from the time we occupied it until the evening of the 31st, and the feelings of hopefulness which then pervaded the camp. We all went to sleep that night, listening as usual to the music of the enemy's *tom-toms* at Metammeh, assured that ere long it would be replaced there by the sound of our bugles, for no one anticipated the rude awakening of the coming morning. But it came, nevertheless, in the message brought to us by Lieutenant Stuart Wortley, the sad burden of which was:

Too late, too late! Ye cannot enter now,

..... for he told us Khartoum had fallen, and that, although Gordon was reported to be still holding out in the stone Mission Church there, there was every reason to fear he had been killed. This news fell on us like a thunderbolt, crushing all our hopes, and filling us with sorrow and bitter disappointment. After our daring march across the desert, and fighting our way to the position we had been ordered to occupy on the Nile, and when we thought the object of our mission had been successfully accomplished, to find that we had failed was a crushing blow to our brave little force. And so far as regards the heroism it had displayed in its efforts for the relief of Khartoum, Sir C. Wilson's gallant struggle to reach it was a worthy climax, as will be admitted by those who have read his official report,[4] as well as his personal and graphic account of what took place after he left us on the morning of the 24th.

The drift of our narrative requires us to call the attention of our readers to a few of the leading incidents in what Lord Hartington so appropriately called, in his despatch to Lord Wolseley, the brilliant services of Sir C. Wilson on this occasion.[5]

The steamers made fair progress on the 24th, and on the 25th passed the first narrow passage of the Shabloka Cataract at 3 p.m., when their further progress was arrested for the night by the *Bordein* running on a rock, from which she did not get clear until 9 a.m. on the 26th. She was no sooner got off than she ran aground again and stuck fast for the whole day. A start was made at 6 a.m. on the 27th, and the Shabloka Cataract was passed through a rocky passage only 30 yards wide. Beyond the Jebel Royan, some Arabs shouted from the west bank that a camelman had passed, going north, who reported that Khartoum had fallen, and that Gordon had been killed. The steamers started at 6 a.m., when a Shagiyeh from the east bank confirmed this report, stating that the disaster had occurred two days previously. Discrediting this, Sir C. Wilson therefore prepared to force his way past the enemy's batteries into Khartoum, leading himself in the *Bordein*. The orders he gave to the detachment of the Royal Surrey were, to fire volleys at the embrasures of their batteries, while the Sudanese troops kept up an independent fire; and that the four guns of the steamers were to reply to those of the enemy.

On nearing Halfiyeh Sir Charles noticed that the large palm grove there had been burned, and that several large *nuggars* were lying alongside the bank. This latter circumstance led Khasm-el-Mus to conclude that Gordon's troops must be there, for the *Mahdi* had no boats. This impression was, however, immediately dispelled by the hot fire which

---
4. Egypt, No. 13 (1885), pp. 26-34.
5. Egypt, No. 18 (1885), p. 3, Telegraphic. 'To General Lord Wolseley. Express warm recognition of Government of brilliant services of Sir C. Wilson, and gallant rescue of his party.'

was opened upon the steamers from four guns and from rifles, at ranges of from 600 to 900 yards.

After passing Shamba just above Halfiyeh on the left bank, two guns opened on the little flotilla from the right bank with a heavy rifle fire from both banks, which was sustained until it came within range of the guns of Omdurman.

When abreast of Tuti Island, which Sir Charles expected to find in Gordon's possession, he says:

> We were received by a sharp musketry fire at from 75 to 200 yards range; three or four guns, of which one was certainly a Krupp, opened upon us from the upper end of Tuti, or from Khartoum, two guns from the fort at Omdurman, and a well-sustained rifle fire from the left bank.

When halfway up Tuti Island, under the impression that it was still in Gordon's hands, the steamers were run within sixty or seventy yards from the shore, ceased firing and asked for news. The only reply was a sharper and better directed fire. While it was thus made evident that the island was held by the enemy, Sir Charles thought that Khartoum might nevertheless be holding out, and still went on. No sooner, however, did they 'start upwards,' he states:

> Than we got into such a fire as I hope never to pass through again in a penny steamer. Two or more guns opened on us from Omdurman, and three or four from Khartoum, or from the upper end of Tuti; the roll of musketry from each side was continuous, and high above that could be heard the grunting of a Nordenfeldt or a *mitrailleuse*, and the loud noise of the Krupp shells.

Sir Charles still bravely kept on until the junction of the two Niles was reached, when it was apparent to everyone on the steamers that Khartoum had fallen into the hands of the *Mahdi*. He then ordered them to turn round and run full speed down the river, as it was hopeless to attempt a landing or communicate with the shore under such a fire as that to which they were now exposed. The scene at this moment is described by Sir Charles as very grand:

> The masses of the enemy with their fluttering banners near Khartoum; the long rows of riflemen in the shelter-trenches at Omdurman; the numerous groups of men on Tuti; the bursting of shells, and the water torn up by hundreds of bullets and

occasionally heavier shot, making an impression never to be forgotten. Looking out over the stormy scene, it seemed almost impossible that we should escape.[6]

After the steamers had moored in the evening. Sir Charles, in order to make assurance doubly sure, sent out two messengers, one to go to Khartoum and the other to collect information. The latter, on his return, stated that he had been told by a Jaalin Arab that Khartoum had fallen on the night of the 26th through the treachery of Farag Pasha and the *mudir* of the town, and that General Gordon was dead.

---

6. From Korti to Khartoum, 2nd Ed., pp. 176-177.

Chapter 20

Gordon's Faithfulness to the End

No one can read the thrilling account given by Sir C. Wilson of the danger to which his steamers were exposed in again running the gauntlet of the enemy's batteries and riflemen when he turned their heads down stream, without admiring his coolness and unflinching courage. The position in which he was then placed was at first most critical, for when the Sudanese troops realised that Khartoum had fallen they completely collapsed; and well they might, poor fellows, for now they knew they had lost wives, families, and all they possessed! Khasm-el-Mus, overpowered with grief, sank down into a corner of the turret and covered his head, and the brave gunner-captain of the *Bordein* forsook his gun, exclaiming, 'What is the use of firing now, for I have lost all?' With some trouble and not a few strong expletives they at length got him to fire again, and now, thoroughly roused, he served his gun with redoubled energy, until the steamers passed out of range of those of the enemy at Halfiyeh.

To Sir Charles the news that Khartoum had fallen, and Gordon was dead, was naturally a crushing blow, and seemed at first 'too cruel to be true,' he says:

> I think I should have collapsed like Khasm-el-Mus, if I had not had to think of getting the steamers down the cataracts, which I knew, from what the captains said coming up, would be a difficult and dangerous business.

And this it proved to be, for both of them, as our readers know, were wrecked as follows.

The *Talahawiyeh* struck a rock at 4.30 p.m. on the 29th, when nearly abreast of Jebel Royan, which made so large a hole in her bottom that she sank very rapidly between the rocks. Captain Trafford and Lieutenant Stuart-Wortley managed with great difficulty to get the men, with their arms, two guns, the rations, and small-arm ammunition, into a large *nuggar* which the steamer had in tow. About sunset they dropped down to a small island where the *Bordein* had been brought up, after the accident had occurred to her sister ship. The natives were landed on the island, but the British officers and soldiers went on board of the steamer.

On the 31st, after having cleared the cataracts, and when Sir Charles was speculating on his chances of safely passing the enemy's battery at Wad-Habeshi, the *Bordein* ran upon a rock, and immediately began rapidly to fill with water. The steamer was then brought up alongside a small island about fifty yards from the larger island of Mernat, about thirty miles up the Nile from our camp. The hole made by the rock in the steamer's bow was unfortunately below the waterline, and in a place so difficult to get at that all attempts to stop it failed. The men, guns, ammunition, and such stores as could be reached were landed on the small island. As Mernat, by which it was commanded, was found to be a miserable place for defence. Sir Charles decided to make a forced march down the right bank by moonlight with the Sussex and Sudanese soldiers, and to send the *nuggar* down the river with the sailors and a small guard.

When the order was given to the native crews and soldiers to prepare to start for the mainland in order to commence the proposed march down the river, they showed such a disinclination to obey it that Sir Charles decided to remain where he was until relief came to him from Gubat. In fact, the men were so demoralised by recent events that he did not know how far he could depend upon them. At 6.45 p.m. he therefore sent Lieutenant Stuart-Wortley in a small boat to report what had occurred, and to ask that a steamer might be sent to his assistance.

On February 1, leaving a guard of twenty natives on the small island, he moved the rest of the force over to Mernat with all the guns and stores, and formed a *zereba*. On the 2nd a friendly Shagiyeh brought news that a steamer had left Gubat on the previous day for his relief, and about 7 a.m. on the 3rd he heard the steamer *Es Safia* come into action with the enemy's battery at Wad-Habeshi; and shortly afterwards Captain Trafford, who was on the 'look out' at the end of the island, reported that he had seen her enveloped in smoke, and feared she had met with a serious accident. As the steamer continued to fire on the battery, and could be seen swinging at anchor, Sir Charles broke up his *zereba* and prepared to march down to her.

In response to Sir Charles's request through Lieut. Stuart-Wortley for assistance. Lord Charles Beresford was despatched by Colonel Mildmay Willson in this steamer at 2 p.m. on February 1. He took with him Lieut. Van Koughnet, and part of the 2nd division of the Naval Brigade which had so opportunely arrived on the previous day, twenty non-commissioned officers and men of the Mounted Infantry under Lieut. Bower, two Gardners, and two 4-pounder brass mountain guns. We watched the *Es Safia* with much interest as she steamed away from us up the river flying the St. George ensign, feeling assured that her gallant commander would on this occasion make as good a fight under it as he had done in the *Condor* at Alexandria in 1882.

The *Es Safia* came in sight of the enemy's battery at Wad-Habeshi at 8 a.m. on February 3, and immediately opened fire on it with her bow gun at 1,200 yards. On nearing it the Arabs opened a heavy rifle fire on her, and also from their gun in the embrasure facing down the river, to which Lord Charles replied with the Gardners and rifles when opposite the central embrasure; the enemy fired their gun from it, but the shot passed over the steamer, although owing to the depth of water she had to pass within 80 yards of it. When the *Es Safia* had got 200 yards beyond the fort, the Gardners could not be got to bear, and only a few of the riflemen were able to continue their fire on the embrasures.

The enemy then sent a shot from the gun on their embrasure facing up the river into the boiler, and let the steam escape in such a volume as to attract the attention of Captain Trafford on Mernat Island, nearly three miles up the river. Sufficient, however, was left to propel the steamer 300 yards further on, when she anchored. The enemy now redoubled their fire, until Lord Charles got one of the Gardners into action upon them through a hole he made in the after side of the steamer's battery, where he was able also to place one of the 9-pounder brass guns by cutting off about a foot of its trail with a saw. The latter, however, having no recoil, capsized every time it was fired.

The fire from this gun and the Gardner, and from as many rifles as could be got to bear upon it, was concentrated on the embrasure facing up the river, and upon the enemy's rifle trenches, from 8 a.m. until 8.30 p.m., and kept up without intermission by reliefs of men told off for the purpose. This prevented the Arabs from getting their gun to bear effectively on the steamer, and also from taking it from the earthwork to put it in another position in which they could do so.

The enemy managed nevertheless to keep up a hot rifle fire, and their bullets, Lord Charles says in his report, 'rattled like hail all over the ship.' They also fired several rounds from their gun, but owing to the hot fire kept up on them from the steamer they could not train it properly, and their shots travelled a hundred yards to the right of the *Es Safia*.

Sir Charles, after breaking up his *zereba* on Mernat Island, crossed over to the mainland from its lower end without opposition from the enemy, and embarked the women, the wounded, and the sailors and stores, &c., in the *nuggar*, with a small guard under Captain Gascoigne. He then marched his men down the right bank until opposite to where the steamer was anchored, when he learned by signal what had happened to her boiler. Bringing up one of the 9-pounder brass guns from the *nuggar*, which in the meanwhile had drifted down the river to where he had halted, the 'gun-captain' Abdullah Effendi and his black artillerymen soon brought it into action against the centre embrasure of the enemy's battery. Sir Charles also lined the bank with his black riflemen, and sent four of the best marksmen of the Sussex down to the river's edge, where they lay down on the sand and made excellent practice at 1,100 yards range.

Having arranged with Lord Charles to embark his party next morning at a more favourable point about two miles further down the river. Sir Charles, after sunset, sent Captain Trafford with the Sussex and part of the Sudanese soldiers to occupy it and form a *zereba*. He remained behind himself with the gun and a detachment of the latter to cover the *nuggar* while floating past the enemy's works. Unfortunately, the unwieldy craft no sooner began to drift down-stream than she ran on a sandbank and did not get off it until after sunset, and then soon after grounded on two rocks within four hundred yards abreast of the centre embrasure of the enemy's battery. Here she remained stuck fast, under a heavy gun and rifle fire, until 8 a.m. next day, but, singular to say, without a single casualty.

By a skilful ruse, Lord Charles led the enemy to believe he had abandoned the steamer, and at daybreak on February 4 got up steam, ran a short distance up the river to turn round, and then safely passed the enemy's battery; and having got Captain Gascoigne and his stranded *nuggar* afloat, picked up Sir Charles's party where they were waiting for him, and safely arrived at El Gubat shortly after sunset.

Thus ended our last effort to rescue Gordon and relieve Khartoum. It failed, but from no lack of heroism and zeal on the part of its commander or of the officers and men under him. For twelve days they had been under fire, and although, from the admirable manner in which their two steamers had been 'blinded' by the late Colonel Stewart, only two Sudanese had been killed and twenty-five wounded, it was a wonder that they had not been either sunk or disabled by the heavy gun-fire to which they had been then exposed. This speaks volumes for the able manner in which Sir C. Wilson and his officers handled their little flotilla, and for the gallantry shown by Gordon's black soldiers while the steamers were forcing their way past Halfiyeh and Omdurman. Although they had to run the gauntlet of the enemy's batteries at these points, and were under a continuous heavy fire, they never flinched.

It was only when all hope failed them of reaching Khartoum that they lost heart and became demoralised. Then followed intrigues and threatened mutiny, desertions of some to the enemy—including the captain of the *Bordein*—and the treachery which wrecked both steamers. That this demoralisation did not result in a complete disaster must be attributed to the tact, coolness, and courage Sir C. Wilson displayed in the trying circumstances in which he was thus placed. We notice, therefore, with no little surprise that Lord Wolseley, in a despatch to Lord Hartington at the time, almost entirely ignored his services, while he extravagantly eulogised those of Lord C. Beresford in the fight he was forced to make at Wad-Habeshi on February 4 in order to rescue his steamer from the perilous position in which no prudent 'leader of men,' however rare his fighting qualities, would have ventured to place her.

We have no wish to detract from the bravery exhibited by him on that occasion, for with Sir C. Wilson we heartily admit there have been few pluckier actions than that sustained by the *Safia* whilst her boiler was being repaired. But was it fair for Lord Wolseley in the above despatch merely to allude to Sir C. Wilson's gallant effort to communicate with General Gordon as 'his endeavour to reach Khartoum in a steamer,' and to refer to the detailed account of his twelve days' fighting, which he enclosed to Lord Hartington at the same time, only as 'an interesting diary of events and of Sir Charles Wilson's proceedings on that occasion'?

We can only account for this ungenerous treatment of a brave and able officer on the ground that Lord Wolseley wrote this despatch when he was almost bewildered through bitter disappointment at the entire failure of his own plans for the rescue of Gordon and the relief of Khartoum. After relying upon their successful issue, it was too cruel to be true, as he appears at the moment to have thought, that he had perished and that Khartoum had fallen. Therefore he expressed his dissatisfaction to Lord Hartington that Sir Charles had not pressed on to the beleaguered city when he had approached so near it. Though Omdurman and Tuti Island had fallen into the hands of the *Mahdi*, he expressed the opinion in a previous despatch that, as it was not clear that any shots had been fired from the place itself on Sir Charles Wilson's steamers, there was a gleam of hope that Khartoum remained uncaptured.

This view of matters he seems to have thought corroborated by the fact that no rumour as to the fall of the city or the death of Gordon had then (February 9) reached any of the villages near Korti. He also seems to have given undue weight in this connection to the rumour brought to him by young Stuart-Wortley that Gordon had shut himself up with a few determined men in a stone mission church, for he points out to Lord Hartington its position in Khartoum, on a map of the place enclosed in his despatch.

Lord Wolseley, misled by these and other conflicting reports, and by the state of his own feelings at the time, even blames Sir Charles for the failure of the expedition, by suggesting that he should have reached Khartoum on January 25, and that if he had done so the place would not have been surrendered. The ground upon which he bases this opinion is that Gordon had said that the presence of a few British soldiers in his steamers at Khartoum would ensure his safety and that of the place.

We have already shown that it was impossible for Sir C. Wilson to have left Gubat under any circumstances early enough to reach Khartoum on that date, and from no fault of his own. It is true, as Lord Wolseley remarks, that Gordon did say that the presence of a few British troops on board of his steamers would save him and Khartoum. But he said this on December 13, in these words:—

> All that is absolutely necessary is for fifty of the expeditionary force to get on board a steamer and come up to Halfiyeh, and thus let their presence be felt; that is not asking too much, but it must happen *at once*, or it will be (as usual) too late.

And in the last entry in his journal, on December 14, he said it again in these emphatic words:—

> Now *MARK THIS!* If the expeditionary force, and I ask for no more than two hundred men, does not come in ten days, the

town may fall, and I have done my best for the honour of our country.

This last warning and sad appeal for help only confirms other warnings and appeals Lord Wolseley had received from Gordon on previous occasions. We refer specially to his letter of November 4, in which he informed him that he could hold out easily until December 14, but that after that it would be difficult. But this warning was not heeded. In an entry in his journal on November 8 Gordon seems to have understood the way in which his appeals for speedy help were being acted upon, for he wrote as follows:—

> If Lord Wolseley did say he hoped to relieve Khartoum before *many months*, he must have a wonderful confidence in our powers of endurance, considering that when he is said to have made this utterance we had been blockaded six and a half months, and are now in our ninth month.

Lord Wolseley must since have learned from Gordon's published journals and Colonel Kitchener's *Notes on the Fall of Khartoum* what good reasons there were for anticipating any day after December 24 the catastrophe which happened at Khartoum on January 26.

From all sources of information we learn that on December 14 the town was in such a critical state as to warrant the fear that it might fall in ten days, for there was then in store an amount of food which represented eighteen days' rations for the garrison alone. On January 1 this supply would have been exhausted.

The fort of Omdurman had been provisioned for six weeks on November 3, and this supply would therefore be exhausted on December 20. All communication with it had been cut off since Gordon's steamers had been sent away to meet our expedition; and there is good reason to fear that it was short of ammunition, from the same reasons, for the supply asked for by its commander, Farag Pasha, could not be sent over to it

The *Mahdi* had learned from deserters the straits for food in which the garrison now was, and he hoped the town would fall into his hands without fighting. Until, therefore, he heard of our approach, he quietly waited for this result

Stewart's first half-dash across the desert seems, however, to have roused him to action, for Omdurman fell into his hands between January 6 and 13.

This was a serious matter for Khartoum, for it enabled the Arabs, by the erection of batteries on the left bank, to close the White Nile to Gordon's steamers and to complete the investment of the place through the establishment of ferries south of it, by which a constant and rapid communication with their positions on that front could be carried on.

On January 18 the state of the garrison was desperate from want of food. All the dogs, cats, donkeys, and even the rats had been eaten up. A ration of gum was now issued daily to the troops, with bread made from the pounded fibre of the palm-tree. Gordon, it is said, during these days never slept, but constantly went round the various posts encouraging the soldiers to stand firm by the assurance that a British army was coming to their rescue. His state of mind is expressed with sad eloquence in the following telegram:—

> From Gordon Pasha to the Sovereigns of the Powers.
>
> Khartoum, December 29, 1884.
>
> (*After salutations.*) I would at once, calling to mind what I have gone through, inform their Majesties the Rulers of Great Britain and the Ottoman Empire, who appointed me Governor-General of the Sudan for the purpose of appeasing the rebellion in that country, that during the twelve months I have been here, these two Powers—the one remarkable for her wealth, and the other for her military force—have remained unaffected by my situation, perhaps relying too much on the news sent by Hassan Pasha Khalifa, who surrendered of his own accord.
>
> Although I am personally too insignificant to be taken into account, the Powers were bound nevertheless to fulfil the engagements upon which my appointment was based, so as to shield the honour of their Governments.
>
> What I have gone through I cannot describe. The Almighty God will help me.[1]

On January 20 the news of our defeat of the *Mahdi*'s picked troops at Abu-Klea created consternation in his camp. Hearing on the 22nd that our column had reached the Nile at Metammeh, which it was supposed he had captured, he decided at once to attack Khartoum before reinforcements could enter it

Rumours were also prevalent in Khartoum itself of the fighting

---

1. This is from the copy of a telegram brought down from Khartoum by a telegraph clerk, who was for some time held prisoner by the Dervishes, but escaped. The original, he says, was concealed in a rifle cartridge and sent down to Dongola. Its authenticity, which was at first doubted, is now admitted by Sir C. Wilson, Colonel Watson, and Sir Henry W. Gordon.

at Abu-Klea and of our arrival at Metammeh. On the 23rd it seems that Gordon had a stormy interview with Farag Pasha, when the latter probably made proposals to him for the surrender of the town. On the following day the question of its surrender was discussed. Some on the Council were of opinion that it could hold out no longer and should be surrendered on the terms offered by the *Mahdi*, apparently through Farag Pasha. Gordon would not, however, listen to the proposal. On the 25th he was slightly ill, and, although he did not appear in public, had several interviews with leading men, and evidently knew the end was near. That night many of the famished troops left their posts in search of food in the town, and many of them were too weak for duty through want of food. This caused considerable alarm in the town, and many of the principal inhabitants with their slaves replaced these famished soldiers on the fortifications.

About 3.30 a.m. on Monday, the 26th, the *Mahdi* made his pre-determined assault on the town, making his principal attacks on the Boori Gate, at the extreme east end of the line of defences on the Blue Nile, and on the Messalamieh Gate on the west side, near the White Nile. The attack on the former place was repulsed, but at the latter, having filled the ditch with bundles of straw, brushwood, beds, &c., they penetrated the fortifications. The defenders of the Boori Gate, taken thus in the rear, retired, leaving the town at the mercy of the enemy.

It is doubtful whether Farag Pasha was guilty of the treachery which has been ascribed to him; but Hassan Bey Balmasawy, who commanded at the Messalamieh Gate, did not, Colonel Kitchener thinks, make a proper defence, and failed to warn Gordon of the attack by the enemy.

There are also some grounds for suspecting that Farag Pasha interfered with the existing telegraphic communication between the palace and the parts along the line of fortifications, so as to prevent General Gordon from being promptly warned of the attack of the enemy on the town.

That he opened the gate to the enemy has, however, been distinctly denied by the colonel of a battalion of irregulars, when the town fell, and by a number of refugee soldiers who came to Dongola before it was evacuated by our troops. In fact, all the accusations of treachery against him seem to have been based on mere supposition.

A careful consideration, however, of all the information yet obtained bearing upon the subject, confirms the opinion that the town fell 'from sudden assault, when the garrison was too exhausted by privations to make a proper resistance,' and that Gordon was killed while on his way to the stone mission church, which, it is known, contained all his ammunition, and had been prepared for defence in case of such a contingency as had now occurred.

And so fell Khartoum, after its noble resistance of 317 days; maintained by the indomitable resolution and resource of one Englishman, who, from a sense of duty, and in defence of the national honour, fell with it rather than desert his post.

He told Sir Evelyn Baring in a telegram on March 1 1884:

> I will do my best to carry out my instructions, but feel convinced that I shall be caught in Khartoum.

In the entry in his journal of November 8, after complaining of Lord Wolseley's alleged wonderful confidence in the further powers of endurance of the people's garrison of Khartoum, he further writes:—

> I am quite sure of one thing, that the policy followed up till lately is one which will act detrimentally on our army, for what officer, if he was in a fortress, could have any confidence that it might not be advisable to abandon him?

Her Majesty's Government told me, or, rather, my friend Baring told me, I was not to leave Khartoum for the equator until I had permission. I have his telegram saying if I leave Khartoum I should be acting against orders.[2]

In a previous entry, October 13, 1884, he had written as follows:—

> We are a wonderful people; it was never our government which made us a great nation; our government has been ever the drag on our wheels. It is, of course, on the cards that Khartoum is taken under the nose of the expeditionary force, which will be *just too late.*

How sadly justified by the event were these instinctive forebodings of General Gordon, and how accurate, also, was his estimate of the causes which brought it about!

To these causes, so far as the Gladstone Cabinet is concerned, I have from the very first specially called attention.

---

2. Egypt, No. 12 (1884).

So far as the forces engaged on the expedition are concerned, I have shown that it was not their fault that Gordon and Khartoum perished.

Although I have felt called upon to differ from Lord Wolseley on the views he expressed in his despatch of February 15, as to the ultimate cause of the failure of the expedition, I agree with him that it was not from any lack of energy on their part, for my narrative confirms this declaration:

> All ranks worked as hard as human beings could, hoping to render the earliest possible assistance to their comrade who was besieged in Khartoum.

At the same time the fact cannot be disguised that several mistakes were made in the conduct of the expedition, which contributed to its failure.

Amongst these the most serious, perhaps, was that made in the middle of November, when the information was received from Gordon that, after December 14, he would be in a most difficult if not desperate position.

Instead of then waiting until the whole force had passed up the cataracts by the whalers, all efforts should have been concentrated upon despatching the Camel Corps, or part of it, across the desert to Khartoum.

This, as we have shown, could easily have been accomplished, for any number of camels could have been obtained from the Kabbabish, and Sir Evelyn Wood had accumulated a good supply of (British) commissariat stores at Hannek.

Unfortunately, the opinions of General Butler and the other Red River men, who had pledged themselves before leaving England to the success of the boat-transport scheme, prevailed, camel transport was neglected, and consequently it was December 30 before Lord Wolseley, as he himself admits, was in a position to make a dash across the Bayuda desert[3] Even then, from lack of camel transport, he could

---

3. Lord Hartington, in submitting the Supplementary Estimates to Parliament for the expedition on November 13, 1884, stated that Lord Wolseley had determined to concentrate 2,000 troops at Debbeh, whence he could send them as a mounted force across the desert to Khartoum. (See map.) This operation may, he further said, supersede the very considerable one of sending five or six thousand men in boats all the distance. He characterised the former as a 'much smaller and more rapid' operation than the latter, which had only been provided for in the event of greater resistance being encountered than was anticipated.

only send with General Stewart a part of the Camel Corps on the expedition, for he had to dismount the heavy camel regiment, as we have seen, and to supply the transport for the stores the Guards took with them.

Had a thousand more camels then been available, General Stewart could have gone on to Metammeh and reached it on January 6 without firing a shot. Yet Lord Wolseley tells us in view of all these facts, in the despatch referred to, that ' no time was lost in pushing across the desert to Jakdul, because he left Korti for there almost a month before the last regiment to arrive had reached Korti.'

As a set-off against our expedition being too late to relieve Khartoum, it has been alleged that the place might, or indeed would, have fallen through treachery on the approach of a British force, even if it had been despatched for its relief at an earlier date. But, as my readers will remember, this was the danger which confronted Gordon on his arrival at Khartoum, and which was increased by the delay of the Government in sending the aid he needed in order successfully to cope with it. In a despatch from which I have already quoted he told the Gladstone Cabinet that conspiracy was more to be feared in Khartoum than open revolt. And yet in face of such a peril they left him alone month after month to contend against it, until at last he was hemmed in by the *Mahdi*, and his garrison reduced to the last extremity from want of food, and then turned round and pleaded as an excuse the inevitable nature of a catastrophe which their own neglect of duty had chiefly contributed to bring about.

Although we have no conclusive evidence that Khartoum did fall through treachery, as is implied by the allegation referred to, the danger arising from its known existence in the town should have been guarded against in the conduct of the expedition. This was specially important with respect to the despatch of the Desert Column. In order to avert danger from this source, in place of being first sent to occupy Jakdul, it ought to have rapidly pushed on to Metammeh. Had this been done, the *Mahdi* would not have had the eleven days' notice he had of our advance by that route in which to avail himself of any treachery he knew to exist in Khartoum, or to take the measures he did to prevent our communicating with the place.

Merawi might have been occupied, but not another soldier nor a biscuit should have been sent up the Nile beyond Korti until we had joined hands with Gordon. If camel-transport was lacking, the whole or part of the intended Desert Column should have been marched on foot in order to secure this object.

The crisis of the expedition was now reached, and every possible effort should have been made to meet it successfully. Late as the expedition had been started, and delayed as it had been by unforeseen obstacles in its ascent of the Nile, it was now within measurable distance, as regards both time and space, of Khartoum, and not an hour should have been lost in reaching it. I have already explained how we failed in a previous chapter, and will only further remark here that, in the opinion of competent military authorities, all the other mistakes made in the conduct of the expedition sink into insignificance compared with this one. It is so sad to think that after the heroic struggles made by Lord Wolseley and the force under his command, he was thus too late to rescue Gordon and relieve Khartoum.

That success was so nearly attained despite all the difficulties with which it had to contend, proves conclusively that Lord Wolseley could have successfully accomplished the object for which he was sent, had the expedition been despatched a month, or, as he himself asserts, a fortnight, earlier. This is abundantly borne out by the facts I have given with respect to its cause and issue. It was indeed a triumph of military skill, in face of all the difficulties with which he had to contend, for a general to have transported supplies for an army of 10,000 men so far inland in so short a time. In fact, the whole plan of the expedition in this and other respects was thoroughly British in its boldness of conception, and could only have been adopted by Lord Wolseley from a full reliance upon the troops who were to be employed in its execution. Foreign military critics, especially those of Germany, have enthusiastically acknowledged all this, and have rightly accounted for its failure by the dilatoriness of H.M. Government in authorising its despatch. This was, indeed, the unfortunate cause which, despite the heroic efforts of its chief and the forces engaged under him in it, made the Nile Expedition too late for Gordon and Khartoum.

Appendices

Appendix A.

Note.—In all their correspondence with General Gordon, both Sir Evelyn Baring and Mr. Egerton merely carried out instructions sent them by Lord Granville. A careful perusal of the Blue Books will show that both these able officials often demurred to the course being pursued towards Gordon by Her Majesty's Government.

Extract from Gordon's Journal (September 23, 1884).

I am sure I should like that fellow Egerton; there is a bighearted jocularity about his communications, and I should think the cares of life sat easily on him. He wishes to know exactly 'day, hour, and minute,' that I expect to be in difficulties as to provisions and ammunition. Now I really think that if —— were to turn over the 'archives' (a delicious word) of his office, he would see we had been in difficulties for provisions for some months. It is as if a man on the bank, having seen his friend in river already bobbed down two or three times, hails, 'I say, old fellow, let us know when we are to throw you the life-buoy. I know you have bobbed down two or three times, hut it is a pity to throw you the life-buoy until you really are *in extremis*, and I want to know exactly, for I am a man brought up in a school of exactitude, though I did forget (?) to date my June telegram about that Bedouin escort contract.

Anyone reading the telegram May 5, Suakim; April 29, Massowah; and, without date, Egerton saying, 'Her Majesty's Government does not entertain your proposals to supply Turkish or other troops in order to undertake military operations in Sudan, and consequently if you stay at Khartoum you should state your reasons,' might imagine one was luxuriating up here, whereas I am sure no one wishes more to be out of it than myself. The 'reasons' are those horridly plucky Arabs. I own to having been very insubordinate to her Majesty's Government and its official, but it is my nature, and I cannot help it I fear I have not even tried to play battledore and shuttlecock with them. I know if I was chief I would never employ myself, for I am incorrigible. To men like Dilke, who weigh every word, I must be perfect poison. I wonder what the telegrams about Sudan have cost Her Majesty's Government.'

APPENDIX B.

In the following entry in his journal, on October 5, 1884, General Gordon summed up the situation:

> Let us consider dispassionately the state of affairs. Does her Majesty's Government consider they are responsible for the extrication of the Sudan garrisons and Cairo inhabitants? We can only judge that her Majesty's Government does recognise this responsibility, for otherwise why did they send me up, and why did they relieve Tokar? Once this responsibility is assumed, I see no outlet for it but to relieve the garrisons, *coûte que coûte*. It may be said that the object of the present expedition is for my relief personally. But how is it possible for me to go away and leave men whom I have egged on to fight for the last six months? How could I leave after encouraging Sennaar to hold out? No one could possibly wish me to do so. No government could take the responsibility of so ordering me.
> There is this difficulty; perhaps it would be patriotic to bolt; but even if I could get my mind to do it I doubt if it is possible to get my body out of this place. Had Baring said in March, 'Shift for yourself as best you can,' which he could have done, the affair could have been arranged, and we could have bolted to the Equator; but if you look over my telegrams, you will see I ask him what he will do, and he never answered. The people had not then endured any privation, and I was, as it were, not much engaged to them; but now it is different, especially as we have communicated with Sennaar.
> No one can judge the waste of money and expense of life in the present expedition—it is an utter waste of both—but it is simply due to the indecisions of our government Had they said from the first, 'We do not care—we will do nothing for the garrisons of the Sudan, they may perish;' had they not relieved Tokar; had they not telegraphed to me as to the force to

relieve me (*vide* telegrams. May 5, from Suakim; April 29, from Massowah); had they telegraphed (when Baring telegraphed to Cuzzi, March 29, which arrived here saying, 'No British troops are coming to Berber, negotiations going on about opening road—Graham was about to attack Osman Digna'), 'Shift for yourself,' why nothing could have been said; but Her Majesty's Government would not say they were going to abandon the garrisons, and, therefore, 'shift for yourself.' It is that which has hampered us so much.

On the one hand, if I bolted I deserted them (Her Majesty's Government); on the other hand, by staying I have brought about this expedition. Baring gave me distinct orders not to go to the Equator without the permission of her Majesty's Government (*vide* telegrams with Stewart's *Journal*). I do not question the policy of her Majesty's Government in not keeping the Sudan. It is a wretched country, and not worth keeping. I do not pretend even to judge the policy of letting the garrisons, &c., &c., perish; but I do say, I think that her Majesty's Government ought to have taken the bold step of speaking out and saying 'Shift for yourself' in March, when I could have done so, and not now, when I am in honour bound to the people after six months' bothering warfare.

Not only did Baring not say, 'Shift for yourself,' but he put a veto upon my going to the Equator—*vide* his telegrams in Stewart's *Journal*. I say this because no one deplores more the waste of money and life in this expedition, and no one can realise its difficulties better than myself, but owing to what has passed, owing to indecision, we are in for it, and the only thing now to do is to see how to get out of it with honour and the least expense possible— and I see no other way than by giving the country to the Turks.

Appendix C

Suez, February 19, 1877.

My dear Mr. Janson,—Could you, if the viceroy gave you them, utilise the four elephants he has on the railway works? You would have to see the *mahouts* and arrange for their pay, and bear them on your budget, and also see to their transport to Wady Halfa. I have asked about them.—Yours sincerely,

C. E. Gordon.

Reply Telegram.
Animals cannot be used; there is no proper food for them.

Janson.

Suez, February 21, 1877.

My dear Mr. Janson,—I count on your helping me in many other ways than as engineer of railway, and, therefore, send you the enclosed note.—Yours sincerely,

C E. Gordon.

(Enclosure.)

1. Report on nature, cost, &c., of placing two strong towing tugs on river between Hannek and Ambukol, either by taking them up in sections and putting them together at Hannek, or else by taking them up at high Nile (this latter course is practicable, for I have steamers at Khartoum of 250 tons, which came up Nile from Alexandria). (Enquire about this.)

N.B.—I should ask you to see to the working of these steamers, when in position, and put them under your orders.

2. Report on river from Ambukol to Berber; I must see in any reports if the river has ever been examined on this length. With respect to No. 2 report on river 'from Ambukol to Berber,' have you a sharp fellow who can undertake this work, and what would be the cost of the same? Nowadays we can get steamers which are powerful and draw but little water.

Massowah, March 11, 1877.

My dear Mr. Janson,—Thanks for your letter and the contents and the information. Mind and keep all my letters to you. Let us clear up all our debts, even if it causes a stop to the works; anything is better than debts unpaid.—Yours sincerely,

C. E. Gordon.

En route to Khartoum, November 16, 1877.

My dear Mr. Janson,—It is of the greatest import to me to get steamers on the river all the way up to Khartoum, so pray consider your time not lost in going carefully over the arsenals at Cairo and Alexandria. Look on the railway as finished with respect to its future, *i.e.* it will eventually go up to Dahl, but never beyond it. I want you to get all information you can about the small steamers, and also to study the question how to get them up. If the Arabs, with one Frenchman, a Count some one, took up seven 200-ton steamers from Cairo to Khartoum, surely you, with so much greater means, can take up smaller steamers. Now what I would do would be—

1. Enquire well into the cost of the coal; bricks 3*l*. 6*s*. per ton, you said.
2. Try and pass up to Hannek one of the screw steamers at Wady Halfa; then,
3. Go up to Merowa and examine that rapid, and pass up a steamer through that, then you can go up in that steamer to Habou Hamed and examine that, and so on, building up as you go, till you reach Berber, where Khartoum steamers can meet you. You said there was between Halfa and Hannek a bit of open river for forty miles; put one screw steamer on that, and the other above Hannek: that will take us without expense to Merowa. You have little idea of the importance of this work, and it *must be done in 1878 right up to Berber;* you may want, perhaps, three largish steam launches, make an effort in it, and let the railway be quiet to some degree.

Think over those rock borers with compressed air; we can at any rate remedy the cataracts with them. Tell me some men you do not want, and I will *congé* them, and take on some men like Baird, your engineer, but with no wretched contract for any length of time. I wish I had told you more of how important the putting of the steamers on the river is. Now kindly have all the extraordinary expenses made out in Arabic and sanctioned by me, also all removals of men of any position. I do not want two kings. Send home for me kindly, as soon as you can, the gunstock I gave you. Johannis is delighted to come with me to take Wahad El Michael, so says a telegram from Sinkat I have no further news of the attack on Fazogli. Do not stay longer at Cairo than necessary, if you think you can do anything at Wady Halfa about the rock borers or the steamers, but if you cannot you might wait for me till about the beginning of February, when I might, if I escape all my foes, come to Cairo, but you will always be able to know my whereabouts from Burrot Bey, and whether I am coming or not to Cairo. Do not say much about putting the steamers on Nile. When they are placed on it we will run them once a month, and charge a great price from Wady Halfa to Khartoum. I calculate it would only take fourteen days from Cairo to Khartoum.—Yours sincerely,

C. E. Gordon.

Debbé, November 14, 1877.

My dear Mr. Janson,—I arrived here yesterday. No further news from Khartoum since I left you. I enclose a letter to Burrot Bey to ask His Highnesses permission to examine the steam launches &c., &c., at Cairo and Alexandria You can make a good inspection, and I feel sure we may pick up some useful boats. Take the letter yourself to Burrot Bey some leisure day.— Yours sincerely,

C. E. Gordon.

Grummur, halfway to Khartoum from Debbé, November 17, 1877.

My dear Mr. Janson,—I wrote to you two days ago, but I fear the letter may not reach you. 1st. Kindly send the gunstock to England by the first chance you have. 2nd. I want all appointments or dismissals on the railway staff notified to me for approval, at least of any of the superior *employés*. I want all extraordinary expenses, such as travelling bills, stationery, postage, &c., made out in Arabic and submitted to me. 3rd. Consider the railway question as settled. I want you to attend to something more important to me, which is—4. To plan in 1878 a chain of steamers on the Nile from Wady Halfa to Berber. Put one of your screw steamers on the open water you told me exists for forty miles between Wady Halfa or Dalule and Hannek rapids, keep the other screw steamer above Hannek rapid to run to Merowe rapids. This will dispose of the two screw steamers, and will cost us only a trifle (you will surely be able to get them up, for one Frenchman (a Count something) and the Arabs got up 250-ton steamers right up to Khartoum).

Now when in Cairo and Alexandria devote your time to seeing if there are any launches or steam tugs likely to suit in the arsenals or owned privately, and prepare a note of their prices. We shall want four to make a chain of steamers up to Berber. Never mind even if they are small; to make the chain of steamers is *all important to me*. However slight and frail the chain may be, it will at any rate enable us to go and examine the river, which now would require months to do, and which examination has never been made as yet. I may come to Cairo about February 1, but I am not certain if I shall do so. However, have all papers about these steamers ready. You can surely form an idea of how I want this chain of steamers completed by 1878. If you see any things which might be useful in Sudan and which are useless at arsenals at Cairo and Alexandria, take a note of them for me.

I think about utilising the rock borers; they may remedy the falls or rapids even if they do not cure them. Think about marking out the deepest channels in the rapids, by beacons either on shore or on the rocks. I will send official orders for the taking up of the two screw steamers, &c., &c., at a later period. Kindly get me a 3s. 6d, penknife (English), and send it to me at Massowah. I hope to get the chain of steamers on Nile in 1878, and in 1879 to commence tramways around such of the rapids as require it (placing camels, about twenty, at each rapid in the meantime) and making good houses at each rapid.

I shall charge 60l. per passage with 10 cwt. of goods (and I think I shall gain) from Assouan to Khartoum; when I succeed I shall ask His Highness to give me the steamers below Assouan, and then I shall charge 80l. from Siout to Khartoum, and run the steamers once a fortnight, or once in three weeks.

Goodbye, and believe me, yours sincerely,

C. E. Gordon,

Tor Desert, November 19, 1877.

My dear Mr. Janson,—(Such a pen and such ink!!!) Camels will do well enough for tramway draught. I used one for drawing a cannon in Darfour, and they plough with them in Turkey. Find out all about tramway, the inclines, curves, &c., &c., any prices of tramway plant—we shall not need much. I feel sure that His Highness will be glad of it. It will be a great thing to utilise the Nile. It is by far the simpler mode; a railway is too exotic a plant to flourish in these countries. Said Pacha had a screw steamer at Debbé twenty years ago. If you have any spare engine power, we could work a wire rope railway or tramway around the rapids. Next winter you must take the rails around the rapids for the tramways by your officers at Wady Halfa. I count on your putting the chain of steamers right up to Berber in 1878.—Yours sincerely,

C. E. Gordon.

P.S.— I can get sleepers up along the river for the tramways.

Abou Karey, November 27, 1877.

My dear Mr. Janson,— Will you send me by post, to await me at Massowah, a packet of clips such as you use to bind papers together, and oblige me? Fazogli alarm was all rubbish, and I am going to be down upon the authors of the report. I want no such luxuries as cushions in the steamers intended for the Nile. I wish you to have made out in Arabic and sent to Khartoum by the Vakeel simple tabular forms to be used quarterly and yearly and to contain the information—

ASSOUAN RAILWAY.
Quarter ending ——

Expenditure.	£ s. d.	Credit.	£ s. d.
Administration		Freight of goods	
Coal, &c.		Freight of passengers	
Incidentals		A. Government account, freight of goods	
		B. Government account, freight of passengers	

A and B of course will not be paid in cash, but it will show in it if the railway pays.

   Railway from Wady Halfa to X Station.
Ditto Form,

   Steamers from Assouan to Wady Halfa.
Ditto Form,

You will, at once, catch my idea, and beware of making any intricate form, for it will be no use. The form must be as simple as it is possible to make it—Yours sincerely,

C. E. Gordon.

March 14, 1878.

My dear Mr. Janson,—What you seemed to say tonight was equivalent to a recommendation to give up the railway altogether, and to draw off the whole affair. Though I see very little prospect of getting any money, I don't agree to this view, and shall do this, *viz.*, finish off the workshops in a satisfactory way, build the bridges, blast out the rock, and do the earthwork up to Ambukol. This done, I may work on further, say for three or four years; then I may be out of my troubles, and able to buy the railway plant, for I am in the Sudan for my life, or until His Highness leaves it, or discharges me. This is my determination; tell me yours. Believe me, yours sincerely,

C E. Gordon.

Appendix D.

Journal of Company H, L Batt., Royal Irish Regiment.
Sarras to Korti.

December 18.—Started from Sarras at 10.30 a.m. No wind. Halted at 11.30 a.m. at a place where towing was necessary, as about twenty boats had to go in their turn before us. Hauled boat until 5 p.m., when another short stop occurred, then hauled on till 6 p.m. when halted for night at lower gate of Semneh Cataract.

December 19.—Hauled through lower gate after C and half of A Companies. Then were stopped by another block. Pro ceeded. Rowed and hauled to first rapid by Semneh Gate where the Voyageurs were stationed.

December 20.—Started unloading at 6 a.m. and then had to wait for the upper line to be clear before the Voyageurs would take us up. Started hauling up about 9 a.m. and having got six boats through were stopped by the Naval Brigade cutting in. They took seven boats up, thus delaying us about three hours.

Two of my four last boats were injured coming up in charge of the Voyageurs. I had to take one of them out of the water for repairs. It took the whole afternoon to plank her inside and patch her with tin outside.

December 21,—Started loading the injured boat at 4 a.m., and got away about 6 a.m. My leading boat. No. 567, was upset in the next rapid while being towed up; the two men in her escaped, but lost tool-box and stores and all my own papers. Hauled up the boat and repaired her and started again about 11.30 a.m., reaching Semneh about 12.30 p.m., finding our first section were through the gate. We unloaded and our boats were passed through.

December 22.—Portaged all our stores and started again at 2.30 p.m. Wind unsteady. Had to track almost all the way. Hauled up for night three miles above Semneh at 5.30 p.m. No. 566 boat was (mended by R.E. at Ambigol) condemned as unsafe, but as we could not get a better we patched her up.

December 23.—Rowed all morning till we came to high precipitous rocks on left bank of river. F Company in front. Had a very long and arduous 'track' along the shore and camped in bay beyond with F Company.

December 24.—Hauled up two bad rapids. At the second one of F Company's boats was injured and half stayed behind to repair it. A Company had also lost a boat and rifles here. The natives, for 3*s*., gave us great assistance, and we got over the rapid safely and then rowed, tracked, and sailed with stronger breeze until we reached the first of the big rapids at Ambigol, where we halted for the night.

December 25 (Christmas Day).—I read service for the men in Wilson's camp. Father Brindle said Mass at 6.30 a.m.

We then worked our boats up to near the portage point.

December 26.—Took the boats round the point, unloaded, carried the stores up the hill, where we bivouacked.

December 27.—Natives began to portage the stores, but only took over four boatloads during the day. Sent a man back to W. Halfa, one of whose legs had been badly cut by rocks.

December 28 (Sunday).—Father Brindle said Mass at 6.30 a.m. The remaining six boatloads of stores were carried over the portage by camels. Loaded up and started about 12.30 p.m. Passing a bend in the rapids, boat 761 was swept back on to a rock and so damaged that I spent till afternoon mending her. Colonel Wynn said he would give me a certificate showing how I was unavoidably delayed at Ambigol. Camped for the night at Mar Island.

December 29.—Found this morning that boat 761, repaired yesterday, was still leaking badly. So we unloaded her at 8 a.m., hauled her up on the shore, and put two more tin patches on her. This made three of my patches, besides nine others put on this 'whaler' by her previous occupants. Delayed consequently three hours. Caught up to Wilson and the other six boats about the long rapid. One of the boats (617) had been injured, and the Voyageurs said she could not go on. Her keel had been taken dean off; the iron strap was bent, keeping it from coming to again. *Upon examination I found the keel had only been fastened to the bottom by small nails.* Went to work and removed the iron strap, when the keel came back into its place. Then we found out that we had no long nails, so took some out of the bottom board (fourteen) and drove them through the keelson into the keel and made it tight, turned her over, caulked and poured pitch all along her seams, making her apparently better than ever. We worked on her until late into the night.

January 2.—Passed the second Okmeh rapid all right, and then sailed or rowed for two or three miles. At one rapid three boats got up rowing, and the other two could not as the wind failed. Tried to haul one up, but it stuck fast on the rocks, right out in the stream, as it was all shallow water. Had to unload her and bring the boxes through the water on land, and then took the boat back. Then took eight good men to row and pulled each boat up, then tracked all afternoon. Three boats camped together near Akasheh, and the two others a mile further on. Mended 742 boat here.

January 3.—Started early, but was delayed a long time at one place by the rope being caught by a rock far out in a dangerous rapid. Eventually we had to cut the rope and take the boat back. All the men got wet crossing to some rocks today. Reached Akasheh at 2 p.m. and hauled through the rapid five miles towards Dal, camping at sundown.

January 4.—Reached Dal at 11.30, put boats through rapids and reached Saremato by evening, leaving three boats behind, one having to be repaired.

January 5.—Had to recaulk 617 again, as its keel had started again, and reached station about noon. Rowed against a strong current for four miles, when boat 742 was forced by the current on to a rock near the islands, and had to haul her up on one of them for repairs. Camped there.

January 6.—Had a long tiring row against a strong current. Rocks numerous until we reached Awara about 3.30 p.m. Wind very light. Put through the rapids in half an hour by the Canadians and went on about two miles, and camped.

January 7.—Father Brindle walked back to get tidings of Wilson and his boats. I had bathing and washing parade and then parade with rifles and accoutrements.

Heard that Wilson had repaired his boat below the cataract. Sent him some nails. Started again about 1 p.m. Very hot. No wind. Rowed and tracked till sunset. Very hard work. Wind ahead.

January 8.—Started at 5 a.m. without cooking. Rowed and hauled till 8 a.m., then halted for breakfast. About 9 a.m., a breeze having sprung up, sailed for Say Island and camped opposite to it.

January 9.—Sailed half an hour before sunrise with splendid breeze, which kept on the whole day. About noon boat 761 struck a rock, and lost three hours repairing her. C, E, D, and G Companies joined me, and Wilson also came up. Started again with six boats about 3 p.m. and sailed till sunset, camping near an old Egyptian temple.[1]

January 10.—Sailed at sunrise with high wind. Sailed, rowed, tracked all day and caught up my own section at Absarat. Left two men in hospital with ophthalmia.

January 11.—Sailed at sunrise with a slight breeze, which gradually died away. Sailed, rowed, and tracked all day, until within two miles of Kaibar, and camped.

January 12.—Sailed a little after sunrise. No wind all day. Rowed and tracked past Kaibar rapid to a little above, and Wilson and five boats below cataract.

January 13.—Sailed. Wind all day. Reached foot of Hannek rapids at 4.30 p.m. The Voyageurs told us nothing about them, so we went on until it got dark. Three boats got over, but two were left behind in a very dangerous place.

January 14.—Father Brindle went on with two boats. I came back along the shore to look for the boats left behind. Found one about halfway. Got the men to track, and reached camp in about an hour's time. Got both boats over and started for Hannek. The men had a tremendous hard time of it, pulling and rowing all day, as there was no wind. River here very bad, strong currents and rocks, and with no one to guide us. Camped at sunset.

January 15.—Found we could neither haul nor sail, so put ten men in each boat to row and go over the Hannek rapid. Worked very hard all day, rowing and tracking. Water very shallow till we reached Hannek, from whence the Canadians piloted us round to Abou Fatmeh, where we camped for the night. Drew three days' rations to complete twelve days from here.

January 16.—Found we had to patch up three boats here, Nos. 567, 654, and 357, all injured in the cataract. Commandant ordered one boat to be given up for Canadians' return voyage, gave up 617, and distributed her crew among my section. Camped in same place.

January 17.—Sailed at 6 a.m. with a high wind, which died away

---

1. Left bank opposite Knotungo.

about midday. Rowed rest of the day and camped on Argo Island.

January 18.—Father Brindle held divine service at 6.30 a.m. Wind ahead and very hot. Rowed and tracked all day and camped on another part of the Island of Argo. People very civil. Plenty of eggs, milk, and dates. Sheik Mustapha gave us bread, dates, and pumpkins.

January 19.—Rowed and tracked in the morning until a dust-storm came on, which helped us very much till wind got ahead. Camped opposite Dongola that night I went over and stayed in Colonel Blundell's tent and dined with him and Sir I. Arthur and Colonel Quirk.

January 20.—Went out into the town at 6.30 a.m. and bought pipes, matches, and onions for the men, and butter for myself, and sailed again at 9 a.m. with a strong breeze which continued till sunset, when we camped on the desert side (right bank).

January 21.—Sailed at 6.30, with a nice breeze, which grew stronger towards noon and lasted till evening. Camped with seven boats, and one other in front and another behind us.

January 22.—Fresh breeze all day, but in the afternoon the river turned, so that the wind was of little use to us. Camped on E. bank with seven boats.

January 23.—Reached Debbeh at 9 a.m. and drew rations, and sailed at 11 a.m., but found breeze a good deal ahead. The whole company camped together again to-night—nine boats, three officers and eighty men.

January 24.—Wind ahead. Tracked all day and camped at night about eighteen miles from Korti.

January 25.—Tracked all day and camped five or six miles from Korti.

January 26.—All my nine boats arrived together at Korti at 11.30 a. m., and Lord Wolseley sent to ask whose boats they were, and said he was pleased.

February 1.—Marched for Gakdul and Metammeh.

Appendix E.
Hard Work for the Boat Corps.

The following letter from an officer of one of the regiments forming the 'Boat Corps' graphically illustrates how arduous its work was.

Writing from Dal on New Year's Day, 1885, he says:—

Here we are, having been only fifteen days on the way between Sarras and Ambigol, so we have not therefore done badly, for some of the companies took twenty-four days and others even more. But I am awfully fagged out with the hard work and the responsibility of the men's lives. On the 22nd I was at Ambigol, a very bad cataract which extends nearly three miles, and as there were heaps of boats waiting to be hauled through, and as nearly all the stores had to be taken out of the boats and carried by "niggers" and camels three miles round, you may imagine what this entailed. We were lucky to get away in two days. That night I slept among the rocks, as it was too steep to pitch any tent. On the 23rd we had a very hard and harassing day's work, only moving the lot about 800 yards.

On the 24th we shoved the things on again nearly three miles to the end of the obstruction. I worked all the while like a common soldier—not that there was any necessity, but it encouraged the men. You can imagine the strength of the rapids when I tell you that the whole company of seventy-nine men generally assists in hauling one boat through; the boat must be kept head to the current, or she is nearly sure to be lost. It is very exciting when the boat reaches the middle of a boiling rushing cataract In accordance with orders we all wear lifeboat belts, so dangerous is the work.

The 27th was a most wretched day's work, and we had some nasty pieces of water to get through; one of our boats got broadside in a rapid, capsized, struck on a rock and stuck there. One of the men in her was swept out, but caught hold of a biscuit-box and landed safely a mile lower down; the other, a Canadian, got ashore by means of a line. We lost all the stores except the rifles and ammunition. We generally see a boat or fragment of one floating down stream every second day. Up to this date there have been forty-nine men drowned, ten of them Canadians. When I got to the head of the Tanjour Cataract, the commandant told me he had orders to push all boats through as they came in, so on I went, but not in my own boat, and consequently without my kit

Both of the Canadians were attacked by dysentery, and we had to leave them in the hospital at Tanjour; obeying orders, I had to go on without my kit, and, worse still, *minus* my Canadians. As soon as I got four boats together, I pushed on, fearful every moment of going on some hidden rock. It is a great responsibility feeling one's way up a dangerous river, with little or no knowledge of it, and with men in the boat, some of whom don't know the stern from the bow. I had a rather narrow squeak at one place.

I was steering my boat through a decently strong rapid, with the man in the bows with a pushing pole to keep her as much as possible off the rocks, when, not having enough men on the rope, the current caught her head and swung her round, and she struck on a rock and all but capsized That was an exciting five minutes. The boat sprung a bad leak, which necessitated baling all the way here, where she is being repaired. Just fancy only going two miles after a very hard day's work!

The 30th was also a very hard day. We saw a man of the 18th Regiment drowned in a rapid, and this did not put our men into better spirits, one man in my boat actually refusing to get in and row her through a rather rapid bit of water. I had to make an example of somebody, for the men were getting demoralised, so I made a prisoner of him and had him hauled into the boat. On the 31st we did better, and got through Ambigol Cataract, with the aid of Canadians stationed there. The worst was now over, and we had a jolly eight miles sail to this place, and I am most thankful that we have arrived safely, when so many good men had gone down.

Our daily routine is as follows. We rise at dawn—about 5.30—tents packed by 6, tea or coffee ready by 6.30, breakfast eaten by 6.50, start by 7, struggle on until 12, when we get an hour for dinner and a ration of limejuice, then go on until sunset, when we halt, pitch tents, and sup. Our fare consists entirely of what the men call "bully beef" and biscuits; so our menu is not complicated.

We move to the head of the cataract here tomorrow, our boats being hauled through by Egyptian soldiers, and our stores (100 days, which each boat carries) carried round by camels and Dongolese labourers. The worst is over now, and our journey to Dongola will be free to a great extent of the cares and dangers of our awful work.

General Gordon
"For all men recommend patience; few, however, they are who are willing to suffer."—Thomas à Kempis

The Battles of Abu Klea & Abu Kru

Chapter 1
The Khartoum Relief Expedition—Abu Klea—Before the Battle.

There was on 31st December, 1884, a brief message dated from Khartoum on December 14, brought into the camp at Korti:

Khartoum all right. Signed, C. G. Gordon.

Verbal answers given by the messenger seemed to prove that Khartoum was not quite so well to do as was here represented, and that the cheerful tone of the message was, perhaps, meant to deceive the *Mahdi* should it fall into his hands. At any rate the execution of the plans for relieving Khartoum was pushed forward as speedily as possible. An expeditionary force under two divisions was moved on to Gakdul wells, in preparation to the move on Metemmeh. The next move was to the wells at Abu Klea, but before they could reach them a great battle had to be fought, for the enemy had collected in great force. Mr. Burleigh, who was present at the battle, tells us that:

"Just before dark on Friday, January 16th, 1885, as we turned in within our *zareba*, we fired two shells at a group of two hundred or so of the enemy gathered upon the top of the black hills on our left face. The missiles fell among the Arabs, who quickly dropped out of sight, leaving, however, two white banners standing out boldly on the sky line. Their sharpshooters meanwhile having crept to within 1,200 yards of our right flank, and their fire proving annoying, a half company of the Mounted Infantry went out to drive them back. The Arabs at the same time were also potting at us from their front at long range, which subjected the square to a transverse fire. The long range and the high trajectory of their Remingtons left scarcely any place safe from their bullets, many of which dropped down almost perpendicularly.

"We soon, consequently, had our first wounded to attend to, and many of the camels were also struck. After nightfall our pickets and sentries, who were posted outside the square or *zareba*, were all drawn in to seventy-five yards from our lines. As the moonless hours wore on the enemy increased their fire, and bands of them marched about from point to point, banging their battle-drums and making a most execrable din. The Hadendowas at Tamai were good enough not to treat us to so much '*tom-toming*,' which is beyond all discordant noises successful in irritating and worrying a sensitive ear. If anything deserve future punishment, and can insure it, then it surely is the constant performance before battle of a full orchestra of 'one-ended drums,' such as the *Mahdi's* force possessed. The savage sounds rose and swelled all through the night, forming a fitting accompaniment to the wail of their bullets. Our crack shots were permitted to reply occasionally to the Arab fire whenever it became too inquisitively searching.

"Evidently we were in for an uncomfortable time, and the officers were enjoined to see that their men were at their posts with bayonets fixed, ready to spring to their feet on the first alarm. With their overcoats on and their blankets wrapped round them the men lay down close behind the low walls and line of bushes, with their heads to the front. All lights were put out after dark, and talking and smoking even were forbidden. A stillness broken only by the *whizz, ping,* or thud of the enemy's lead hung over the square, even the tired camels grunting far less than customary. During the earlier part of the night I had a long chat with Colonel Fred. Burnaby, who expressed his delight at having arrived in time for the coming battle. He had been appointed, he said, by General Stewart to the command of the left face and rear of the square, and on the morrow would be virtually discharging the duties of a brigadier-general. He had got to that stage of life, he continued, when the two things that interested him most were war and politics; and, whether it was 'slating' an unworthy politician or fighting against his country's foes, he expressed himself equally exhilarated and happy.

"Much more he confided to me, but neither time nor the occasion now avail for the repetition of that chat, destined to be the 'last words' of a noble and fearless gentleman. About ten p.m. on Friday, January 16, our sentries came running into the lines, and there instantly arose that indescribable murmur—half-shout, half-inarticulate roar—that heralds 'a night scare' and an attack upon a camp of armed men. The officers called out, 'Stand to your arms, men.' There was little need for the order, for all except a very few sluggards were promptly ready at the first sound to repel the expected attack and rush of the Arabs. It turned out, however, a false 'alarm,' or, at any rate, if any numbers of the enemy had been threatening a nocturnal assault nothing came of the movement. Ere day broke we had three more of these 'alerts,' each terminating as the first had done; that is to say, the men were kept on the *qui vive* for a quarter to half an hour, and then were allowed to go to sleep again, which not all the whizzing of the enemy's bullets could keep the tired soldiers from doing Before the first rosy tints of day tinged the eastern sky, or, as General Stewart's orders defined it, 'when the planet Venus rose, the troops were all to get up and stand to their arms till daylight'

"Towards morning the air became sharp and cold, and it was with little reluctance the troops left their chill bivouac. When it became light enough Captain Norton, of the Royal Artillery, fired three rounds of shrapnel at a party of the enemy's sharpshooters, who had been worrying the square all night by shooting from a hill 1,500 yards on our right flank. After this there was a brief lull, only a few dropping shots falling in the *zareba*. Our total loss during the night was comparatively light—not more than five or six wounded, of whom three were natives and one a hussar—but many camels were wounded and several killed. An early breakfast was now prepared, and with hot tea and coffee, beef and biscuit, the soldiers regaled themselves. Before they had finished their meal the Arabs, to the number of two hundred, had again come down from the knife-edge of the range of hills on our right flank, and were delivering a well-aimed fire from a distance of 1,100 yards at our position.

"A troop of the Hussars and some of the Mounted Infantry were at once sent out as skirmishers. They succeeded in driving the enemy towards the east, in the direction of their main force. A little later five hundred spearmen, with a few *Baggara* (cavalry), came sweeping down as if to attack our right; but a round of shrapnel, which was burst over their heads, knocked over three or four Arabs, and scattered the others. Still, their rifle-fire was being well maintained; the number of our wounded was steadily increasing, and many camels and horses were being hit.

"As the Arabs still showed a disposition to attack us, bands of them continually appearing and disappearing on our front and right, it was determined to try a ruse to draw them on. At about 1,800 to 1,900 yards on our left front could be seen masses and lines of rebels, their bright broad spear-heads and two-edged swords glittering in the sun's rays. With *tom-toms* fiercely thumming, and scores of heathenish banners fluttering in the fresh northerly breeze, they swarmed everywhere along the crests of the rolling foothills, and threatened to rush us. Close to the *wady* on our left there were probably 3,000 or 4,000 of them, deployed in two not very irregular lines of men four to five deep. Their leaders, sheiks or dervishes clad in conspicuously embroidered *Mahdi* shirts, were stationed at intervals of about twenty-five yards apart, and mounted on fleet little horses. The lines were at least half a mile long, whereas our front barely extended, when in square, to 150 yards. A strong force of skirmishers, Guards and Mounted Infantry, were now sent out by General Stewart, and they engaged the enemy at 1,200 yards range, gradually reducing the distance to 1,000 yards.

"At a preconcerted signal our skirmishers rose together and ran back upon the *zareba*. It was all to no purpose, however, as the enemy did not pursue for more than 200 yards. The stratagem was repeated without better success; so, despairing of inducing them to assault our position, the screw guns were turned upon the Arabs on our front, and they were treated to a few rounds of shrapnel, which quickly sent them to cover."

Such were the preliminaries to the battle.

Chapter 2
The Battle of Abu Klea.

"At seven o'clock General Stewart began his preparations for sending forth an attacking column, which was to march in square and on foot as if ours had been an infantry force. The object was naturally to drive the enemy from Abu Klea wells, which were four or five miles on our front. The enemy, it will be observed, had taken up ground three miles to the west of the wells. Their position was strong, but they could have chosen a much better one had they defended the crest of the hills two miles or so behind our *zareba*, where begins the descent into the *wady* which leads to the wells. There they would have had complete shelter for their men until our troops got within thirty or forty yards of them, and at the same time could have witnessed all our operations and movements, which must have taken place on the open plain below. As the camels were to be left behind, their packs were unloaded, and saddles and stores were taken to strengthen the detached works surrounding the *zareba*.

"The animals themselves were herded closer together in the centre of the enclosure, and securely tied down. Shortly after seven a.m. the troops were marched to a position close behind the ridge on our front, surmounted by the low stone wall. Each detachment as it came up was ordered to lie down to await the moment for the advance. About one hundred beasts only were included in the 'fighting square,' fifty-two for carrying *cacolets* and litters for the wounded, the rest for medical stores, water, and ammunition. I was glad there were so few camels going, and sorry there were not fewer, for although by his size he is a good breastwork against bullets, the camel obstructs vision, impedes mobility, destroys symmetry, and is an unsettling element in a square of men.

"Precisely at 7.35 a.m. the troops marched forward in the following order: Front face (left to right), Mounted Infantry, Royal Artillery with three guns, Guards. Right face (front to rear), Guards, Royal Sussex. Left face (front to rear), Mounted Infantry, Heavy Cavalry Regiment. Rear (left to right), Heavy Cavalry Regiment, Naval Brigade (with Gardner), Heavy Cavalry Regiment, part of Sussex Regiment. The 19th Hussars, under Colonel Barrow, numbering ninety sabres, were sent to our left flank to advance along the spur of land on the north of the *wady*, and in front of the stone outwork held by the company of the Royal Sussex. Their duty was to move forward on a line parallel with the square and prevent the enemy attacking our left from the high ground across the little *wady*. A squadron of the 19th, counting thirty sabres, followed the square, marching by the front right to assist the skirmishers, Mounted Infantry and Guards, who were sent out seventy-five yards from the square to keep the enemy's sharpshooters from coming too near.

"The Heavies were commanded by Colonel Talbot, the Guards by Colonel Boscawen, the Mounted Infantry by Major Barrow, the Naval Brigade by Lord Charles Beresford, the Royal Sussex by Major Sunderland, the Royal Artillery by Captain Norton, and the Royal Engineers by Major Dorward. The command of the Mounted Infantry devolved upon Major Barrow—a brother of Colonel Barrow. At the last moment Major Gough, the commanding officer of the Mounted Infantry, had been lying down behind the ridge on the crest of which was the stone wall protecting our front, awaiting the order to march, when a spent ball struck him on the back of the head. The '*crack*' was audible for yards around, and we who were near thought

BATTLE OF ABU KLEA—DEATH OF BURNABY.

he was killed.

"In a few minutes, nevertheless, he recovered consciousness, and it was seen he had only received a severe contusion. Several others were struck at the same time, and one of the gunners lost his finger, and owed his life to carrying an iron key in his hand at the moment a bullet struck him. Altogether the situation was exciting and serious, and narrow escapes were becoming much too frequent. As the men rose from the ground, and the square advanced at slow march, our front showed above the slope, and the enemy promptly saluted us with a brisk rifle fire. In lines two deep—not of four men, as squares ordinarily are formed—our 1,400 or thereby of fighting men advanced. Major Gern, of the Sussex, with a company of men and details, was left in command of the *zareba*, in which were over fifty sick and nearly a score of wounded. With frequent halts to pick up our wounded—the dead were left where they fell—the square trudged on, the men as steady as if on parade. Our line of route was parallel to the little *wady* on which the left of our *zareba* rested.

"Onward we marched, keeping the *wady* eight hundred yards to our left. One moment we tramped along the stony upland crests or slopes, and then we would make an abrupt descent into some little gully or watercourse, climbing again up the opposite bank. Our progress was like that of some huge machine, slow, regular, compact, despite the hail of bullets pouring in from front, right, and left, and ultimately from the rear. A mile from the *zareba* the square halted to pour in a few volleys at a force of 1,500 Arabs demonstrating on our right. We anticipated their main attack would fall upon our front or left, and it was thought best to clear the flank threatened before going further on. Altogether there were perhaps 10,000 to 12,000 Arabs gathered to oppose us. They swarmed upon our front, and for two or three miles on either flank groups of their horsemen and spearmen could be seen watching us from the rocky peaks. There was no avenue of retreat; it was now '*do or die.*'

"Colonel Barrow, with his small force of Hussars, became engaged about the same time as the square. He took ground in advance of the outwork upon the circular hill held by the Sussex, dismounted the greater portion of his men, and opened fire at a body of 200 horsemen and 200 or 300 footmen trying to creep around our left. They gave him all he could do with his small force, for the ground offered ready shelter from the fire of the troopers' carbines, and his advance lagged behind the march of the square. When our flanks became comparatively clear, with our ranks well drawn together, the square once more advanced, but slower and more cautiously than before. We were rapidly passing to the flank of the enemy's outlying position. The Arabs appeared more numerous every moment, sometimes showing in lines of battle array as if they meant to charge the square, and *anon* disappearing behind a ridge, or sinking out of sight in the water-scored lumpy ground, covered with scrub and bunch grass just as Roderick Dhu's clansmen vanished at a wave of their chieftain's hand.

"There was no questioning now among old campaigners whether the Arabs would fight, and General Stewart and his personal staff, consisting of Major Wardrop, Lord Airlie, and Captain Rhodes, galloped to right and left to keep the force in readiness to repel any attack. With all deference to the gallant Heavies, it was felt to be a trial for them, a much mixed cavalry force, fighting on foot as infantry and with the long rifle, to which they were unused. Onward our fighting square moved, the enemy forming up as if to charge, and after a volley or two, given by companies, getting again out of sight By half-past nine our left face was well abreast of their right, or the position it had held, and we could see before us that the stony upland along which we marched sloped down a mile ahead into the vast flat plain that reached away right clear to the Nile. The hilly, rocky ground was being left behind, and, with the exception of a low ridge or two a mile east of the wells, the *sabas*-covered land stretched forward, unbroken, by a single hillock, far to the east and south-east

"At 9.50 a.m., just as the front of the square had crossed a narrow depression and gained the top of the little crest on the opposite side, we saw a force of 4,000 to 5,000 of the enemy echeloned in two lines on our left, or opposite the side of the square maintained by part of the Mounted Infantry and the Heavy Cavalry regiments. They were four hundred, or perhaps five hundred, yards distant, and looked like coming on. Dervishes on horseback and on foot marshalled them, standing a few paces in front of the fanatic host. With fluttering of banners, clamour of '*tom-toms*,' and shoutings of '*Allah*,' they began to move towards our square.

"At first they came slowly, not quicker than a fast walk. Our skirmishers' fire appeared to have little or no effect upon them, and the whole left face of the square, which now halted upon the high ground, turned their rifles upon the Arabs, with, however, not much better results. Very few of the *Mahdi's* force fell, their lines were scarcely marred, and the miscarriage of our bullets must have inspired them with the hope that Mohammed Ahmed had at last conferred upon them charmed lives. They were soon within three hundred and fifty yards of the square, and now they commenced to run towards us, coming over the rolling ground like a vast wave of black surf.

"At first their direction was towards the left face front corner of the square, but as they came nearer the great mass of them swung round, so as to strike the rear corner of our left face. The skirmishers along our left came running home at full speed towards the square, closely pressed by a fringe of bloodthirsty Sudanese. At this moment the Gardner gun, under Lord Charles Beresford's superintendence, was moved to the left face rear corner, to be brought into action. During the advance it had been fired occasionally at groups of the enemy, and performed good service in clearing them off some strong positions upon dominating ridges. When it was now most wanted, before three rounds had been fired the cartridges stuck, and the weapon was rendered temporarily useless, an accident to which, as Lord Charles afterwards declared, all machine guns with a rotary feed motion are perpetually liable.

"Still down upon us the dark Arab wave rolled. It had arrived within three hundred yards almost undiminished in volume, unbroken in strength. It was a rush of spearmen and swordsmen, scarcely any carrying guns. Their rifle fire had practically ceased; and the other Arab forces surrounding us—*Mahdi's* troops, plundering Bedouins, and pillaging villagers from the riverside—all stood eager on the hillsides watching the charge upon the British square. In wild excitement, their white teeth glistening, and the sheen of their brandished weapons flashing like thousands of mirrors, onward they came against us.

"By twos and threes our skirmishers had now reached our lines, and, the left face being nearly clear, a volley was sent into the enemy at one hundred and fifty yards: as they rose over the last crest between our opposing lines. A hundred or more Arabs dropped, and for a moment I saw their force waver and halt, as a man stops to gasp for breath or at any sudden surprise. Had that volley been promptly repeated there would have been little more of the Battle of Abu Klea to tell except the rout and slaughter of the *Mahdi's* troops, for *Mahdi's* troops they were, and not mere villagers or swarming tribesmen arrayed against us. But, somehow, the firing that followed from our ranks was dropping, irregular, scattering, wild, without visible effect; and the Arabs, who had barely checked their run, leaped over their falling brethren and came charging straight into our ranks.

"I was at that instant inside the square, not far from the Gardner gun, when I saw our men beginning to shuffle a little backward. Some say Colonel Burnaby issued an order for the men to 'fall back;' but—I can speak confidently on this point—though near him, I never heard it. That, however, is a small matter, and it may have been issued all the same. At any rate, the left face moved somewhat backwards, and slightly towards the *zareba*. Colonel Burnaby himself, whose every action at the time I saw from a distance of about thirty yards, rode out in front of the rear of the left face, apparently to assist two or three of our skirmishers, who were running in hard pressed. I think all but one man of them succeeded in reaching our lines. Burnaby went forward to the men's assistance sword in hand. He told me he had given to his servant to carry that double-barrelled shotgun which he had used so well against the Hadendowas at El Teb, in deference to the noise made in England by so-called humanitarians against its use. Had it been in his hands Burnaby would easily have saved other lives as well as his own, but they would have been English lives at the expense of Arabs'.

"As the dauntless colonel rode forward on a borrowed nag—for his own had been shot that morning—he put himself in the way of a sheik charging down on horseback. Ere the Arab closed with him a bullet from some one in our ranks, and not Burnaby's sword-thrust, brought the sheik headlong to the ground. The enemy's spearmen were close behind, and one of them suddenly dashed at Colonel Burnaby, pointing the long blade of his spear at his throat. Checking his horse and slowly pulling it backward, Burnaby leant forward in his saddle and parried the Moslem's rapid and ferocious thrusts; but the length of the man's weapon, eight feet, put it out of his power to return with interest the Arab's murderous intent. Once or twice I think the Colonel just touched his man, only to make him more wary and eager. The affray was the work of three or four seconds only, for the savage horde of swarthy negroes from Kordofan, and the straight-haired, tawny-complexioned Arabs of the Bayuda *steepe*, were fast closing in; upon our square.

"Burnaby fenced smartly, just as if he were playing in an assault at arms, and there was a smile on his features as he drove off the man's awkward points. The scene was taken in at a glance with that lightning instinct which I have seen the desert warriors before now display in battle whilst coming to one another's aid—by an Arab who, pursuing a soldier, had passed five paces to Burnaby's right and rear. Turning with a sudden spring, this second Arab ran his spear-point into the colonel's right shoulder. It was but a slight wound—enough, though, to cause Burnaby to twist around in his saddle to defend himself from this unexpected attack. Before the savage could repeat his unlooked-for blow—so near the ranks of the square was the scene now being enacted—a soldier ran out and drove his sword-bayonet through the second assailant. As the Englishman withdrew the steel, the ferocious Arab wriggled round and sought to reach him. The effort was too much, however, even for his delirium of hatred against the Christian, and the rebel reeled and fell.

"Brief as was Burnaby's glance backward at this fatal episode, it was long enough to enable the first Arab to deliver his spear-point full in the brave officer's throat. The blow drove Burnaby out of the saddle, but it required a second one before he let go his grip of the reins and tumbled upon the ground. Half a dozen Arabs were now about him. With the blood gushing in streams from his gashed throat the dauntless Guardsman leapt to his feet, sword in hand, and slashed at the ferocious group. They were the wild strokes of a proud, brave man dying hard, and he was quickly overborne, and left helpless and dying. The heroic soldier who sprang to his rescue was, I fear, also slain in the *mêlée*, for—though I watched for him—I never saw him get back to his place in the ranks."

Chapter 3
Abu Klea— Close of the Battle.

"But what of the square? We had fallen back one hundred yards, and the foremost Arabs were driving their spears at our men's breasts. They were yet too few, however, to make any serious break in our ranks, and, desperately as they charged and fought, rifle and revolver bullet, and more rarely bayonet point, stopped their career. Then the great onrush came, and with spear poised and sword uplifted straight into our left face, rear corner, the Arab horde struck us like a tempest. The Heavies were thrown into confusion, for the enemy were right among them, killing and wounding with demoniacal fury. Backward from the left face the square fell, staggering and irregular. Officers exerted themselves to keep their men together, and General Stewart himself rode to the broken corner to assist. His horse was here killed, and he himself was with difficulty extricated and saved from Arab spears.

"Lord Airlie received two slight spear wounds, and so did Lord Charles Beresford. The enemy's rush swept clean over where the

Gardner gun had been placed, and the small naval contingent lost two officers and six men killed, defending their gun as at Tamai. It was actually one of the same weapons that was used in that equally terrible fight. Confusion for the instant reigned supreme as the men fell back towards a low circular mound.

"The charge of the Arabs carried many of them into the centre of our square and among the camels. There death and havoc rioted for two or three minutes, whilst our men moved off from the inextricable mass of wounded, dying, and dead camels. It was an awful scene, for many, alas! of the wounded left behind on the *cacolets* and litters perished by the hands of the merciless Arabs, infuriated by their sheiks, whose wild hoarse cries rent the air, whilst the black spearmen, entangled among the animals, ran hither and thither thirsting for blood. Amid the general calamity there were many providential escapes. Lord St Vincent, who, with another wounded man, was being borne upon a pair of camel-litters, was overturned with his camel, and fell underneath; the wounded man, who was on the opposite side, was killed, and St. Vincent owed his life to the accident. Trifling as was the obstacle offered by the heap of helpless animals, it was enough to break and disorganise the rush of the Arabs. So great at this moment was the peril of the situation that officers in the Guards and Mounted Infantry placed their men back to back to make a desperate battle for life.

"The Martini-Henrys had never ceased, for hundreds of men kept firing steadily and with good aim at the enemy. There were others, I regret, who were neither discreet nor careful as to the direction of their fire. Possibly much of the wildness of aim was occasioned by the excitement of finding that hundreds of the cartridges jammed fast after the second or third shot. I have since been told by officers that this year our mongrel cartridge sticks worse than ever. Positively, at Abu Klea, and later at Metemmeh, I saw scores of weapons rendered temporarily useless. At this stage, seeing the Arabs were no respecters of persons, I myself took up a Martini-Henry, but the third cartridge stuck, and I had to resort to my revolver.

"Our men were now nearly all clustered around the circular mound, with a swarm of Arabs fighting upon what was originally the left and rear faces of the square; the others were still hanging back undecided among the wreck of camels. The column kept backing with their faces outward towards the top of the low mound, until they were wedged in a compact mass. To me, who was outside on the right face, they appeared to spin and turn slowly around the mound, a whirlpool of human beings. The position luckily enabled them to deliver a heavy and withering fire into the dense mass of Arabs. Soon the enemy showed signs of wavering, and with cheers and shouts our men redoubled their fire.

"A young officer, whose name I did not learn, rallied a number of men on the right rear, and these being soon joined by others were able to deliver an excellent and most telling transverse fire into the enemy's ranks. The strained tension of the situation had lasted nearly ten minutes, when at last the Arabs, two or three at first, then in twenties and fifties, began to trot off the field. In five minutes more there was not an enemy to be seen standing within three hundred yards of us. With cheer upon cheer, shouting ourselves hoarse, we hailed our victory, dearly won as all knew it to be. Parting volley after parting volley was sent into the now flying foemen, and we had the satisfaction of noting that all around they were taking ground to the rear.

"Colonel Barrow, who had been holding the enemy about three-quarters of a mile on our left rear, was now able to push on, and soon three long streams of Arabs, afoot and on horse, camel, and donkey back, were making off, one in the direction of Berber, another towards Metemmeh, and a third for Khartoum. Our skirmishers were again pushed forward, and the screw guns brought into action to quicken their flight. Details of men were sent out to search for our wounded among the heap of slain lying to our left face. As at Teb and Tamai, the wounded Arabs refused to be made prisoners, and great caution had to be exercised in moving about the field, not only to avoid the covert stabs dealt by the bleeding Arabs, but the rushes and cuts of the fanatics who shammed death in order that they might the more surely get a chance of burying their weapons in one of us.

"Our men were drawn forward one hundred and fifty yards from the battlefield, and then, after great delay in getting the soldiers into their proper places, the square was re-formed. We found our losses during the day were, roughly, including native camel drivers, over one hundred killed and about two hundred wounded. Of the enemy, five or six hundred lay heaped in front of and around our dead camels, and I think nearly as many more fell on the hill-sides and in the *wady*. I should have sent you by telegraph as accurate a list as possible, but that, I knew, was forbidden, and at any rate my statement would not have gone on until the official returns were sent. The latter will, therefore, have told you enough, but still with many inaccuracies, no doubt, on account of the hurry and confusion.

"The greatest sufferers were the Heavy Cavalry regiment, which had six officers and over fifty men killed, whereas the Guards and the Mounted Infantry had each but five men killed. It took till ten minutes past noon to get the force again in order. Our Aden cameldrivers, many of whom were killed and wounded, and who displayed a loyalty, courage, and pluck conspicuous alongside the few cowardly Egyptians, scoured the battle-field, and brought in such of the camels as were able to travel. *Cacolets* and litters were put upon the animals, and the lost baggage was left to be recovered later on. The reserve ammunition, which could not then be transported, as over fifty camels were killed, was set fire to and destroyed. While this was taking place the Hussars came up and opened communications, and were sent ahead to take possession of the wells and hasten the enemy's evacuation of their camp.

"Meanwhile small knots of *dervishes* hung about, longing to charge the square. I was unfortunate enough to precipitate one of these rushes on the part of six concealed fanatics. Riding one hundred yards to our left, in a little hollow I saw some men ' stretched on the ground in attitudes not assumed by the dead. A soldier fired at one of the halfdozen who moved his head to peep, missed him, and brought five Arabs to their feet, who rushed for the square. There was a rattle of many rifles. None of them ran more than eighty yards! About one p.m. the force received orders to again advance. As we descended into the *wady* on our left we saw hundreds of Arabs dead and dying. In the dry watercourse they left behind them many water-skins, water-bottles, earthenware pots and bags of *dhurra*. There were even a score of *tomtoms*, the heads of which were instantly burst in. On the northern side of the shallow *khor* they had dug numerous rifle-pits and trenches.

"There were one or two castaway *Mahdi* uniforms and lots of flags, but no shields, for the False Prophet had bade his adherents neither wear their ancient chain armour nor seek the protection of thick rhinoceros hide bucklers. Exploring along this *wady* a party of our men came upon six dead and four wounded Arabs lying under a bushy dwarf mimosa tree. The soldiers had an interpreter with them, and the Arabs were called upon to surrender and come out. That they said they could not do; would the soldiers, therefore, come and take them? The four wounded men still held their spears in their hands. 'Very good,' said our soldiers, 'put down your spears, and we will see you are well treated, and do all we can to cure your wounds.' The answer of the four Arabs came fierce and concise, 'Put down our spears, *infidel* dogs! By God and the Prophet, never!' There was a crack of Martini-Henrys. You can guess the rest.

"It was again, at Teb and Tamai, almost impossible to take prisoners, and we secured but two of their wounded alive. The third prisoner I assisted to bring in, but he was hardly a capture, for the man gave himself up. He had a Remington and over one hundred rounds of ammunition. His story was that he had been one of the Berber-Egyptian garrison, and since the fall of that place had been forced into the *Mahdi's* army. He was glad to escape from them, he declared, and I must say the fellow looked cheerful at being taken. A trooper of the 19th conducted him to General Stewart! He was our one unwounded prisoner!

"Choked and parched with thirst after the day's turmoil, we got to the wells at four p.m., delighted to find an inexhaustible supply of cold pure water. Men and horses gathered around some one or other of the fifty wells sunk in the level plain, quenching their thirst by deep draughts. An hour later fires were being lit to prepare our evening meal. Hands were sent to cut bushes and construct a small *zareba*, and a detachment of troopers was ordered to occupy the hill on our left front. Rifle firing had ceased, and the doctors, who had shared, with a courage and zeal beyond all praise, in all the dangers of the day, had got a temporary hospital in order, and were each doing their utmost to alleviate the sufferings of our wounded. Surgeon-Major Ferguson, the principal medical officer, Surgeons Briggs, Parke, Dick, Maconochie, and others, with the regimental surgeons, worked untiringly through the night, helping the wounded.

"At eight p.m. a force of two hundred and fifty of the Mounted Infantry, under Major Phipps, with fifteen pairs of *cacolets*, was sent back to the *zareba* to order its evacuation, and to bring on to the wells the wounded and all the men and stores. I set out with the Major's detachment, and on our way back we heard the groans of wounded Arabs who had hidden themselves in the bushes to die. Riding ahead, I got into the *zareba* half an hour in front of the Mounted Infantry. When the square advanced, those left in the *zareba* had fired for over an hour at small bands of Arabs who came down from the hills on the right to join in the attack upon our men. In a high wind, and by a guttering candle-light, I wrote my telegram describing the battle of Abu Klea, and sent it you by special messenger, hours ahead of anybody else. I trust it reached you in good time, for I had contrived relays at Gakdul.

"By daylight next morning all the stores were packed on the camels, and the wounded men placed in the litters and *cacolets*. As soon as it was light the *zareba* was abandoned, the force marching to Abu Klea wells, which were reached about eight a.m. without accident or attack from the enemy, small bodies of whom were still, however, visible on the hills to the north and south."

Chapter 4
The Khartoum Relief Expedition—On Towards the Nile!

It was at first thought that after the great victory of Abu Klea the Arabs would give no further trouble. This was not the case, however. A still more terrible battle had to be fought before the Nile could be reached. Mr. Burleigh was again present. He tells us that:—

"History records no military events of a more stirring character, or situations more thrilling and dramatic, than those through which Sir Herbert Stewart's flying column has passed during the past week. Had the British soldier not once more proved a splendid fighter, the story of Stewart's march would have had to be gathered from other sources than the pens or lips of those who accompanied it.

"On the 16th inst., when the column crossed the ridge of foothills that sloped into a *wady*, wherein Abu Klea wells lay six miles to the eastward, few among the troops expected any fighting. The prevailing fear was that the Arabs would bolt, and that there would be neither rewards nor honours to be won.

"On Friday I saw the first shot fired by an Arab scout, and was glad that I persuaded the outpost of the 19th Hussars to let the enemy open the battle. The skirmish that ensued was more disastrous to the rebels than to ourselves, and revealed to us the strength of their force in horse and foot, as well as the position they had taken up.

"By nightfall our column was drawn up inside a rather weak, irregular, and incomplete *zareba*. The front face, instead of being formed of cut brushwood, was protected by low walls of rough stones. An undulation in the ground left an opening in the wall twenty-five yards wide. The wall itself was twenty inches high, and the *zareba* was nearly two hundred yards square.

"Each man had his pint of water served out—half his day's supply—and on that quantity he had to work, march, and fight in a thirst-provoking country. Lights were all ordered out at dusk, and the troops lay down in square formation, with their arms beside them ready for instant use.

"During their much-needed respite, I may recall the fact that after we had undergone a night of alarms, following the memorable events of Abu Klea, and had had several men injured by the enemy's fire, the column moved out of the *zareba* in square, lightly equipped for fighting. A small garrison was left behind to guard the stores and animals. Nearly one hundred camels were taken with the column to carry water, ammunition, and *cacolets*. These were all inside the square. Just before the force set out, Major Gough received a contusion on the skull from a bullet, and the command of the Mounted Infantry devolved on Major Barrow. A fierce battle and hard-won victory had secured to us Klea wells, giving the troops an abundant supply of water, with something for the horses and camels.

"A bath or even a wash in the desert was too great a luxury, only to be indulged in alongside the well or at a reservoir like Gakdul. By dint of hard work and going without sleep the column was ready to resume its forward march on Sunday at four p.m. The old *zareba* was emptied, all the supplies having been transported to the wells by working overnight, and a new small *zareba* and fort were built at Abu Klea, which a detachment of the Sussex Regiment and a few men of the Royal Engineers were left to hold. It was given out by General Stewart that the force should only go five miles out and encamp till morning.

"The column got off punctually, tired though the men and animals were. It was with pleasure that we set our faces for another forced march so that we might get to the river. Instead of making a protracted halt at sunset, the column rested for a few minutes only in order to allow the darkness to settle down. And then, altering our course so as to avoid Shebacat wells and the Arabs posted there to intercept or hinder us, we struck due south into the desert, attempting to reach the Nile before daylight, and before the Arabs could stop us. The general sought to avoid another battle until the force should have entrenched itself, or, at any rate, packed its baggage by the water's edge.

"Night marches are always difficult, if not dangerous, and with our overworked animals the energies of men and officers were taxed to the utmost to keep the column together. In spite of everything the column often extended for two or three miles, that distance separating the van from the rear. This necessitated frequent halts. Completely done up, the men dropped asleep in their saddles, and came tumbling to the ground. Those who undertook to rest on the desert while the column closed up had to be roughly aroused to get them to remount.

"Part of the way the force moved in columns of regiments, the Mounted Infantry leading, with the Hussars in advance and on the flanks. Although this increased the width of our front, it did not diminish the length of the column. Apparently Ali Gobah, the outlaw robber chief, directed our course, which was at times rather circuitous—now south, then south by west, and again south by east. Sir Charles Wilson and Captain Verner, of the Rifles, looked after Ali, in whose experience as a pathfinder they both trusted. I was inclined to regard Gobah as a failure; he lengthened our way and wasted hours.

"Silence was enjoined upon all on the march. The camels, as usual, disregarded this order, and made night awful with their groans and cries. Smoking likewise was forbidden.

"Daylight broke, finding the column six miles from the river, and about the same distance south of Metemmeh. The objective point was to occupy a position on the Nile four miles south of Metemmeh. An hour before sunrise we had altered our course, turning more to the east.

"Before the sun was up we saw that the enemy were on the alert all along our front. Streams of men on horseback and on foot came from Metemmeh, interposing themselves between the column and the water we so longed to gain. For a short interval of time Sir Herbert Stewart deliberated whether to push on two miles nearer the Nile. As the Arabs mustered in force sufficient to seriously threaten our advance, he decided to halt upon a ridge of desert covered with sparkling pebbles, four miles from the river. To our right and rear lay a few low black hills, one mile to two miles distant; on our front the desert rolled downward towards the green flats bordering the Nile; for here, as at Dongola, the belt of cultivation is rich and wide.

"Turning with a light smile to his staff, General Stewart said, 'Tell the officers and men we will have breakfast first, and then go out and fight.'

"The column was closed up with the baggage animals to the centre as usual; the boxes and pack saddles being taken off to make an enclosure to protect the square from rifle fire. In less than ten minutes the Arabs were not only all over our front and flanks, but had drawn a line around our rear. Groups bearing the fantastic *Koran*-inscribed banners of the False Prophet, similar to those of which we had taken two or three score at Klea, could be seen occupying vantage-points all around.

"The enemy's fire grew hotter and more deadly every minute. Evidently their Remingtons were in the hands of Kordofan hunters. Mimosa bushes were ordered to be cut at once, and breakfast preparations were peremptorily suspended for an hour, whilst most of the troops lay flat Fatigue parties strengthened our position.

"In going towards a low mound, a hundred yards on our right front, where we had a few skirmishers, General Stewart was shot in the stomach. The command thereupon devolved upon Lord Charles Beresford by seniority, but he, being a naval officer, declined it, and Sir Charles Wilson took it over.

"The mound on our front was quickly turned into a detached work, forty volunteers, carrying boxes and pack-saddles, rushing out, and, in a short space of time, converting it into a strongly defensible post.

"The situation appeared to me so threatening that I took part in this enterprise.

"Gradually the enemy's riflemen crept nearer, and our skirmishers were sent out to engage them. They were too numerous to drive away, and the nature of the ground and the high trajectory of their Remingtons enabled the Arabs to drop their bullets into the square at all points. Soldiers lying behind camels and saddle-packs were shot in the head by dropping bullets. Mr. Cameron, the Standard correspondent, was hit in the back and killed whilst sitting behind a camel, just as he was going to have lunch. Later on I received a graze on the neck and a blow on the foot from bullets. The enemy were firing at ranges of from 700 to 2,000 yards, and their practice was excellent.

"The *zip, ping,* and *thud* of the leaden hail was continuous, and, whilst the camels were being killed by fifties, our soldiers did not escape, over forty having to be carried to the hospital, sheltered as well as possible in the centre of the square behind a wall of saddles, bags, and boxes. As a precaution against stampede the poor camels were tied down, both their knees and necks being securely bound by ropes in order to prevent their getting upon their legs. At Klea, I remember, the camels' pack-saddles caught fire from the guns.

"The 10,000 *dervishes* whom the *Mahdi* has sent from Omdurman to annihilate us were blocking our road to the Nile; and over a hundred *Baggara*, the horsemen of the Soudan, and crowds of villagers, who had joined Mohammed Ahmed's crusade, hung like famished wolves on our rear and flanks, awaiting an opportunity to slay. Apparently they were emboldened by our defensive preparations, for their numbers swelled and their fire increased in intensity; and, as stretcher after stretcher with its gory load was taken to the hospital, the space was found too little, and the wounded had to be laid outside. Surgeon-Major Ferguson, Dr. Briggs, and their colleagues had their skill and time taxed to the utmost. Want of water hampered their operations; doctors and patients were alike exposed to the enemy's fire. More harrowing battle scenes in the course of a long experience I never saw.

"One of the most touching incidents in the *zareba* on the 19th was the wounded general being tended by his friends, two or three of whom wept like men, silently. Poor St. Leger Herbert, the *Morning Post* correspondent, one of these latter, was himself shot dead shortly afterwards.

"Our situation had become unbearable. We were being fired at without a chance of returning blows with or without interest.

"There were three courses open to us—to sally forth and fight our way to the Nile; to fight for the river, advancing stage by stage, with the help of *zarebas* and temporary works; or to strengthen our position and try to withstand the Arabs and lack of water till Wolseley should send a force to our assistance, we meanwhile sending a messenger or two back to Korti with the news.

"It was bravely decided to go out and engage the enemy at close quarters. At two p.m. the force was to march out in square, carrying nothing except ammunition and stretchers. Each man was to take a hundred rounds and to have his water-bottle full. Everything was put in most thorough readiness for the enterprise. Lord Charles Beresford, who had been 'seedy' since we left Abu Klea, with Colonel Barrow, remained in command of the enclosure, or *zareba*, containing the animals and stores. They had under them the naval contingent, the 19th Hussars, a party of Royal Engineers, and Captain Norton's detachment of Royal Artillery, with three screw guns, and details from regiments and men of the Commissariat and Transport Corps.

"All day long Lord Charles and Captain Norton had been pounding the enemy whenever the Arabs gave them a chance, the former at the Gardner gun, and the latter with two of his light guns."

Chapter 5
Battle of Gubat (Abu Kru)—The Nile Reached.

"It was nearly three before the square started, Sir Charles Wilson in command, and Colonel Boscawen acting as executive officer. Lord Airlie, who had been slightly wounded at Abu Klea, and again on the

19th, together with Major Wardrop, served upon Sir Charles's staff, as they had done upon General Stewart's. The square was joined to the east of our enclosed defence, the troops lying down as they were assigned their stations. The Guards formed the front, with the Marines on the right front corner, the Heavies on the right and right rear, the Sussex in the rear, and the Mounted Infantry on the left rear and left flank. Colonel Talbot led the Heavies, Major Barrow the Hussars, Colonel Rowley the Guards, Major Poe the Marines, and Major Sunderland the Sussex Regiment. Captain Verner, of the Rifle Brigade, was told off to direct the square in its march towards the river. When the order was given for the square to rise and advance, it moved off to the west to clear the outlying work.

"The instant the Arabs detected the forward movement on our part they opened a terrific rifle fire upon the square from the scrub on all sides.

"For the first few minutes many of our men were hit and fell. The wounded were with difficulty picked up and carried.

"When the square slowly marched, as if upon parade, down into the grass and scrub-covered hollow, intervening between the works we had constructed, and the line of bare rising desert that bounded our view towards the south and east—shutting out of sight the river and the fertile border slopes—All felt the critical moment had come.

"Steadily the square descended into the valley. Gaps were made in our force by the enemy's fire. As man after man staggered and fell, these gaps were doggedly closed; and without quickening the pace by one beat, onward our soldiers went. All were resolved to sell their lives dearly. Every now and again the square would halt, and the men would lie down, firing at their foes hidden in the valley. Those sheltered behind the desert crest were too safely screened to waste ammunition upon at that stage. Wheeling to the right and swinging to the left our men fought like gladiators, without unnecessarily wasting strength or dealing a blow too many.

"A more glorious spectacle was never seen than this little band in broad daylight, on an open plain, seeking hand-to-hand conflict with the courageous, savage, and fanatical foe, who outnumbered us by twelve to one.

"As the square moved over the rolling ground, keeping its best fighting side—or rather, I should say, its firing side—towards the great onrushes of the Arabs, the soldiers swung around, as though the square pivoted on its centre. Once it entered ground too thickly covered

Battle of Gubat (Abu Kru) "The Thick of the Fight."

by grass and scrub, halted, and coolly swung round and marched out upon the more open ground, with the Arabs to the right front, their '*tom-toms*' beating, and their sacred battle-flags of red, white, and green, flying in the air.

"Bearing banners lettered with verses from the Koran, a host of fanatic Arabs was the first to hurl its swordsmen and spearmen upon the square. The column wheeled to receive them, and the men, by their officers' direction, fired volleys by companies, scarcely any independent firing being permitted.

The wild *dervishes* and fanatics who led the charge went down in scores before our fire, which was opened on them at 700 yards, and none of the enemy got within two yards of the square. This checked their ardour, which had been excited by seeing the gaps in our ranks.

"Three more charges were attempted by the enemy at other points along the line of the square's advance.

"At half-past four, after nearly two hours' incessant fighting, as the column neared the south-easterly edge of the valley to pass out of it, the Arabs made their final grand onrush. Nearly 10,000 of them swept down from three sides towards the square, their main body—numbering not fewer than 5,000—coming upon our left face.

"It was a critical time. Their fire had made fresh gaps in our ranks, and fierce human waves were rolling in upon every side to overwhelm our force.

"Down the Arabs came from behind the ridge at a trot, and not at the top of their speed, as the Hadendowas charged. Gallant horsemen and wild dervishes led them, and shouted to their followers to rush on in *Allah's* name and destroy us.

"Firm as a rock, the square stood steadily, aimed deliberately, and fired.

"Again and again had volleys to be sent into the yelling hordes as down they poured. The feeling was—Could they be stopped before closing with us?

"Their fleetest and luckiest dervishes, however, did not get within twenty-five yards before death overtook them; whilst the bulk of the enemy were still a hundred yards away.

"At last—God be thanked!—they hesitate, stop, turn, and run back. Victory is ours, and the British column is safe!

"The broken lines of Arabs sullenly retreated towards Metemmeh, but our square had to gain the ridge before escaping from their sharpshooters' fire, and getting a chance of punishing the daring foe.

"Without further opposition, the British advanced to the river, and encamped in a sheltered ravine for the night, the men lying down with their arms, and strong outposts being on the alert against any surprises.

"Every man drank freely of the refreshing water, and, exhausted by the hardships endured, slept soundly, grateful that the enemy left them undisturbed for that night.

"Whilst the square was marching to gain the Nile, the garrisons left in charge of the hastily-constructed works sought to render our men all the help possible.

"Skirmishers were thrown out about two hundred yards all round, and the enemy on the right, left, and rear, were kept behind the sheltering ridges as much as possible by good shooting.

"The *Baggara* horsemen and the Arabs on our left and rear were looked after by Lord Charles Beresford with his sailors and their Gardner, and were kept from joining their force with that on the left, when the grand onrush was made upon the square. The 19th Hussars watched our rear; and threatened attacks upon the works were provided against on our front and right.

"Captain Norton and Lieut. Duboulay, R.A., with two screw guns, pitched shell and caseshot, at ranges varying from 1,500 to 2,300 yards, into the dense groups of Arabs gathered around the *Mahdi's* standards. The practice made was excellent, and not only did it prevent the Arabs from forming their attacking columns in dense lines, but the exploding shells indicated to the square the points where the enemy was mustering in force to attack.

"Our approximate loss in the day's fighting was, in and about the works, sixteen killed and sixty wounded; with the square, twelve killed and forty wounded.

"The enemy lost a thousand killed.

"Official returns now going home will give you the names of the officers.

"On Tuesday morning, Jan. 20, the square returned to the works, after having left a small garrison guarding the wounded in a deserted village near the river.

"On their way back they drove the enemy out of the villages of Abu Kru and Gubat, and partly burned these places.

"During the night the garrison at the works had two alarms; but, altogether, there was little firing, and the dark hours passed quietly.

"The return of the square was signalled by great cheering from all the troops. The soldiers grasped one another warmly by the hand, and heartily congratulated each other. It was a scene of sincere enjoyment and earnest triumph.

"In a few hours the camels left alive were repacked, our dead were buried, and, bearing our wounded on stretchers, the column, with its baggage as before, in the centre, marched towards the Nile at Abu Kru—the Arabs passively watching us from the distant ridges.

"We, the correspondents, carried poor Cameron to his grave, and there we laid him with St. Leger Herbert, Lima, and Quartermaster Jewell. It was but a soldier's funeral. Lord Charles Beresford read the burial service; and then we turned away sorrowfully, each of us to help in the task of bearing wounded men to a safe shelter on the banks of the Nile, which we gained about four p.m.

"On Wednesday, Jan. 21st, a column, composed much like that of the 19th, advanced to attack Metemmeh, and we found the enemy had loopholed most of the mud walls, and were holding the place in force.

"After we had manoeuvred on the plain to the south-east of the town, firing at the fugitives running towards the north, the enemy unmasked a battery of Krupp guns and played upon us.

"We could see the flags of the dervishes as they waited for us behind the walls, and it was deemed prudent not to attempt an assault

"About eleven in the forenoon, four of Gordon's steamers, under Nousha Pasha, steamed down abreast of the place where we were.

"I rode forward and got aboard one of these steamers, and afterwards carried back a message to Sir Charles Wilson that the Pasha would land 500 men and five guns to assist us.

"This they did, and for several hours we poured shot and shell into Metemmeh. But mud walls take much of this sort oi thing with but little hurt, and at three o'clock the entire force withdrew.

"Our loss was one killed and nine wounded.

"Our Egyptian friends appeared overjoyed to see us. They told us that Khartoum and Gordon were safe and well.

"We further learned that all was safe six days ago, and that the *Mahdi* had sent 2,000 men on the 17th instant to reinforce Metemmeh, within which were 1,000 riflemen and 10,000 spearmen.

"Olivier Pain, the French renegade, we were informed, was in command there.

"The *Mahdi* himself was said to be at Omdurman with 12,000

Water at Last! First sight of the Nile after the Battle of Gubat.

troops.

"The steamers had not been in Khartoum for one month, but had been awaiting us at an island above Metemmeh. The vessels, or three of them, at any rate, are rather larger than Greenwich steamers. They are covered with heavy boards of hard wood, and, inside, with thin iron plates. The hulls are of iron, and the general appearance of the craft is very battered, resembling nothing so much as an old hoarding in a shabby London street. Bullet marks have pitted them from the funnel top to the water line, just as a virulent attack of smallpox disfigures a man's face.

"On board there are several hundreds of plucky blacks, led by a few Turks. As usual they have their wives and families with them. The vessels are more like floating houses than war-ships.

"Yesterday evening the steamers threw fifty shells into Shendy, and have promised to return again unless the people submit. This they do not seem inclined to do.

"We have been improving our defences, as we learn that an Arab force from Berber is on the way to attack us.

"Tonight a convoy, under Colonel Talbot, proceeds back to Gakdul with unloaded camels to bring up supplies and reinforcements. My messages go by it.

"This is my first opportunity. As we all have been so busy, there has been but little leisure, even for writing.

"Today the troops were put on half-ration scale. Tomorrow (Saturday, Jan. 24), Sir Charles Wilson, with Stewart Wortley, Captain Gascoigne, Captain Trafford, and twenty men of the Sussex Regiment, sail in two of Gordon's steamers for Khartoum. The other two stay here."

Such were the plans of our leaders.

ALSO FROM LEONAUR
AVAILABLE IN SOFTCOVER OR HARDCOVER WITH DUST JACKET

THE 9TH—THE KING'S (LIVERPOOL REGIMENT) IN THE GREAT WAR 1914 - 1918 *by Enos H. G. Roberts*—Mersey to mud—war and Liverpool men.

THE GAMBARDIER *by Mark Severn*—The experiences of a battery of Heavy artillery on the Western Front during the First World War.

FROM MESSINES TO THIRD YPRES *by Thomas Floyd*—A personal account of the First World War on the Western front by a 2/5th Lancashire Fusilier.

THE IRISH GUARDS IN THE GREAT WAR - VOLUME 1 *by Rudyard Kipling*—Edited and Compiled from Their Diaries and Papers—The First Battalion.

THE IRISH GUARDS IN THE GREAT WAR - VOLUME 1 *by Rudyard Kipling*—Edited and Compiled from Their Diaries and Papers—The Second Battalion.

ARMOURED CARS IN EDEN *by K. Roosevelt*—An American President's son serving in Rolls Royce armoured cars with the British in Mesopotamia & with the American Artillery in France during the First World War.

CHASSEUR OF 1914 *by Marcel Dupont*—Experiences of the twilight of the French Light Cavalry by a young officer during the early battles of the great war in Europe.

TROOP HORSE & TRENCH *by R.A. Lloyd*—The experiences of a British Lifeguardsman of the household cavalry fighting on the western front during the First World War 1914-18.

THE EAST AFRICAN MOUNTED RIFLES *by C.J. Wilson*—Experiences of the campaign in the East African bush during the First World War.

THE LONG PATROL *by George Berrie*—A Novel of Light Horsemen from Gallipoli to the Palestine campaign of the First World War.

THE FIGHTING CAMELIERS *by Frank Reid*—The exploits of the Imperial Camel Corps in the desert and Palestine campaigns of the First World War.

STEEL CHARIOTS IN THE DESERT *by S. C. Rolls*—The first world war experiences of a Rolls Royce armoured car driver with the Duke of Westminster in Libya and in Arabia with T.E. Lawrence.

WITH THE IMPERIAL CAMEL CORPS IN THE GREAT WAR *by Geoffrey Inchbald*—The story of a serving officer with the British 2nd battalion against the Senussi and during the Palestine campaign.

AVAILABLE ONLINE AT **www.leonaur.com**
AND FROM ALL GOOD BOOK STORES

www.ingramcontent.com/pod-product-compliance
Lightning Source LLC
Chambersburg PA
CBHW031619160426
43196CB00006B/193